Organising Knowledge: Taxonomies, Knowledge and Organisational Effectiveness

CHANDOS
KNOWLEDGE MANAGEMENT SERIES

Series Editor: Melinda Taylor
(email: melindataylor@chandospublishing.com)

Chandos' new series of books are aimed at the busy information professional. They have been specially commissioned to provide the reader with an authoritative view of current thinking. They are designed to provide easy-to-read and (most importantly) practical coverage of topics that are of interest to librarians and other information professionals. If you would like a full listing of current and forthcoming titles, please visit our web site www.chandospublishing.com or email info@chandospublishing.com or telephone +44 (0) 1223 891358.

New authors: we are always pleased to receive ideas for new titles; if you would like to write a book for Chandos, please contact Dr Glyn Jones on email gjones@chandospublishing.com or telephone number +44 (0) 1993 848726.

Bulk orders: some organisations buy a number of copies of our books. If you are interested in doing this, we would be pleased to discuss a discount. Please email info@chandospublishing.com or telephone +44 (0) 1223 891358.

Chandos Publishing
TBAC Business Centre
Avenue 4
Station Lane
Witney
Oxford OX28 4BN
UK
Tel: +44 (0) 1993 848726
Email: info@chandospublishing.com
www.chandospublishing.com

Chandos Publishing is an imprint of Woodhead Publishing Limited

Woodhead Publishing Limited
80 High Street
Sawston
Cambridge CB22 3HJ
UK
Tel: +44 (0) 1223 499140
Fax: +44 (0) 1223 832819
www.woodheadpublishing.com

First published in 2007

ISBN:
978 1 84334 227 4

British Library Cataloguing-in-Publication Data.
A catalogue record for this book is available from the British Library.

Typeset by Domex e-Data Pvt. Ltd.
Printed in the UK and USA.

Printed in the UK by 4edge Limited - www.4edge.co.uk

Organising Knowledge: Taxonomies, Knowledge and Organisational Effectiveness

PATRICK LAMBE

CP

CHANDOS
PUBLISHING

Oxford Cambridge New Delhi

Contents

List of abbreviations   *ix*

List of figures and tables   *xi*

Preface   *xiii*

Introduction   *xv*

About the author   *xix*

1   **Defining our terms**   **1**

    Can we organise knowledge?   1

    What are taxonomies?   4

    Taxonomy as artificial memory   8

    Taxonomy work   11

2   **Taxonomies can take many forms**   **13**

    Lists   14

    Tree structures   15

    Hierarchies   18

    Polyhierarchies   25

    Matrices   25

    Facets   33

    System maps   42

    Practical implications of different taxonomy forms   45

3   **Taxonomies and infrastructure for organisational effectiveness**   **49**

    Organisational ineffectiveness   50

    The problem of Babel   57

    Taxonomies as boundary objects   61

Information and knowledge structure   64

4   Taxonomies and activities for organisational effectiveness   67

     Risk   68

     Case study 4.1 Department of Homeland Security digital library   *72*

     Costs   74

     Case study 4.2 Unilever's brand simplification exercise   *80*

     Customers and markets   81

     Case study 4.3 Club Med, storytelling and archetypes   *88*

     Innovation   90

     Case study 4.4 Unilever Research and disposable taxonomies   *92*

5   Taxonomies and knowledge management   97

     Taxonomies and findability   98

     Taxonomies and content management   100

     Taxonomies and knowledge management   102

     Logos/Information   105

     Sophos/Expertise and learning   106

     Case study 5.1 The British Council maps its competencies   *108*

     Pathos/Collaboration   112

     *Case study 5.2 Cabot Corporation builds a taxonomy to
     coordinate global quality*   *114*

     Ethos/Culture   115

     *Case study 5.3 The Civil Aviation Authority of Singapore uses a
     typology to structure and communicate its knowledge
     management strategy*   *118*

6   What do we want our taxonomies to do?   123

     What taxonomies do   124

     Making sense of taxonomy work   134

     When taxonomies go bad   140

7   Preparing for a taxonomy project   153

     Step 1: Meet project sponsor   155

     Step 2: Engage stakeholders   166

Step 3: Refine project purpose   167

Case study 7.1 The structure-and-organise taxonomy   168

Case study 7.2 Losing clarity of purpose   170

Case study 7.3 Evolving purpose   173

Step 4: Design the approach   175

Step 5: Build the communication plan   177

Step 6: Start the governance process   181

8   Designing your taxonomy   **185**

The cognitive constraints on taxonomy design   186

Step 7: Collect vocabularies and organising principles   193

Step 8: Facet analysis   197

Step 9: Test and observe   198

Case study 8.1 Facet analysis for a sports organisation   203

9   Implementing your taxonomy   **207**

Step 10: Plan the instantiation of your taxonomy   209

*Case study 9.1 Metadata strategies and vocabulary control at
the BBC*   215

Step 11: Integrate your taxonomy into the infrastructure   217

Step 12: Secure the governance process   234

10   The future of taxonomy work   **237**

Ontologies and machine intelligence   238

Folksonomies and rich serendipity   240

Enhancing usefulness in folksonomies   245

Taxonomies vs folksonomies?   249

Towards an array of knowledge infrastructure tools   253

The benefits of diversity in knowledge and information
infrastructure   255

Spimes and the future of taxonomies   260

Bibliography   **263**

Index   273

List of abbreviations

AIDS	acquired immune deficiency syndrome
APQC	American Productivity and Quality Center
ASHEN	Artefacts, Skills, Heuristics, Experience, Natural talent (Snowden, 2000b)
BCG	Boston Consulting Group
BCS	business classification scheme
BPR	business process re-engineering
CAAS	Civil Aviation Authority of Singapore
CEO	chief executive officer
CIO	chief information officer
DDC	Dewey Decimal Classification
DIMIA	Australian Department of Immigration
DIRKS	Designing and Implementing Recordkeeping Systems
GPS	geographical positioning systems
HIV	human immunodeficiency virus
HR	human resources
ICD	International Classification of Diseases
IP	intellectual property
ISO	International Standards Organisation
IT	information technology
KM	knowledge management
NAA	National Archives of Australia
NAICS	North American Industry Classification
OLAP	online analytical processing
RDF	Resource Description Framework
RFID	radio frequency identification
SARS	severe acute respiratory syndrome
SIA	strategic information alignment (Marchand, 2000)
SIPOC	suppliers, inputs, processes, outputs, customers (Rath & Strong, 2000)
W3C	World Wide Web Consortium
WHO	World Health Organisation

List of figures and tables

Figures

1.1	Relationships in a thesaurus	7
2.1	Effective and ineffective ways of representing caste	19
2.2	Maslow's hierarchy of needs	20
2.3	Hierarchical tree used to represent a corporate structure	21
2.4	Periodic table in Mendeleev's format	27
2.5	Boston Consulting Group Matrix	28
2.6	Three-dimensional Alexander periodic table	30
2.7	Matrix representation for an engineering project taxonomy	31
2.8	Career advice matrix from LearnDirect UK	32
2.9	Detail from Epicurious.com enhanced search page showing facets as lists	39
2.10	Taxonomy of arteries shown as a map	43
2.11	Concept map of taxonomy attributes	44
2.12	Example of a project roadmap with knowledge assets	45
3.1	Public and private taxonomies	60
3.2	Incident report – facet analysis	63
3.3	The elements of information and knowledge infrastructure	65
4.1	Marchand's strategic information alignment framework	67
4.2	SIPOC process map	75
4.3	SIPOC knowledge mapping template	76
4.4	Crop rotation plan for a kitchen garden	79
4.5	Unilever's taxonomy of brands	81
5.1	Knowledge lens framework	103
5.2	Knowledge lens framework and taxonomy work	105
5.3	Example archetypes from CAAS	120
6.1	The Cynefin framework	134
6.2	Taxonomy functions as sense-making responses	137

6.3	Where taxonomies go wrong	140
7.1	Preparing for a taxonomy project	154
7.2	Detail from a human resource concept map	157
8.1	Designing a taxonomy	186
8.2	Cognitive constraints in navigating a taxonomy	191
8.3	Example of input-output knowledge map	195
9.1	The full taxonomy development cycle with implementation steps	208
9.2	Checklist for building an information neighbourhood	225
10.1	Person-mediated serendipity trails in folksonomies	243
10.2	Social tagging as a complement to taxonomy work	253
10.3	An array of knowledge infrastructure tools	254
10.4	Thinkmap's Visual Thesaurus	256

Tables

2.1	Kinds of relationship expressed in a tree structure	17
2.2	Practical implications of taxonomy forms	46
7.1	Examples of important cues to taxonomy types and construction approaches	158
7.2	Key decision factors in choosing your design approach	175
7.3	Example statements of taxonomy purpose and benefits	180
8.1	Knowledge asset types	194
8.2	Candidates for facet analysis	198
8.3	Key criteria for taxonomy validation	199
9.1	Example of a metadata framework	211
9.2	Extract from a thesaurus for a training institution	213

Preface

This has been a long pregnancy. I started preparing my notes for this book in early 2004 but didn't start writing until late 2005. It has been a challenging task to write in the midst of client projects and an exciting period of growth for my firm, Straits Knowledge.

The book has been challenging for another reason. There is very little systematic literature but a good deal of opinion on taxonomy work within a knowledge management context. In the consequent uncertainty we have suffered from an overreliance on classification theory from the library and information studies domain – a field that can only partially address the organisational contexts and issues with which knowledge management has to deal. As so often in knowledge management, technology developers have also seized the field and sown it with competing concepts and vocabularies. Behind them all lies the great Linnaean myth of the perfect structured hierarchy, where every document has its unique identifiable position.

The book has therefore required a wide review of literature and practice from several different disciplines, and the weaving of a serviceable cloth from such rich and diverse stuff has at times felt like wrestling several angels at once.

The observant reader will detect several significant influences on my thought. Probably the most pervasive is David Snowden, who brings to knowledge management theoretical rigour combined with a keen awareness of the naturalistic settings within which ordinary people do their knowledge work. His generosity in sharing his insights and supporting his fellow travellers is legendary. Gary Klein taught me how to use concept maps and opened my eyes to the ways in which simple tools and frameworks can be used to make sense out of the complexity of human knowledge activity. Geoffrey Bowker and Susan Leigh Star had a huge impact on my understanding of information infrastructure. Barbara Kwasnik's seminal paper on knowledge representation showed me how malleable and adaptive taxonomy work can be. She liberated me from the Linnaean prison. Less obviously perhaps, Etienne Wenger's work on communities of practice gave me a way of understanding the fluid boundaries between social and individual knowledge use, and the variety of ways in which we transmute information into knowledge and back again. Maish Nichani and James Robertson have educated me on the point where the taxonomy rubber hits the working road – the user experience of information and knowledge use in everyday work contexts. Marita Keenan initiated me into the mysteries of records management with grace, clarity and humour. I inherited a taxonomy project mid-way from my former pupil Patricia Wong Bao Bao after her death, and learned from her far more than I could have taught her. Lee Henn taught me by example that a steady hand, limitless patience and nerves of steel are essential in a taxonomy project.

Several people have had a more direct hand in this book. I have been a mostly silent lurker in two communities, Seth Earley's TaxoCoP community and Jean Graef's Montague Institute. I've learned from both, and am grateful for the help and support they provided for the early chapters in this book. I'd like to thank Jean Graef, Angela Pitts, Adrian Dale, John Mackenzie and Daniel Ng for their support in providing case studies for Chapters 4 and 5, and Karen Loasby for the case study material in Chapter 9. Liam Brown, who consistently provides me with food for thought, first pointed me to the Victoria Climbié tragedy, which illustrates so graphically what can happen when information and knowledge infrastructure fails.

Marita Keenan, Dave Snowden, David Eddy, Kim Sbarcea, Maish Nichani, Edgar Tan and Paolina Martin have all read and commented on various drafts of this book. Maish Nichani, Kim Sbarcea and Marita Keenan made suggestions that substantially influenced the structure of Chapter 9, though the responsibility for any infelicity must remain mine.

I owe an enormous debt of gratitude to my colleagues Edgar Tan and Paolina Martin, who have tolerated both my presences and my absences with generosity, good cheer and perfect honesty. Without their encouragement and support I could not have completed the task. And my final thanks must go to the clients with whom I've had the privilege to work. Without them, this book would have been far less pragmatic.

This book is dedicated to the memory of my Aunt Mary and Uncle Jimmy, in whose home, looking out over the fields, I wrote much of it.

Balcunnin, Skerries
September 2006

Introduction

No classification system, any more than any representation, may specify
completely the wildness and complexity of what is represented.
(Bowker and Star, 1999: 232)

Taxonomies are at the same time deceptively simple and fiendishly complicated. They are simple because they are absolutely basic to human consciousness, so everybody manipulates and creates them with great ease. Our world is populated with categories, of family, friends, social groups, things, concepts, activities, feelings, places, times and many other things besides.

Taxonomies are complicated because we use them for the most part unreflectingly – they are simply part of our mental and social background – and we use categories in a huge variety of ways, often in competing and inconsistent ways.

This makes it difficult to be consciously consistent and consistently conscious in our use of categories, and the implicit taxonomies of which they are a part. And yet to manage our knowledge we do need to be both conscious and consistent.

Consider the case of going for a drive. To achieve this relatively simple task we need to be able to manipulate a category system involving cars and parts of cars (at least the parts that we manipulate); categories of road sign; rules of the road and their relative importance; types of traffic conditions and appropriate responses; categories of other drivers and appropriate responses; categories of vehicles and their capabilities. Except among chauvinists who like to complain about women drivers, or among driving test candidates, very little of this taxonomic knowledge comes consciously to the surface. Our daily taxonomies remain largely tacit. As we'll see later on, most of the taxonomy work we do in organisations is also invisible and not consciously organised.

Moreover, human beings are programmed with the 'Babel Instinct'. If we can organise things around us differently from other people, we will do so. Sometimes this is for pragmatic working needs – we like our things organised in such and such a way because it suits the tasks we have to do. Different people with different tasks will order their knowledge assets differently to suit the tasks they have to do. Sometimes we just organise them differently because we feel like it. We don't always know how to discriminate between pragmatic need and arbitrary inclination.

These few factors are what make taxonomy work difficult. Our clients can and do categorise continually. They are confident about knowing how to sort things out. It is easy for them to find fault with the taxonomies we design for them. They can be fluent in critique. But they are not skilled at conscious, strategic organisation of their knowledge assets to suit collective needs. In knowledge management, much of the work of a taxonomist is not in analysis, but in 'reading' the varying information perspectives of different groups in the client organisation, 'collecting' their languages and labels, and helping them reach a negotiated, well-structured compromise. It goes beyond that, to working within an organisation's information environment to make sure that the taxonomy is understood pragmatically, adopted consistently, applied productively and managed sustainably.

There are many contradictions in taxonomy work. It is intensely democratic, yet it is also a highly specialised art – everyone can do it, but few can do it well. Good taxonomies are simple; they become invisible and taken for granted, because they reflect so well the contours of their users' knowledge world – but only complex, difficult taxonomies are held to represent the true art of taxonomy building. Taxonomies work on principles of consistency and predictability, yet they must also accommodate inconsistency, contradiction and ambiguity, because so do the knowledge worlds that we are trying to navigate. Taxonomies are a losing battle, sandcastles shored up against the rising tide of change – but we fight nevertheless, because they give temporary respite from advancing chaos. Taxonomies are commissioned, constructed and managed as products, yet the most important part of taxonomies lies in the processes and environments that produce them, and the processes and environments where they are employed. Taxonomies make knowledge visible, but while they reveal, they also conceal – the 'stuff' that is not accommodated at all, and the attributes of our knowledge that our taxonomy builders considered of secondary importance. A taxonomy is a standard, and yet it is also highly contingent on current circumstance.

It's no wonder that such a confusing picture gives rise to popular assumptions about taxonomies that are only partially true, misleading, or just plain wrong. One of these, that it's a highly arcane domain inaccessible to the ordinary human being, we've already dealt with. Another, that only librarians and biologists understand taxonomies, is misleading – biological taxonomies are paragons of consistency and purity of principle, but they are totally unlike taxonomies for knowledge work. Our messy, confused world of knowledge and information artefacts does not follow the simpler laws of genetics. And while they are usually well-schooled in their own specific sets of classification principles, neither biologists nor librarians, for the most part, ever have to build taxonomies. In their professional roles, they will at most be passive users of existing taxonomic schemes. There is no ready reservoir of taxonomy construction experts – we are all muddling through.

In the first half of this book we'll challenge a number of assumptions about taxonomies and the work of taxonomy building, and relate this work to organisation effectiveness and knowledge management. Chapter 1 defines our terminology and introduces the basic concepts we'll be working with throughout the book. In Chapter 2, we tackle the assumption that a taxonomy has to look like a hierarchical tree. In Chapter 3 we show that taxonomy work is an integral part of information infrastructure development going far beyond information retrieval. In Chapter 4 we look in more detail at how taxonomy work influences the basic things that organisations do to be effective. Chapter 5 traces the history of taxonomies in knowledge management and challenges the assumption that taxonomy work is just a specialised area of work within knowledge management associated with content management and information retrieval. In that chapter too we look in more detail at the variety of contributions that taxonomy work can make to knowledge management initiatives.

In the second half of this book, we take a more practical approach and guide you through the steps involved in a 'typical' taxonomy project. Here we challenge the assumption that taxonomy development can be done in the abstract, by a consultant, sitting apart from the information and knowledge world of the organisation it is intended for. Very few taxonomies for knowledge management can be developed in that distant, unengaged way.

In Chapter 6 we look at the practical things that taxonomies can do for us in organisations, and how different taxonomies work towards different results. It is possible to do a lot of damage by applying taxonomies badly. Chapter 7 outlines the key steps that need to be walked through in planning and preparing for a taxonomy project. Chapter 8 looks at the typical activities in designing and validating a taxonomy, while Chapter 9 looks at implementation and change management issues.

To close, in Chapter 10 we take a forward look at issues and challenges on the horizon for knowledge managers. What do the semantic web, folksonomies, ontologies and social tagging mean for taxonomy work? Will we need taxonomies at all? Here we challenge the assumption that taxonomies are the only 'true' way to organise and connect to information content.

About the author

Patrick Lambe is co-founder and Principal Consultant of Straits Knowledge, a Singapore-based firm specialising in Knowledge and Information Management. He holds a Master's degree from University College London in Information Studies and Librarianship, and he has worked as a professional librarian, as a trainer and instructional designer, and as a business manager in operational and strategic roles. He has been active in the field of knowledge management and e-learning since 1998, and is former President of the Information and Knowledge Society. He is also Adjunct Professor at Hong Kong Polytechnic University. Patrick speaks and writes internationally on knowledge management, and has conducted a number of taxonomy projects, usually as an integral part of larger knowledge management initiatives. Patrick is the author of *The Blind Tour Guide: Surviving and Prospering in the New Economy* (Times, 2002). His knowledge management writings are posted at *www.greenchameleon.com*.

The author may be contacted at:

E-mail: *plambe@straitsknowledge.com*

Defining our terms

To organise is to impose order, counteract deviations, simplify, and connect.
(Weick, 1995: 82)

This book is primarily written for knowledge and information managers, or for those responsible for knowledge and information management in their organisations. It is intended to help you commission, build and maintain taxonomies to aid you in your knowledge management efforts. As such, we'll focus more on the pragmatic than the pure. This is not as easy as it sounds; rigour and purity are two of the most intense seductions of taxonomy work.

Let's start with some working principles and definitions.

Can we organise knowledge?

Organising knowledge: what do we mean by this?

Karl Weick's definition of 'organise' given at the head of this chapter relates organising activity to sense-making activity. The same things that help us organise also help us make sense of the world around us. But organising goes further than sense-making. It enables us to act systematically and intentionally in relation to our environment and this is one of the primary activities of management.

It's not immediately obvious that you can organise knowledge unless you have a clear definition of what knowledge is, and knowledge is notoriously difficult to define without fear of contradiction or counter-proposal. Many would say that knowledge cannot be organised because it resides in people's minds and abilities. What *can* be organised is information, which resides in documents or other artefacts apart from people (Taylor, 2004: 3).

In a limited sense, such writers say, we can be said to organise our own private knowledge in the sense that we 'collect our thoughts' and 'structure' our thinking when preparing to express our knowledge, and we frequently plan how to 'deploy' our knowledge in specific situations. So there is a limited, mental sense of knowledge organisation, we are told, but not a public, objective one.

To a degree, these writers have a point. A great deal of so-called 'knowledge' management is simply information or data management in disguise. The confusion of knowledge with information and data has led to some of knowledge management's worst failures – overreliance on information processing technology and ignoring the issues of people, process, culture and trust that influence how knowledge actually gets created, shared and applied in human social groups. The overly simple distinction between tacit and explicit knowledge compounds this confusion, because it is all too easy to assume that information is simply explicit knowledge.

On the other hand, information management is not completely distinct from knowledge management. It's a very important part of knowledge management (Davenport and Marchand, 2000). Knowledge is externalised and communicated most obviously via information. So information organisation is also, by extension, knowledge organisation.

But if we step back from formal definitions for a moment and think about normal human knowledge activities, we can easily see that knowledge is also transferred or acquired through other means, such as observation, emulation, experimentation, the exercise of imagination in combination with memory, and the application of experience embodied in memory and habits.

Knowledge is not just expressed in documents containing information. It can be embedded in tools and designed artefacts (chairs 'teach' us how to sit, hammers 'teach' us how to hit a nail square and true). It can also be embedded in designed environments (an auditorium 'teaches us' how to project our voice, a coffee corner 'encourages us' to have conversations). It is found in ways of doing things, processes, unwritten scripts, routines, well-worn paths and habits.

Knowledge does not sit as an abstract, idealised entity inside people's heads, waiting to be consulted like a mysterious oracle, apart from the world of objects and documents, situations and customs, expressions and communications. It is inextricably mingled with this embodied, social world.

When we apply our knowledge we do so in a world that is mental, physical, emotional and social, and we do so using information and memory and tools and routines and observation. Much of this knowledge-world *can* be managed to support whatever objectives we have in mind. But to manage it, we need to have effective ways of organising it.

So information management, and the organisation of information, are important parts of knowledge management, but do not complete it. If we limit ourselves to the organisation of information and exclude other manifestations of knowledge, we also limit what we can achieve.

'We organise because we need to retrieve,' says Arlene Taylor in her textbook *The Organisation of Information*, and so far as information is concerned she's mostly right (Taylor, 2004: 1).

But when we broaden the scope to knowledge organisation, *we organise so that we can manage*. This includes retrieval, but it goes beyond retrieval and enables other interesting and useful tasks such as knowledge-building, identifying novel knowledge relationships, sense-making, managing complexity, diagnosis and decision-making, pushing knowledge assets in useful directions, and controlling the flow of knowledge and information. We'll look at some of these applications in more detail later on in this book.

The term 'knowledge' is still a slippery word. It's hard to pin down. But this doesn't mean that conscious organisational strategies cannot be applied to it. As we've seen, knowledge comes to the surface in a variety of guises: in people, in documents and artefacts, in memories and stories, in activities and patterns of behaviour. Many of these *can* be organised, and they *are* subject to management strategies.

We don't only use taxonomies to organise our knowledge; we have other devices as well. Theories and mental models provide structure and organise our knowledge for flexible application in the real world. Narratives and stories organise cultural and social knowledge, among other things. Tools and designed environments structure knowledge for particular operations. In building our social networks we organise our collective knowledge by giving everyone potential access to the knowledge distributed across the network. The knowledge we manipulate is fluid, touched by all these devices in different ways and at different times. These ways of organising form an ecology, within which taxonomies play an integral role.

For now, our main point is that knowledge organisation is not simply about locating and retrieving relevant knowledge, although this is important. *Knowledge organisation is a fundamental precondition for managing knowledge effectively.*

What are taxonomies?

Tell the ordinary person in the street that you build taxonomies for a living and you are likely to get the wary, half-respecting look of someone who has no idea what you do but is intimidated by the sound of what you say.

The more knowledgeable will associate you with an arcane branch of library science or biology, or less often with social anthropology. But whether your audience is ignorant or informed, you will have been labelled mentally as a specialist practising a rare and difficult art. The root 'tax' doesn't help – it suggests to the innocent hearer 'taxing' and 'taxes', neither very attractive ideas.

In fact, this impression manages to combine a grain of truth with a large quantity of misapprehension. Far from being a specialist art, the classification or taxonomic impulse is a fundamental ingredient of the way humans visualise and understand the world. Taxonomic activity exists in almost every domain of human activity – in fact, taxonomies provide the lenses by which we perceive and talk about the world we live in.

> [Classification] is almost the methodological equivalent of electricity – we use it every day, yet often consider it to be rather mysterious. (Bailey, 1994: 1)

The word taxonomy itself derives from two Greek stems: *taxis* and *nomos*. Liddell and Scott's *Greek–English Lexicon* describes the meaning of *nomos* as: 'anything assigned, usage or custom, law or ordinance'.

Taxis, broadly, means the arrangement or ordering of things, but it is used in ancient Greek quite flexibly to encompass the disposition of soldiers in military formation, a battle array, a body of soldiers, the arrangement, order or disposition of objects, order or regularity in general, ordinances, prescriptions or recipes, assessment of tributes or assigned rations (whence comes taxation), political order or constitution, rank, position or station in society, an order or class of men, lists, registers, accounts, payments, and land types, a treatise, a fixed point of time or a term of office.

So the term taxonomy means in general *the rules or conventions of order or arrangement*, and the variety of usage we've just seen reflects the extent to which taxonomies can enter daily life, from classes of people to the disposition of things, ideas, times and places.

This somewhat loose description will form our background definition, instead of the much narrower sense of taxonomy as it has evolved in the biological sciences (which we will discuss later).

However, for our purposes in knowledge management, this loose definition is not quite enough. We need slightly more specific guidance. In this chapter we'll be defining three key attributes of an effective taxonomy in knowledge management:

1. A taxonomy is a classification scheme.

2. A taxonomy is semantic.

3. A taxonomy is a knowledge map.

Let's examine each of these attributes in turn.

A taxonomy is a form of classification scheme

Classification schemes are designed to group related things together, so that if you find one thing within a category, it is easy to find other related things in that category. Notice that I am deliberately not using the term 'similar' things. Many classification schemes are indeed based on similarity of attributes, but we organise things in our world on the basis of many kinds of relationship, not just similarity. Examples might be functional proximity (things we do around the same time such as when we go shopping), causal relationships, the relationships embedded in organisational structures, and so on. Again, we are deliberately keeping our definitions broad and flexible, so as not to get trapped into a narrow and unnecessarily limited set of applications for taxonomies.

We use classification in every aspect of our lives. When we go to the supermarket for oranges, we know we are on the right track when we can see vegetables. When our e-mail inbox starts to get overwhelmed with e-mails, we create named subfolders and sort our e-mails into them for ease of retrieval later.

Classification schemes can be very informal and ad hoc, such as when we organise our bathroom cabinet or line up our music CDs by genre. They can also be highly formal and standardised. We might be familiar with some of the more well-known formal classification schemes, for example the Dewey Decimal Classification (DDC) in libraries, or the North American Industry Classification Scheme (NAICS) used in procurement functions or in official statistics.

Taxonomies are semantic

Taxonomies in knowledge (and records) management are a little different from formal published classification schemes. In libraries, classifications serve to summarise the subject matter of books and articles in an abbreviated code, which is usually also used as a means of locating the physical item in a fixed sequence on the shelves. Shared codes bring related books together physically. Classifications such as NAICS also focus on the use of shorthand codes as a standardised means of enabling information transfer and data manipulation. It can be used in a very wide variety of ways, for example in statistical returns, in company registrations or the provision of procurement services in electronic marketplaces.

Taxonomies in knowledge management do not usually rely on codes. They are primarily *semantic*. That is, they provide a fixed vocabulary to describe their knowledge and information assets, and this vocabulary needs to be meaningful and transparent to ordinary users. When content is labelled 'Project Kickoff', everybody should know what kinds of documents they can expect to find within that category.

In the language of librarianship and information science, a taxonomy also therefore provides *a controlled vocabulary*. It is controlled in the sense that the meaning of each label is carefully considered, and ambiguous, alternate or less precise terms are excluded. A new term is admitted to the taxonomy only when it clearly describes a commonly understood category of content for which there is currently no term.

This usually means that changes to the taxonomy are managed carefully. Changes are not random, and ordinary users cannot change them. This is very different from *folksonomies* which are completely user defined and which we will discuss towards the end of this book.

A taxonomy is also semantic in the sense that it expresses the *relationships* between terms in the taxonomy. In a taxonomy of driving, CAR : STEERING WHEEL would imply the relationship 'is a part of' between STEERING WHEEL and CAR. In the folder structure PROJECT DOCUMENTS : PROJECT KICKOFF we immediately recognise that we will find other types of project documents adjacent to the PROJECT KICKOFF folder, and we expect that they will be linked to the sequence of stages in a project.

If you take all of the labels in a taxonomy and put them into alphabetical order, you have your controlled vocabulary – a kind of dictionary of your taxonomy.

If you then take each term in your controlled vocabulary and describe its relationships with other terms in the taxonomy, you get a *thesaurus*.

In other words, a thesaurus is simply your taxonomy in dictionary format. A taxonomy on the other hand is a thesaurus with all the labels organised by subject. A taxonomy visually represents or maps the subject as a whole, while a thesaurus explains the topics one by one. A thesaurus may also have scope notes attached to each term, explaining what is included or excluded under the term – i.e. giving guidance on how the term should be applied.

A good thesaurus goes beyond your base taxonomy, however – it will also include all the other alternative words we use in common language for your 'controlled' terms – automobiles, for example, as an alternative term for 'CAR' – and point them to the authorised controlled term. These terms will not usually appear in your taxonomy (although they are sometimes included in 'scope notes' – explanatory notes describing the meaning of each category label). A good thesaurus will also highlight any other relevant relationships (see Figure 1.1).

Figure 1.1   Relationships in a thesaurus

CAR	broader term	MOTOR VEHICLES
	narrower term	STEERING WHEEL
	related term	VAN
	use for	MOTOR CAR
MOTOR CAR	use	CAR
MOTOR VEHICLES	narrower term	CAR
STEERING WHEEL	broader term	CAR
VAN	related term	CAR

An immediate and obvious use for a thesaurus is in a search engine. A good thesaurus can ensure that a whole range of commonly used synonyms that are *not* part of your controlled vocabulary can still retrieve relevant taxonomy categories. If a synonym means the same thing as a term in your taxonomy and has been associated with that term in the thesaurus, your non-taxonomy keyword will still be recognised and retrieve valid results.

A thesaurus can also help you deal with nasty homonyms – when the same word can mean different things. Let's say I'm searching for cheap flights to Ireland, and I type 'Dublin' into the box for destination airport. The page reloads with the question, 'Do you mean Dublin Ohio or Dublin Ireland?' The site has a thesaurus, and it is using that thesaurus to disambiguate two homonymous terms.

A taxonomy is a kind of knowledge map

The great military writer von Clausewitz speaks of the importance of the 'coup d'oeuil' for the experienced general. By this he means that with one 'cast of the eye' over the military situation, the general can immediately grasp its implications and start to anticipate appropriate courses of action (von Clausewitz, 1999: ch. 3). A good taxonomy should enable the same feat with regard to a knowledge domain for any of its users. With one 'coup d'oueil' any user of the taxonomy should immediately have a grasp of the overall structure of the knowledge domain covered by the taxonomy and be able to accurately anticipate what resources he or she might find where. The taxonomy should be comprehensive, predictable and easy to navigate.

Taxonomy as artificial memory

These features of a taxonomy (classified, semantic, a map of a knowledge domain that can be grasped as a whole) give it more than just navigational power. A taxonomy also acts as an artificial memory device. Concepts are 'located' in taxonomy structures and locked in place by association with their neighbours through their classification relationships, and this affords considerable mnemonic power.

There is a story told from antiquity of the poet Simonides, who supposedly invented the art of artificial memory – an important art for poets, storytellers, lawyers and politicians in mostly oral cultures. Simonides had been invited to entertain at a banquet, but failed to sufficiently flatter his host, preferring to honour the gods Castor and Pollux. Irritated, his client, Scopas, told him he'd better collect half his fee from the gods themselves. A few moments after, Simonides was asked to step outside to see two young men who were asking for him. He found nobody there, and was turning to go back inside when the roof of the banqueting chamber suddenly collapsed, killing all inside – including the god-mocking Scopas.

This is not just a story about paying your consultants their proper dues, however. Simonides' expertise was about to migrate from theologically efficacious poetry to memory. The corpses had all been crushed beyond recognition, and their families were distraught that they could not claim their own. However, Simonides was able to recall exactly where everybody had been sitting in the room, so from the location of the bodies was able to identify each one accurately.

The story of Simonides began a tradition of associating artificial memorisation with physical locations that was to last throughout antiquity and the Middle Ages and flowered in the late Renaissance into universal representations of mystical and earthly knowledge, before entering a steady decline as the printed book became a more public form of memory (Yates, 1984).

In the classical form of the art of memory, aspiring students of mnemonics were asked to recall a building with which they were familiar, and then imagine their progress through this building, passing from room to room. As they went, they were to associate the concepts they wished to remember with features of the rooms – perhaps a statue, or an arch, or a corner. An image for each of the concepts is imprinted on the spaces of their chosen building, so that they can recall with complete accuracy, in the exact sequence of memorisation, each of those concepts whenever they make an imaginary journey through their chosen building.

By the late sixteenth century, this technique had been modified to include imaginary buildings and not just buildings with which the memory artist is already familiar. In this version, the buildings are constructed by the imagination, and imprinted with images in the classical way. The Jesuit explorer Matteo Ricci taught a version of this mnemonic device which he called a 'memory palace' to the Chinese. In this method, you imagine entering a palace, and as you go from atrium to room to room, you populate the palace with images and objects representing the memories you wish to recall (Spence, 1984).

But as Ricci was teaching the Chinese, the memory tradition had already taken a more experimental turn, much closer to the role that taxonomy plays in organising knowledge.

Born in 1480, the eccentric scholar Giulio Camillo became the wonder of Europe after he devoted decades of his life to constructing a wooden 'memory theatre'. This was a physical structure, based upon the semi-circular classical theatre, which from contemporary accounts was large enough to accommodate at least two persons. The theatre was built to house the entirety of occult knowledge, and to the modern eye looked very much like a physical expression of a taxonomy. It was, for his time, revolutionary. Erasmus's correspondents gossiped to him about it, and the king of France paid Camillo a small fortune to have a copy constructed for him in Paris.

Camillo's structure was called a theatre, but it was also an inversion of a theatre – here, the visitor (the audience) stands on the central stage, and the dramatic presentation of the knowledge stored within happens in the divisions and tiers of the structure surrounding him. Camillo's theatre had seven divisions and seven levels and was supported by seven central pillars. Each division was named after the gods Diana, Mercury, Venus, Mars, Jupiter, Saturn and so on, representing the different divisions of occult knowledge. Each of the tiers represented a progression from earthly to heavenly knowledge.

In each of the classes so defined, Camillo had mnemonic images and representations to signify key concepts in the classical memory style, but he also stored behind each image writings and papers that explained the meanings and concepts being represented (Yates, 1984: ch. 6). Memory structures had become taxonomy structures. This was more than a library, where organisational structure follows collection of content. For Camillo, taxonomy came first and population followed. He had invented the world's first content management system, and his work demonstrates more than any other the powerful role that taxonomic structures can play in acting as memory aids as well as organisation aids.

Many of the taxonomies you will see look like hierarchies or tree structures, like the folder structure in your computer or the site map in your intranet. The structure of the tree visually represents the nature of the relationships between the categories and sub-categories, and this makes the map predictable, enabling navigation between categories. But a taxonomy doesn't have to be a tree. The simplest form of taxonomy is a list, and there are several other forms of representation. In our next chapter we'll consider the various ways of representing taxonomies such as:

- lists
- trees
- hierarchies
- polyhierarchies
- matrices
- facets
- system maps.

These are all perfectly valid ways of representing taxonomies, and each has its value and function. The primary purpose of a taxonomy representation is to help users understand and navigate the structure of the subject covered by the taxonomy. So long as it does that effectively, we should not be hung up on whether or not it looks like a generic textbook taxonomy tree structure.

Taxonomy work

We need to introduce one more concept that is important for our approach in this book, and that is the notion of *taxonomy work*. Taxonomies are products, things that can be used. But in many ways, the processes that produce our taxonomies are more important than the things themselves. This is because the taxonomies we develop in knowledge management need to reflect the working worlds of the organisations they are created for – and because those working worlds continue to change and evolve, so must our taxonomies. The days have long gone of the classification scheme that is developed and published and applied and forever more holds true. Continuing taxonomy work in an organisation is essential to keep a taxonomy relevant and alive.

Shifting our focus from the product to the processes has an interesting effect. It liberates us from the more conservative, narrower definitions of what taxonomies are and what they are for. It allows us to see the wide range of things we need to be able to do if we are to build relevant taxonomies and keep them working in support of organisational needs.

If taxonomies classify, describe and map knowledge domains, then taxonomy work is made up of the things we must do to achieve that outcome: listing, creating and modifying categories, standardising, mapping, representing, discovering native vocabularies and categories, negotiating common norms. These activities happen naturally in all organisations, more or less consciously. One of the goals of this book is to help make those activities more conscious.

With a more flexible concept of what taxonomies are and how they function in organisations, we are permitted to see the application of taxonomy work on a broader and more productive scale than if we simply see it as a means of organising documents for easy retrieval.

2

Taxonomies can take many forms

A good classification functions in much the same way that a theory does, connecting concepts in a useful structure. If successful, it is, like a theory, descriptive, explanatory, heuristic, fruitful, and perhaps also elegant, parsimonious, and robust.

(Kwasnik, 1999)

We ended our previous chapter by saying that taxonomies do not always need to be in a tree format. Our objective in this chapter is to understand the variety of forms that a taxonomy can take, and to appreciate the strengths and weaknesses of each. This grounding will give us added versatility in putting together our taxonomy development strategy later on. These are the taxonomy forms that we'll examine.

- lists
- trees
- hierarchies
- polyhierarchies
- matrices
- facets
- system maps.

Lists

Lists are the most basic form of taxonomies, and in fact list-making is a foundational activity for most other (more complex) ways of representing taxonomies.

We make lists all the time: when we are going shopping, when we are figuring out how to plan our day, when we want to 'sort things out' or make important decisions.

A list is simply a collection of related things; the relationship, usually, is defined by our purpose in making the list. Hence the name of the list ('shopping list', 'people I dislike', 'to-do list') often defines the relationships between the items of the list. Lists typically describe relationships of similarity or of sequence (e.g. the things we need to do to start a project). So the list satisfies our first two requirements for taxonomies: (1) in classifying related things together, and (2) in making their relationships obvious.

Most other, more complex taxonomy structures are simply about putting lists in relation to each other. Tree structures or system maps often grow from lists that got too complicated to handle – either a collection of lists of different things, or lists that have grown too long to be easily managed. As a general rule of thumb from the usability perspective, we start to have difficulty in easily comprehending and navigating a list that goes above 12–15 items. We'll look at some of the evidence for this in Chapter 8. Long lists require more complex structures to represent the content.

Consider a taxonomy of military rank in the British army. Hierarchy (as power structure) is present, but the rank hierarchy is most straightforwardly represented in the sequence of the list, not in a tree structure.

Field Marshal
General
Lieutenant-General
Brigadier
Colonel
Lieutenant-Colonel
Major
Captain
Lieutenant
Second Lieutenant

A tree structure only becomes relevant in this case when we want to describe an actual command structure with real people at each level – i.e. an organisational structure – or when we want to say numerous types of things about each rank. For example, we may want to define sub-categories for each rank containing lists of their insignias, pay scales, privileges and so on. Then a tree structure might start to emerge, and it will serve an entirely different purpose from the 'tree as command structure'. Trees can serve many different purposes, but the lists from which they grow can be just the same. Lists are the basic building blocks of taxonomies. The function that the taxonomy is intended to serve will guide the structure you adopt.

Taxonomy lists can be compiled based on the following characteristics or relationships:

- commonality in attributes or purpose (e.g. motivational factors, competencies required for jobs, engineers in my firm);
- collocation (e.g. living-room furniture, people in my department);
- sequence (e.g. project start-up activities, regular duties, activity cycles);
- chaining (e.g. cause and effect chains, stages in a manufacturing process);
- genealogy (e.g. parent–child relationships);
- gradients in attributes (e.g. from private to general, from tall to short, relative percentages of market share).

Tree structures

Using a branching tree structure to represent the transition from general to specific or from whole to part (the 'broader term/narrower term' in a thesaurus) is a very powerful way of representing relationships. When we looked at the list of military ranks above, we saw that adopting a tree structure allows us to add a lot of additional information in a structured way to a simple list.

The tree structure mirrors the way we manipulate our ideas of the world. However, it is so common that it often causes problems, because it can serve many different purposes (as we have just seen) and these purposes can easily get confused. For example, tree structures are easily confused with biological taxonomies, which actually work quite differently from knowledge taxonomies. More about that in our next section.

Tree structures are powerful because they reflect the way we think. In human perception we naturally identify 'basic level categories'. These are not, as we might think, the most granular, atomistic elements in our world. They tend to be whole objects that we can identify and act upon in a direct way. Linguistically we usually have shorter and simpler names for them compared to other objects, and they tend to be accessible things that populate our everyday world.

We generalise upwards from these basic level categories (e.g. from the pine tree in my garden to trees in general, or from 'monthly project status report' to 'reports') based on *similarities* or resemblances.

We differentiate downwards from these basic level categories to more specific levels based on discriminating *differences*, distinctions or whole/part relations.

So, in practice, we don't usually reason from most general in the direction of most specific, nor from most specific to most general. Human beings start in the middle, and from there we generalise up, and differentiate down (Lakoff, 1987: 31–8). This has important implications for how people will use our taxonomies, and we will have to consider this later when we look at how a taxonomy should be designed.

The tree structure supports this basic cognitive operation beautifully (with the single exception that the use of a tree wrongly implies we start cognitively at the most general level). It clusters families of related things together bound by a common superordinate label or concept. It mirrors the way we see our families and our tribes and how we organise the 'stuff' of our lives.

The tree structure also works much better than a list does as a mnemonic for the world around us. If we recall the 'memory palace' technique of Matteo Ricci from Chapter 1, you construct your imaginary palace and begin in the entrance hall, which is imprinted with the three or four main classes of things that you want to remember. In each of the rooms branching from this hall, you place further imaginary items representing the more detailed things you want to remember. From each of those rooms, you can have three more doors (in fact, in your own memory palace you can define as many doorways as you want) and so, room by room, you build a memory system of thoughts, all rooted in the first set of ideas represented in your hallway and all branching out from that central node in a classic tree structure (Spence, 1984).

So the tree structure turns out to be a powerful technique for visualising and structuring memory, and it's also a powerful taxonomic representation device. The metaphor of 'containers within containers' with a path leading from one idea to further ideas in a structured and predictable way is exactly mirrored in our ready adoption of the digital folder structure metaphor in our organisations – although the palace metaphor sounds more interesting!

Like the memory palace technique, tree structures are very versatile. They can express several different kinds of relationship: general to specific; concept to example; cause to effect; parent to child; whole to part; group to member; container to contained (see Table 2.1).

Table 2.1   Kinds of relationship expressed in a tree structure

Taxonomy	Superordinate term	Subordinate term	Relationship term
Military rank	General	Colonel	Power/authority
Biology	Genus	Species	Common evolutionary history
Family	Parent	Child	Genealogical
Vehicles	Car	Steering wheel	Whole : part
History	1960s	Assassination of JFK	Period : event
Geography	United States	Alaska	Whole : part
Landscape	Mountain	Everest	General : specific
Terrorism	Al Qaeda	Osama Bin Laden	Group : member
Disease control	Infection	Symptoms	Causality, sequence

In all of the cases in Table 2.1 a tree would be an acceptable means of representing the relationships between superordinates and subordinates, but the relationships being described are sometimes 'contained within', sometimes 'more important than', sometimes 'generated by', sometimes 'caused by', sometimes 'share common history'.

Very often our trees are not 'pure' in the sense that subdivisions in one part of the same tree can mean 'x is a part of y', in another place 'X is a specific instance of the general category Y', and 'xx is a stage in the process yy' in yet another place. Trees are both pragmatic and versatile, and our main caution is simply to ensure that the relationship between a superordinate term and a subordinate term is not ambiguous.

Hierarchies

We earlier showed how a hierarchy can be presented as a list. But in taxonomy work, a hierarchy is a very specific kind of tree structure. It causes problems in taxonomy building for knowledge management because many people think that a taxonomy needs to have the specific features of a hierarchical structure in order to be valid. This is not always a helpful line to take. Trees are one thing, but hierarchies are another.

> Taxonomies are structures that provide a way of classifying things – living organisms, products, books – into a series of hierarchical groups to make them easier to identify, study, or locate. (Graef, 2001)

> In recent years, the business world has fallen in love with the term 'taxonomies'. We use it specifically to refer to a hierarchical arrangement of categories within the user interface of a web site or intranet. (Rosenfeld and Morville, 2002: 65)

Describing taxonomies as hierarchies can be confusing because hierarchy means different things in different disciplines. In sociology and anthropology hierarchy signifies the relative disposition of power and as we saw in the military example, the flow of power is not always best represented as a tree structure.

Take the Indian caste system, for example. Hierarchy is best represented as a pyramid or a list rather than as a tree, because a hierarchical tree would mistakenly suggest that Brahmanic power over Dalits is mediated exclusively through the other castes, or that Dalits are a part of Brahmana, or are a variety of Shudra, and so on (see Figure 2.1).

The same goes for our organisational hierarchies of chief executive officers (CEOs), vice presidents, general managers, supervisors and front-line workers. A front-line worker does not inherit the attributes of a CEO by virtue of being at the end of the hierarchical chain. If we want to express power relationships, then a pyramidical tree works perfectly well. If we want to collect information assets about each level of employee, then a simple list is the most effective way to do it. A hierarchical nested tree of employee types would be misleading and inefficient for collecting together information assets about them but perfectly reasonable for a representation of authority relationships.

Figure 2.1   **Effective and ineffective ways of representing caste**

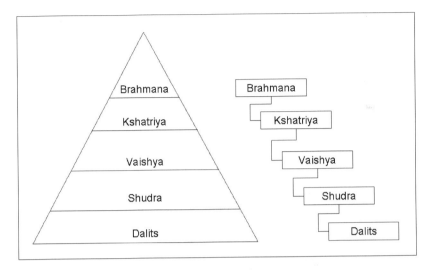

In the humanities such as religion, literature or education, hierarchy can also be ascribed to relative importance. We talk about 'classics' or 'canonical' or 'primary' texts, and we distinguish them from lesser texts, apocrypha, 'secondary' literature, 'popular' literature and commentary (McArthur, 1986: 37). In our teaching bibliographies we hand our students carefully composed taxonomies of reading matter containing 'core' and 'supplementary' reading matter.

In management theory we discriminate (e.g. in Porter's value chain model) between the primary activities of a firm (e.g. procurement, manufacture, marketing, sales and service) and the secondary activities (e.g. human resources, finance, information technology and strategic management). Maslow's 'hierarchy of needs' (see Figure 2.2) is used in human resources to identify motivating/demotivating factors again in terms of their relative importance, except that in his hierarchy Maslow inverts the structure to ascribe 'foundational' importance to the more basic needs at the bottom of his pyramid. Once again, lists are better than trees for this set of distinctions.

In the pure sciences, as well as in information and library science, hierarchy has a very different and a very precise sense. The requirements for a 'scientific' hierarchy include (Kwasnik, 1999: 4–5):

- *Inclusiveness* – the top category 'includes' all subordinate categories in the tree. (So our Indian caste system does not qualify as a scientific

Figure 2.2   Maslow's hierarchy of needs

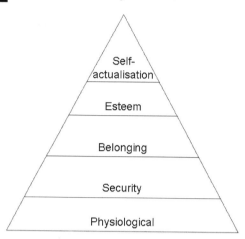

hierarchy because the Brahmana caste does not contain all subordinate castes.)

- *Relational consistency* – the kind of relationship between each level in the hierarchy is exactly the same relationship. (So 'steering wheel *is a part of* a car, which is a *kind of* vehicle' would fail this requirement because the relationships change from *part of* to *kind of* as you move up the tree.)

- *Inheritance* – subordinate categories in a hierarchy inherit all of the attributes of superordinate categories, which makes it easier to focus just on the differentiating attributes and makes hierarchical taxonomies very economical to use – by knowing which branch of the tree we are in we can already say a lot about anything we find in that branch. (Again, our Indian caste hierarchy fails this criterion – all castes are mutually exclusive, and the lower castes inherit nothing from the castes above them in the hierarchy.)

- *Mutual exclusivity* – an entity can belong in one and only one class which is why this strict sense of hierarchy is so attractive – it eliminates ambiguity completely. (Unfortunately for us, while biological objects tend to follow these rules automatically in consequence of the laws of genetics, other manufactured objects and mental objects don't.)

Scientific hierarchies are very attractive in principle because of the way they eliminate ambiguity, enforce consistency, ensure rigorous observation and knowledge of the field, and identify relationship rules that produce predictability. Beautiful, you might think, for making knowledge content easily findable.

Think again. In practice, the world (and especially the world of organisational knowledge) is by no means as tidy or as well-defined as the scientific paradigm would suggest. Many of the categories we work with in normal life overlap with each other and sometimes compete. They rebel furiously against being pinned down.

Take a typical organisational chart. We have a beautiful tree structure which actually says inconsistent things at different points, mixing up 'hierarchy as authority' relations at the upper levels with 'tree as division of parts' relations at the lower levels (see Figure 2.3). Conceptually we have no problem with such transitions in meaning within the same tree structure, just as we have no conceptual problem with the sequence VEHICLE : CAR : STEERING WHEEL moving from 'kind of' relations to 'part of' relations in the same tree structure.

Figure 2.3 Hierarchical tree used to represent a corporate structure

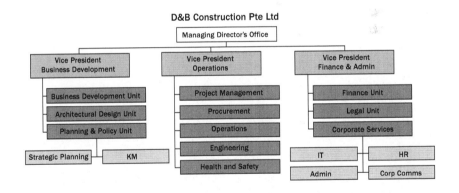

We are not only inconsistent. Our everyday categories are also often ambiguous. Let's say we have a category in our corporate taxonomy for 'presentations'. We know that people go looking for presentations. They say 'I want that presentation we did for so and so ...' So it seems like a useful category to have. Most of our presentation files are meant as communication documents, supporting a spoken delivery. So we make them subordinate to 'Communications' along with corporate brochures and press releases and other internally focused communications.

But we also have training materials which are partially packaged as presentation slides. Do we put them into the Communications folder, or into the Learning and Training folder? Formally they have the same attributes as the communications presentations but functionally they serve different purposes.

What seemed at first like a simple distinction (Communications vs Learning and Training) has been undermined by our very human tendency to mix and match categories and blur boundaries.

Librarians are familiar with this dilemma, as are supermarket managers. Where should a book on the history of economics go – into history, or economics? It cannot in good conscience go into both. Someone has to decide, and you can bet it will not be an objective decision based on matching attributes of the object to the attributes of the category.

Where should ice cream be classified, with slightly chilled dairy products where it will melt, or frozen foods where it jostles with meat and vegetables?

At the end of the day, most of our categorisation decisions are pragmatic ones, which is why information scientists need to forget a lot of their training if they are to design knowledge taxonomies that work in practice.

Inexperienced taxonomists, brought up in the tradition of scientific taxonomic correctness, still believe that there can only be one correct place for any item, and agonise for hours over the correct place for the item to go. Don't. It's not worth it. Put it where it's most likely to be found and used.

The librarian will place the book where he sees it being most easily found by the clients – if it's on the economics faculty reading list and not the history list, the decision is made. The supermarket manager is going to bet on keeping the ice cream frozen. And if the Learning and Training folder has nothing in it, the departmental knowledge manager might well put the training presentation file into the Communications folder, unless he or she expects more training materials to come along soon to join the lonely orphan file.

We have additional problems when we move from the observable attributes of a thing to culturally defined concepts. As human beings we love ambiguity, and we habitually manipulate categories that refuse to play the scientific consistency game. Our taxonomies and our categories are also shaped by what's important to us both individually and culturally – even if these influences are inconsistent or in competition.

A 'bachelor' defined as an unmarried adult male only exists as a category in a society that sees heterosexual marriage as an idealised norm. We are quite comfortable with the term, but we conveniently pass over in silence the counter-examples of divorced men, widowers, gay partners, Catholic priests or Tarzan, none of whom would qualify for the category of bachelor, but all of whom possess all of the necessary attributes to be a bachelor (Lakoff, 1987: 70).

It's hard to define a category 'bachelor' on the basis of intrinsic attributes alone – it can only be defined by knowing the exceptions to the rule and referring to a cultural norm. The categories of 'terrorist' and 'freedom fighter' are just as difficult to pin down based on objective observation of attributes and behaviours alone. Some people formerly described as terrorists become prime ministers and presidents, and history changes their classification even though their internal properties remain the same. Other people do not get reclassified. We need cultural conventions – and cultural *positions* – to help us make the distinction between a terrorist and a freedom fighter. And the fact that different people take different positions at the same time means that our categorisations also diverge and compete.

The world of tidy, mutually exclusive categories evenly distributed across nested hierarchies and based on objective observation of attributes is a pipe dream. As human beings, we manipulate many competing category systems simultaneously, and we often don't care about accurate or complete belonging to categories.

'Climbing' belongs to the category of upward movement (we might think), but we also say 'he climbed out onto the ledge' where horizontal movement is implied, or 'he climbed down from the tree'. We accept 'climbing' in this case because of the grasping and pulling action, not the upward movement. But we also accept 'the aircraft climbed to 20,000 feet' with no grasping and pulling movement involved (Lakoff, 1987: 20).

The key lesson from these 'messy' categories is that the 'scientific' sense of a taxonomy as a strict hierarchy is attractive from a distance, but rarely useful in practice when building knowledge management taxonomies. Here much of the knowledge and information we are working with is not susceptible to scientific observation and does not adhere to predictable or consistent behaviours. Social psychologist Stanley Milgram expressed this well when he was trying to figure out the difference between people's mental perceptions of their city and the objective reality. 'The main problem in investigating a mental entity is to learn how to render it observable. The person's mental image of Paris is not like his driver's license, something he can pull out for inspection' (Milgram, 1992). Our confusions and vaguenesses and ambiguities are reflected in what Peter Morville describes as the 'slippery slope of semantics':

> It's all about words. Words as labels. Words as links. Keywords. And words are messy little critters. Imprecise and undependable, their meaning shifts with context. One man's paradise is another man's oblivion. Synonyms, antonyms, homonyms, contranyms: the challenges of communication are part of the human condition, unsusceptible to the eager advances of technology. (Morville, 2005: 15)

And at the end of the day not even the sciences can resolve all categorisation uncertainty through the discipline of a strict hierarchical model. Even in the supposedly mature taxonomic field of biology, there is vehement debate among those who classify organisms on the basis of their physical characteristics and those who classify based on genetic history. Organisms end up in different taxonomic positions as a result.

Scientific taxonomies are also very different from knowledge management taxonomies in another important way. In a biological taxonomy based on physical characteristics, you will find the things being classified – actual organisms – only towards the ends of the taxonomic tree, at the species level. As you progress up to the genus level and above, you will find no real entities attached to the higher level categories. There is no such thing as a '*Homo*' animal (the genus to which the species *Homo sapiens* belongs) – the genus (and anything above the genus) is an abstraction to describe the family of all '*Homo xxx*' species.

This is different from a library classification scheme, for example, where you will find entities (books) being assigned at very general levels high up in the tree as well as at more specific levels of the taxonomy, and this will be true for your knowledge management and records management taxonomies as well. This sometimes causes problems, when an electronic document management system is designed on the biological model and only allows the assignment of documents to the lowest nodes in the hierarchy.

Knowledge objects can be either general or specific whereas physical objects can only be specific. Your taxonomies will need to accommodate generic content as well as highly specific content. Each level of your taxonomy may well have content attached, and your taxonomy needs to be designed for this – as well as your supporting technology.

Hence biology does not provide a terribly good model for knowledge management taxonomy building, though it teaches us about the virtues of consistency and disambiguation. It's better to stick with trees.

We started this section by saying that a taxonomy is a kind of knowledge map. The way in which it visually represents the relationships between categories should inform you about the structure of the subject area and help you navigate through the subject. We've already seen that trees are powerful devices for helping us do that; in the case of the scientific hierarchy, however, the messy world of knowledge that we deal with is not susceptible to such strict management.

A key objective in representing a taxonomy is to help users understand and navigate the subject area covered. Hence the structure you choose must inform the user about the structure of the subject.

Polyhierarchies

Polyhierarchies are an attempt to cope with the fact that in an untidy ambiguous world, pure hierarchies and even the more versatile tree structure don't do the full job. Sometimes items belong in more than one class, as we have already seen. In a polyhierarchy, items that belong in more than one class have their relationships mapped to more than one superordinate concept. Polyhierarchies are hierarchies that break their own rules.

Polyhierarchies usually arise when you have more than one main organising principle at work. For example, you could organise diseases by body area (diseases of the eye, ear, heart, etc.) or you can organise them by cause (bacterial, viral, genetic, dietary). Viral pneumonia would then be a sub-category under two hierarchies of disease, the body parts classification and the causal agents classification (Rosenfeld and Morville, 2002: 202).

As Rosenfeld and Morville point out, polyhierarchies are problematic for taxonomy representation, because if you cross-connect too many hierarchies, you start to lose your sense of regular, consistent structure – the very thing that a hierarchy is meant to enforce. Far more useful ways of dealing with this same problem (where items belong to more than one category or can be categorised in several alternative ways) are provided by the topics covered in our next two sections, *matrices* and *facets*.

Matrices

One of the most interesting alternative ways of representing a taxonomy is the matrix structure. Matrices are also known in social sciences as typologies (Bailey, 1994: 4), in library sciences as paradigms (Kwasnik, 1999) and sometimes they turn up as interlinked polyhierarchies in information architecture (Rosenfeld and Morville, 2002: 202). Probably the best known taxonomy presented as a matrix is the periodic table of elements (see Figure 2.4).

The horizontal axis of the table is arranged from left to right in rising order of atomic mass. The vertical axis is arranged by similar arrangement of electrons, which happens to give the elements in each column similar chemical properties, despite their wide differences in atomic mass. In fact, Dmitri Mendeleev, who constructed the first periodic table, arranged the elements in columns by similarity of properties before electron structures had been identified. This arrangement was only subsequently explained (and vindicated) by similarity of electron structure.

Arranging the elements in this way did two interesting things for science. First, it helped to make sense of the 'periodicity' of elements – where elements exhibit similar properties at regular intervals of atomic mass increase. Secondly, representing the elements in a matrix enabled scientists to identify gaps in the table where elements that were previously unknown should exist.

Hence the taxonomy helped explain behaviours and gave predictive power by identifying new elements that scientists could hunt for – and were subsequently discovered or manufactured in the laboratory – simply because their 'place' in the taxonomy was unfilled. Discovering and displaying the periodicity of behaviour by organising by mass and electron structure allowed scientists to predict new elements – essentially to create new knowledge.

This turns out to be a strong feature of matrix representations. They are extremely useful for sense-making as well as for new knowledge creation or discovery. Sense-making is important for the theme of this book because, as Karl Weick points out, 'sense-making' and 'organising' are very similar activities – they both involve ordering things, explaining deviations, simplification and explaining relationships (Weick 1995: 82).

In management, the most visible and common use of matrices is in sense-making. The 'two by two' matrix beloved of consultants is beloved for a reason. It gives shape to an ambiguous and uncertain business environment by helping us to classify items into that environment according to (usually) two important dimensions. Let's take the well known Boston Consulting Group (BCG) Matrix as an example (see Figure 2.5). To use this matrix, you take your organisation's products or

Figure 2.4 Periodic table in Mendeleev's format

Group →	1	2	3	4	5	6	7	8	9	10	11	12	13	14	15	16	17	18
↓ Period																		
1	1 H																	2 He
2	3 Li	4 Be											5 B	6 C	7 N	8 O	9 F	10 Ne
3	11 Na	12 Mg											13 Al	14 Si	15 P	16 S	17 Cl	18 Ar
4	19 K	20 Ca	21 Sc	22 Ti	23 V	24 Cr	25 Mn	26 Fe	27 Co	28 Ni	29 Cu	30 Zn	31 Ga	32 Ge	33 As	34 Se	35 Br	36 Kr
5	37 Rb	38 Sr	39 Y	40 Zr	41 Nb	42 Mo	43 Tc	44 Ru	45 Rh	46 Pd	47 Ag	48 Cd	49 In	50 Sn	51 Sb	52 Te	53 I	54 Xe
6	55 Cs	56 Ba	*	72 Hf	73 Ta	74 W	75 Re	76 Os	77 Ir	78 Pt	79 Au	80 Hg	81 Tl	82 Pb	83 Bi	84 Po	85 At	86 Rn
7	87 Fr	88 Ra	**	104 Rf	105 Db	106 Sg	107 Bh	108 Hs	109 Mt	110 Ds	111 Rg	112 Uub	113 Uut	114 Uuq	115 Uup	116 Uuh	117 Uus	118 Uuo

* Lanthanides	57 La	58 Ce	59 Pr	60 Nd	61 Pm	62 Sm	63 Eu	64 Gd	65 Tb	66 Dy	67 Ho	68 Er	69 Tm	70 Yb	71 Lu
** Actinides	89 Ac	90 Th	91 Pa	92 U	93 Np	94 Pu	95 Am	96 Cm	97 Bk	98 Cf	99 Es	100 Fm	101 Md	102 No	103 Lr

services, and you categorise them along two dimensions: market growth rate (vertically) mapped against relative market share (horizontally).

Figure 2.5   Boston Consulting Group Matrix

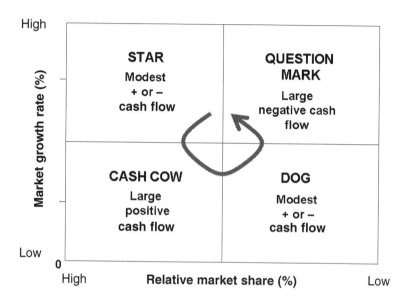

The point of the matrix is to support strategic decisions about your product development cycle, so it includes assumptions about the life cycle of a product or service in the marketplace, and hence the relationships between each of the four main categories. A product life cycle starts as a speculative innovation ('Question mark') and ends with being a drain on resources ('Dog'). 'Cash cows' are your bread and butter, but they will mature and die and they need a pipeline of growing 'Stars' behind them.

To be commercially healthy, you need to be exploring 'Question marks' (for which you can temporarily tolerate negative cash flow) that you might be able to turn into 'Stars' – innovative new products that will be accepted readily by the marketplace. 'Stars' over time need to be turned into 'Cash cows' that can be milked, and the signal that this needs to happen is when the product is considered mature and when market growth slows down. 'Dogs' are products or services that no longer have growth potential but also have low market share. They are a dead weight on the organisation and need to be dropped.

Using this matrix, a whole host of specific decisions can be generated by teaching managers how to 'see' and describe the implications of their product behaviour. It also provides a single, easy-to-comprehend map of an organisation's whole product or service suite so that managers can check the relative health of their overall portfolio.

Just like in the periodic table, by categorising their products into the matrix they also can see if they have gaps that they need to fill. The lack of a 'Star' or a 'Question mark' is a warning signal that product innovation needs to be stepped up. The lack of a 'Dog' is reassuring, and the lack of a 'Cash Cow' explains why you are not profitable and tells you that you need to be commoditising some of your 'Stars'.

Matrices are very good for when you want to categorise your content along multiple dimensions. They allow you to compare things, locate issues, problems or opportunities, create inventories and checklists, identify gaps, and describe complex phenomena. By comparison, a tree structure subdivides a group on the basis of only one dimension at a time (e.g. 'is a part of' or 'is a specific instance of' or 'is produced by'), so really only helps you locate and retrieve things either mentally or physically.

Matrices are most effective when categorising along two dimensions, but they can also be quite useful in three dimensions. Indeed, in physical chemistry, advances in science have determined that the periodicity of the elements is not completely explained just by changes in atomic mass and electron structure, but other factors are at play as well. This has resulted in numerous variations on the original Mendeleev model, including the three-dimensional Alexander version in Figure 2.6.

To put this into an information management context, let's consider a taxonomy structure for an engineering company's project documentation. In this real example, there were three important organising principles at play: the stages of the project, the types of document that need to be available to people and the different project roles that people play.

A three-dimensional matrix could display the taxonomy as shown in Figure 2.7. You can use any of the three axes to navigate to any given set of documents, from the perspective of project stage, project role or type of documentation required. This is a much more flexible presentation than a tree structure, which must decide which dimension takes priority.

If we use a tree structure, we have multiple dilemmas to resolve. Do we subdivide first on project stages (in which case role-specific documents and document types are scattered across the branches of the tree) or by role (which scatters project stages and document types beneath the first layer) or by document type (which hides project structure and roles)? Invariably a decision made on one front means that

Figure 2.6   Three-dimensional Alexander periodic table

alternative approaches to the same content are compromised – which means that people who prefer to approach the content in a different way from the primary organising principle of the tree are not being served.

And in a large collection of content where these simple subdivisions are not enough and you need to subdivide by further sub-stages within each project stage or sub-roles within a project or subdivisions of content type, the complexity produced by a tree structure is magnified enormously, whereas a matrix structure will cope relatively gracefully – at least up to three dimensions of categorisation.

Murphy's Law of taxonomies states that 'Whichever organising principle you choose will automatically be different from that of the majority of taxonomy users'. As Melvil Dewey, creator of the Dewey Decimal Classification is reported to have once said, 'Let me tell you how dangerous it is [to design a classification scheme]. It's very dangerous. I have suffered. People attribute all kinds of motives to you. Apart from that, if anything goes wrong, they will pounce upon you.' He

Figure 2.7 Matrix representation for an engineering project taxonomy

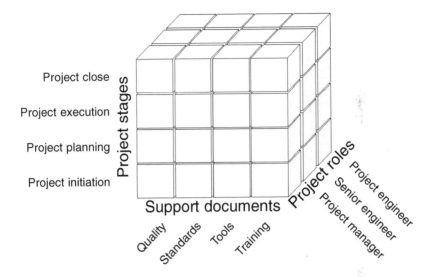

was writing to the creator of an alternative classification scheme at the time, so this may not have been an entirely disinterested statement, but it does smack of bitter experience. Tree structures do not accommodate alternative points of view very effectively. Matrices do so very well, for two to three alternative approaches to the content.

To an extent, our reliance on trees over matrices in knowledge management systems is influenced by the lack of availability of alternative metaphors for visual navigation. The folder structure is a powerful visual metaphor and is deeply embedded in programming conventions as well as user expectations, and this drives taxonomy representation towards the tree structure even when it is not always appropriate to do so.

Above three dimensions of categorisation, it becomes more difficult to represent taxonomies as a matrix. It's difficult to organise the content visually for easy comprehension and navigation – our third basic requirement for a good knowledge management taxonomy.

But clever design can help. Three dimensional does not even always have to be 3D. In Figure 2.8 we see an interactive career map produced by LearnDirect, a learning advice network of the UK's University for Industry. It maps skills, interests and jobs using an overlay of three parallel taxonomy dimensions – one for job categories, one for skill sets and one for interest orientations.

Figure 2.8 Career advice matrix from LearnDirect UK

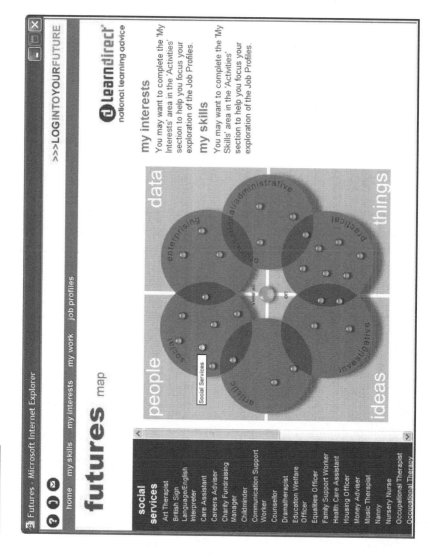

In this case the three dimensions have been overlaid, one on top of the other. Although it doesn't look like a traditional matrix, it works perfectly as a matrix taxonomy – the intersections between dimensions are clearly understood, the relationships between constituent parts are clearly understood, and you can navigate to job lists, or conduct a sense-making exercise (answer questions about your job preferences) or identify training and learning opportunities based on desired jobs. It's an excellent example of clever and innovative design in support of a taxonomy.

Facets

In 1932, Indian librarian S.R. Ranganathan published his *Colon Classification*. In fact, he was the person to whom Melvil Dewey had complained in 1931 about the dangers of developing your own classification scheme. Ever an inveterate self-publicist and intellectual entrepreneur, perhaps Dewey feared competition.

However, Dewey need not have feared, because while Ranganathan's scheme was profoundly innovative, it had to wait some seventy years before its foundational principles found their true medium for success – the digital content collection. To understand why, we need to dip briefly into the history of library science.

The primary function of a library classification scheme has until very recently been to enable clients to find a physical book on a physical shelf. They have been used to serve other subsidiary purposes, but this was their main intent and role for many years. In earlier centuries, with fewer books in libraries, booklists would normally be sufficient, with perhaps distinctions for the different sizes of books. As collections grew, basic categories developed, but with the mechanisation of the publishing industry in the nineteenth century this was no longer enough. More detailed schemes were required to identify an accurate and predictable location for any book that might be produced.

Various library classification schemes were developed throughout the last quarter of the nineteenth century, beginning a struggle for dominance between different classification standards. Broadly speaking, Dewey's Decimal Classification (originally developed in 1876) ended up dominating the public library market, while the Library of Congress Classification dominated the academic library market, with numerous niche classification schemes being developed for specialist libraries.

In library science language, the common feature of all these schemes is that they are *pre-coordinated and enumerative*. This simply means that the entire domain of knowledge needs to be mapped out in advance, and a specific location 'number' identified for any conceivable new book. Furthermore, it presupposes that there is only one place for any book in a classification scheme, resulting in the librarians' dilemmas that we referred to earlier. Where should a book that covers two different categories be placed? A decision always has to be made, and it always has to be one place (though librarians often cheat in the name of pragmatism).

As Ranganathan realised, this approach to classification has a number of problems. First, books are rarely as straightforward as enumerative schemes would like. They frequently cover multiple topics and categories. Second, the universe of knowledge is constantly expanding and producing new knowledge domains, or combining old domains in new ways – life sciences and nanotechnology are good recent examples of this. Pre-coordination is very difficult in new or rapidly changing knowledge domains, because the possible future needs of the classification scheme are not yet known.

Ranganathan's *Colon Classification*, which was based on what he called an *analytico-synthetic method* to contrast it with the enumerative method, rested on two key innovations: *facet analysis* and *post-coordination*. Recognising that a single book often relates to multiple categories, he analysed the content of books into five fundamental types of categories which he called facets. The five fundamental facets, according to Ranganathan's mature theory are (Ranganathan, 1967):

- *Personality* – the main topic or orientation of the book.
- *Matter* – the things or materials that the book talks about.
- *Energy* – the actions or changes discussed in the book.
- *Space* – the places or locations referred to in the book.
- *Time* – the times, periods or chronology covered in the book.

In the *analytic* part of his approach, each facet works like a mini-classification scheme or mini-taxonomy, and the book is analysed into each *relevant* facet (not all books are relevant to all facets). Library students remember this basic set of facets by the acronym PMEST. Remember this acronym – it will be useful later on.

The *synthetic* part of his approach comes when the book has been analysed into the five main facets. Each component is then combined in the citation order P:M:E:S:T. In his original classification, Ranganathan uses colons to separate the facet codes to distinguish his scheme from the decimal points used in Dewey and the punctuation of Library of Congress – hence the name of his classification scheme.

What was so different about Ranganathan's scheme? Well, unlike the other enumerative schemes where librarians had to locate a single 'correct' pre-coordinated number for each book, in Ranganathan's scheme they built a classification code that expressed the precise content of the book from the basic building blocks of the facets.

It was a *post-coordinated* scheme, and therefore by definition theoretically hospitable to whatever new fields of knowledge might emerge. The expressive notation of the scheme also means that every element in the notation of a *Colon Classification* code expresses an aspect of the book's subject – an important precursor of the semantic taxonomies we use today.

The major problem with Ranganathan's scheme, however, was the set of basic limitations imposed by the physical world. A major objective of a library classification scheme is to locate a book in a physical sequence on a shelf in such a way that its location can easily be predicted by library users.

While his scheme enabled precise subject *description*, the added requirement to be able to locate the physical item in a fixed sequence led to the need for complex ways of determining the citation order and compiling his classification code (i.e. which elements are more important than the others, and in what sequence they follow each other). His scheme has always, for that reason, been very difficult to implement in a physical library collection – for both librarians and library users.

At the end of the day, a physical book generally speaking still needs to end up in one and only one precise place in a library, for reasons of reducing ambiguity as much as economics. Ranganthan's scheme accommodated the ambiguity and complexity of much of the content of published books, but the limitations of the physical world meant that the enumerative, pre-coordinated schemes still had a distinct advantage in their simplicity and predictability of use. Dewey need not have worried.

In fact, for its first fifty years of life, Ranganathan's scheme found much more success in the world of subject indexing than in libraries because of its analytical and descriptive power.

All that changed in the late 1990s, when Ranganathan's theory of facet analysis and post-coordination found new life among the people trying to solve the challenges posed by large corporate collections of digital content.

Here, large, deep pre-coordinated taxonomies didn't make sense, because change was a constant force in the information and knowledge landscape. In banking and telecommunications, for example, deregulation opened up markets, redefined markets and business functions, and increased demands for information about the external competitive environment. The development of new products and services spawned their own new worlds of information and knowledge assets.

Major external events could have significant impact on the nature of business, and the nature of information management requirements surrounding that business. Just to take one example, in banking and finance, the aftermath of the 9/11 terrorist attacks in the USA saw increased attention to anti-money laundering measures, on the premise that terrorist groups were using money laundering techniques to conceal their funding channels. Here was a whole new domain that banking, financial and other commercial organisations had to internalise very quickly, just to keep up with new legislative requirements.

In the wake of the same events, under international and internal pressure for better governance infrastructure, national banks in Muslim countries began to take on more oversight and to develop deeper knowledge of Islamic banking operations, many of which had previously remained in the informal banking sector and were therefore at risk of being misused in support of terrorist activities. One influential event rippled into significant new knowledge and information needs.

In corporate life, corporate scandals such as that of Enron brought in the Sarbanes-Oxley legislation in the USA, imposing new information and records management requirements.

Each new move meant new domains of knowledge, required new dimensions of information infrastructure, and placed fresh demands for flexible and hospitable taxonomies. Taxonomies that could not keep up would not reflect the new categories of content, and that meant that this content would remain invisible to the general users of these information systems and content repositories.

If sophisticated pre-coordination didn't make sense, neither did an enumerative approach that said 'one location for every document'. In the physical world, there is a real cost in terms of both ambiguity and replication cost to have a physical document or book in more than one place in a collection. In a digital world, there is no replication cost, because the same document can appear to be in multiple places depending on how it has been tagged or indexed. Ambiguity can be managed by having a set of clearly defined facets, each of which is clearly distinguished from the others.

Faceted taxonomies are also uniquely well positioned to take advantage of the way that metadata works. *We define metadata as the collection of structured information about a document or piece of content.* For example, author, title, subject keywords, date of publication, place of publication, archiving date and access permissions are all individual pieces of metadata that might be associated with a document.

Each facet of your taxonomy can be incorporated as a separate field in your metadata record, and each of these fields can be made searchable by your search engine. This means you are not constrained by a single classification decision ('it's either a presentation document or a training document'), but you will be able to find the content by searching any of the dimensions in which it has been classified (e.g. by function or by document type). To go back to our engineering project example earlier, you will be able to find the same document whether you search by project stage, or project role, or document type – provided it has metadata fields for each facet and provided it has been classified under each facet.

In addition, facets tend to be much simpler and shallower than tree and hierarchy taxonomies, because each facet only takes one aspect of the content into account and does not need to account for different combinations of attributes. This makes them much easier to navigate and use. In fact, many facets are simply lists.

A facet then can be defined as a base taxonomy comprising only one of the fundamental dimensions in which content can be analysed. Working with faceted classification schemes or taxonomies simply means working with a number of base taxonomies, where each document or piece of content is analysed according to one or more base taxonomies at the same time.

Faceted taxonomies avoid ambiguity by ensuring that each facet is inherently and obviously different from all others – i.e. facets are mutually exclusive (the technical term is that facets are *orthogonal* to each other). For example, objects might be classified according to the facets of shape, colour and texture. Shape can never be confused with colour, nor with texture. There is no conceptual overlap. Good faceted taxonomies base their facets on important and easily recognisable attributes of the content being analysed.

It should be obvious by now that when we were discussing matrices and some types of polyhierarchy in earlier sections, we were already prefiguring the discussion of facets. Each 'dimension' of a matrix is in fact a distinct facet. In our polyhierarchy of diseases mentioned earlier, we had one facet by cause of disease and one facet by body part affected.

Facets work best where the main types of organising principle are transparent and well understood by the audience – i.e. in mature, predictable and commonly known subject areas. Some of the best-known faceted schemes on the Internet work with the very accessible areas of food and wine, for example. *Epicurious.com* (see Figure 2.9) provides recipes, and has facets by cuisine, type of meal or course, main ingredients, season and preparation. *Wine.com* allows visitors to search for wine by the facets of grape, geography, vineyard, year and price range. Car auction and car hire sites also benefit from faceted taxonomies – facets can cover engine size, number of doors, manufacturer, price range and so on.

Facets are less effective where the structure of the base taxonomy is not well understood and cannot easily be observed or predicted – such as specialist knowledge domains presented for the general user. Medical information websites are a good example of this issue. Here, for the general user, facets need to be extremely simple and easy to navigate – preferably in simple list formats. The same problem does not exist for specialist users who have been educated into a deeper knowledge of the subject matter – for example trained medical practitioners, who would have no difficulty with a more technical vocabulary, more detail and a deeper tree.

Hence when working with taxonomy facets it is very important to understand the pre-existing knowledge base of your target audience (and any *variation* in knowledge depth among different audience groups), because faceted schemes often do not give as good an overview of the overall structure of the content collection as trees and hierarchies do. They give you a series of perspectives onto the same content instead. Where a tree or hierarchy educates novices and accommodates experts, facets are less informative and find it harder to accommodate both novices and specialists at the same time.

Matrices are a partial exception to this. As we've seen, matrices are faceted presentations of taxonomies comprising two or three major facets, where the facets involved are seen to interact – there is still a degree of pre-coordination to them. Above three facets, however, it is usually too visually complex to show the interaction between the facets, so each facet is normally presented as a single list or a tree structure.

This leads to another major drawback of facets – their post-coordination feature means they pull content together only when each facet element has been specified. In many matrix presentations,

Figure 2.9 Detail from Epicurious.com enhanced search page showing facets as lists

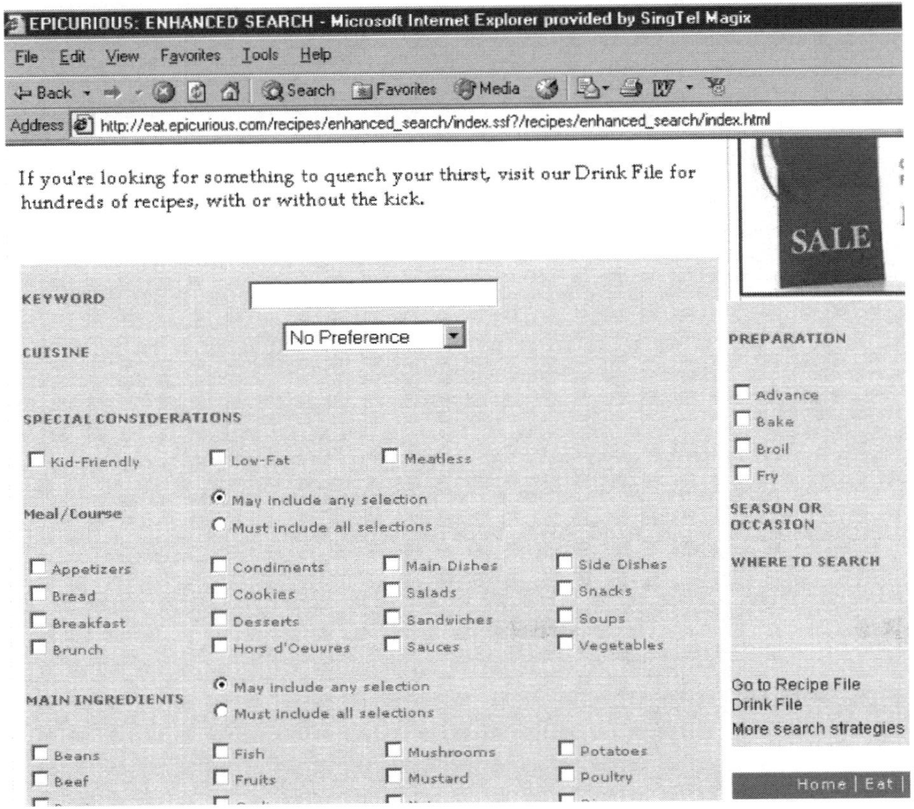

If you're looking for something to quench your thirst, visit our Drink File for hundreds of recipes, with or without the kick.

KEYWORD

CUISINE

No Preference ▶

SPECIAL CONSIDERATIONS

☐ Kid-Friendly   ☐ Low-Fat   ☐ Meatless

◉ May include any selection
Meal/Course
○ Must include all selections

☐ Appetizers   ☐ Condiments   ☐ Main Dishes   ☐ Side Dishes
☐ Bread   ☐ Cookies   ☐ Salads   ☐ Snacks
☐ Breakfast   ☐ Desserts   ☐ Sandwiches   ☐ Soups
☐ Brunch   ☐ Hors d'Oeuvres   ☐ Sauces   ☐ Vegetables

◉ May include any selection
MAIN INGREDIENTS
○ Must include all selections

☐ Beans   ☐ Fish   ☐ Mushrooms   ☐ Potatoes
☐ Beef   ☐ Fruits   ☐ Mustard   ☐ Poultry

PREPARATION

☐ Advance
☐ Bake
☐ Broil
☐ Fry

SEASON OR OCCASION

WHERE TO SEARCH

Go to Recipe File
Drink File
More search strategies

Home | Eat |

EPICURIOUS: ENHANCED SEARCH - Microsoft Internet Explorer provided by SingTel Magix

File   Edit   View   Favorites   Tools   Help

Back ▾ ➔ ▾ ⊗ ⊠ ⟳ Search ⬚ Favorites Media ⊗ ⬚ ▾ ⬚ W ▾

Address ⬚ http://eat.epicurious.com/recipes/enhanced_search/index.ssf?/recipes/enhanced_search/index.html

SALE

especially two-dimensional matrices, you can immediately identify what content exists for each intersection between the two dimensions. This makes it very easy to predict where useful content can be found.

However, when you present a larger number of different facets on a screen you cannot display the relationships or intersections between all of the facets. It is visually too complex and confusing to do so. Multiple facets can only be used in a post-coordination role, i.e. when somebody is conducting a search and deciding which facet combinations they need. The content that matches each of the criteria selected is only pulled together and identified at the click of the search button.

This means that searchers frequently have no sense of whether any content actually matches the precise combination of facet categories they have selected. Facet-driven searches often result in so-called 'false drops' where the facet selection has been overly precise and no exactly matching content exists. There are ways of mitigating this problem, which we will discuss later on.

Despite this drawback, faceted taxonomies are a powerful way of organising knowledge and information assets that need to be accessed in digital formats, simply because they:

- are hospitable to changing or combining knowledge domains;
- deal with very large collections of content using relatively simple and easy-to-understand structures;
- exploit the tools provided by the technology very well (e.g. metadata);
- mitigate some of the technology's faults (e.g. limited number of ways of visualising taxonomy structures and usability problems with browsing complex trees and hierarchies).

Later on in this book, we will be discussing how to build a faceted taxonomy, but the basic principles set out by Ranganathan hold good. In my own company's taxonomy work, we usually start with a baseline set of facets loosely based on Ranganathan's:

- *People and organisations* – often controlled name lists.
- *Things and parts of things* – often general:specific or whole:part tree structures, e.g. document types, factory plant:machinery:parts of machinery.
- *Activity cycles* – often based on business processes and functions and following a sequence:stage:task tree structure.
- *Locations* – often based on plans, maps or geographical zones.

- *Time or sequence* – usually chronological or sequential.

- *Subject matter* – often (and preferably) a well understood and well defined discipline such as engineering, sports or law.

We might build more than one operational facet out of each baseline facet, and we might drop some, depending on the content that needs to be covered. For example, time may not be a significant organising factor for some clients, but there may be several different subject matter disciplines at play, or several distinct types of 'Things' to be mapped and classified.

Rosenfeld and Morville's *Information Architecture for the World Wide Web*, which covers mostly web-based content, suggests the following basic facets (Rosenfeld and Morville, 2002: 205):

- Topic

- Product

- Document type

- Audience

- Geography

- Price.

Amrit Tiwana's *Knowledge Management Toolkit* suggests facets (which he calls 'attribute types') based on research into patterns of corporate knowledge usage in the 1990s (Tiwana, 2002: 151–4):

- Activities – business or functional activities

- Domain – subject matter

- Form – whether document, file, tacit knowledge, etc.

- Type – document type

- Products and services – as in Rosenfeld and Morville

- Time – time of creation

- Location – location relevant to the content of the document.

And Richard Wurman, in his classic *Information Anxiety 2*, states: 'The ways of organising information are finite. It can only be organised by location, alphabet, time, category [type], or hierarchy [scale of magnitude]' (Wurman, 2001: 40–1).

Notice in each of these examples that there is some variation but significant common ground. You will need to choose your facets based on your own perception of needs and the user perspectives that you want to support. Also notice that the number of different facets in each case is limited. Large numbers of facets (above seven or so) are cognitively difficult for users to manipulate.

We'll discuss later on how to design robust facets and the different ways that you can deploy facets in your taxonomy work, but for now we simply need to note with Barbara Kwasnik:

> Decide, in advance, on the important criteria for description. These form the facets or fundamental categories ... The strength of a faceted classification lies in the fundamental categories, which should express the important attributes of the entities being classified. Without knowledge of the domain and of the potential users, this is often difficult to do. (Kwasnik, 1999: 39–41)

System maps

Each of the taxonomy representations we have considered so far works differently with each of the three attributes of a taxonomy: its classification power, its semantic expressiveness and its ability to map the structure of a knowledge domain. Lists up to a certain length provide the simplest overviews of a domain but lack depth and detail. Trees and hierarchies produce strong maps, are very expressive and introduce predictability, but are inhospitable to different approaches to the content. Matrices work well when a domain only has a limited number of perspectives to consider. Facets are expressive, but do not map a whole domain very effectively.

System maps focus, as you might expect from the term, on the knowledge *mapping* character of a taxonomy. For the purposes of this book, I will define system maps as *visual representations of a knowledge domain where proximity and connections between entities are used to express their taxonomic and real-world relationships*. They still use labels and retain their semantic element, but the visual representation takes centre stage.

System maps can be descriptive or they can be conceptual. An example of a descriptive map might be a taxonomy of arteries shown in relation to each other and in their approximate position in the human body. In other words, the system map is an *analogue of a real-world arrangement*. Sometimes this might be quite abstract, as in the famous London

Underground map. System maps are often designed for very specific uses; for example, our artery map (Figure 2.10) was produced for a book on first aid. Notice that these maps are essentially lists that have been given much greater representational power by illustrating the natural relationships between the elements. Nomenclatures may also be represented as descriptive system maps. A nomenclature is a list of all the parts that make up a whole – for example, the nomenclature of a car would include engine, wheels, doors, seats, exhaust, etc. *Descriptive system maps are excellent devices for communicating the knowledge domain in its natural context.*

Figure 2.10   **Taxonomy of arteries shown as a map**

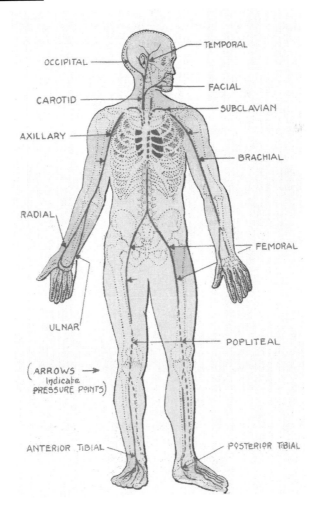

Conceptual system maps deal with mental constructs rather than physical things. The most common form of conceptual system map is a mind-map, where different ideas are linked by branching lines. Mind-maps can also be represented as tree structures, but the 360° format radiating around a central core provides greater representational power. Proximity and cross-linkages are easier to represent than in a tree structure. Mind-maps also frequently employ colour coding to discriminate between different categories.

Concept maps are a more rigorous form of mind-map. In concept mapping the nature of the relationship between any two concepts is made explicit – in fact, you should be able to literally 'read' any two connected nodes as a grammatical sentence, in the format CONCEPT 1 + relationship + CONCEPT 2. The overall visual representation of the knowledge domain should still take primacy over the completeness of the linkages (Crandall et al., 2006: ch. 4). An example of a concept map summarising the three main attributes of a taxonomy is given in Figure 2.11.

Concept maps are extremely useful for cataloguing specialist knowledge domains (often constructed by interviewing subject matter experts) as well as explaining knowledge domains in a summary form for novices. Their taxonomic use can be deepened by attaching further knowledge information resources to each of the nodes in the map.

Figure 2.11   Concept map of taxonomy attributes

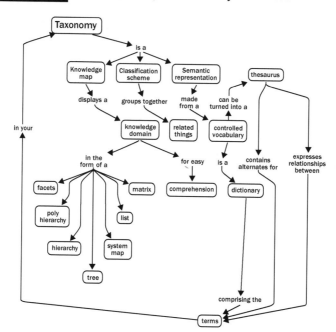

Process maps are another form of system map. They can be as straightforward as a sequenced list of stages or tasks, or they can show complex interrelationships between different activities in the process. Whatever their form, the important thing to note is that they are powerful instruments for organising knowledge assets associated with projects, processes or business systems. In Figure 2.12, we can see a (fictional) knowledge organisation example from an oil industry project. Process maps can be very useful devices when building functional taxonomies – i.e. taxonomies that reflect the business activities of an organisation.

Figure 2.12 Example of a project roadmap with knowledge assets

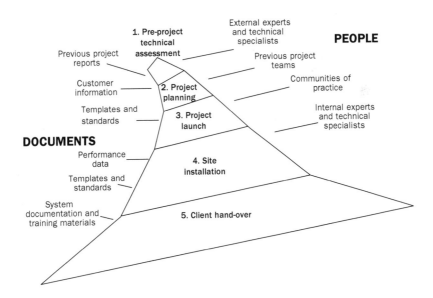

Practical implications of different taxonomy forms

The practical implications of the different taxonomy forms are listed in Table 2.2.

Table 2.2	Practical implications of taxonomy forms	
Form	When to use	Issues to watch
List	Use a list when the knowledge domain is relatively simple and you do not have a large collection of knowledge assets within it. Lists are the basic building blocks of taxonomies so need to be built on regular, consistent principles. Examples of list principles are: • commonality in attributes or purpose; • functional collocation; • regular sequence; • chaining; • gradients in attributes.	If your list is not well constructed, it will not grow in a regular, easy to comprehend way. Lists become unmanageable for users when there are more than 12–15 elements. Above that they typically need to be turned into trees or maps.
Tree	Trees can be used when your lists grow too long; when content can be divided on predictable, well understood principles of subdivision; when content can be clustered into 'natural' generic groups with labels that are easily understood by your user community. Trees are versatile because they can express different relationships between levels at different places. Trees can allow heterogeneous relationships within the same taxonomy. Examples of relationships expressed between superordinate and subordinate terms in a tree can be: • 'contains' • 'is more important than' • 'generates' • 'causes' • 'shares common history' • 'is a generalisation of' • 'controls'.	The strength of a tree is in its predictability. Trees function badly: • when the nature of the relationship between levels is not immediately apparent to the users; • where too many inconsistent principles of subdivision are applied in the same tree; • where different user communities use a range of alternate organising/subdividing principles to that of the tree; • where there are too many levels of detail.
Hierarchy	The real strength of a hierarchy lies in its absolute consistency and predictability. The rules of inheritance and transitivity mean that you can predict from the top layer down what attributes will belong to subordinate layers and how the content there will be organised. Hierarchies work best with very mature, formal logical schemas or with highly structured systems of physical objects. There is only one kind of relationship allowed between superordinate and subordinate terms.	Hierarchies do not deal well with the complexities and ambiguities of the real world, especially in areas that are not easily subject to observation and analysis – such as information and knowledge artefacts. Like trees, they do not deal well with competing principles of organisation. Unlike trees, they do not even admit that competing principles might exist.

Form	When to use	Issues to watch
Poly-hierarchy	Polyhierarchies are compensations for the inability of trees and hierarchies to accommodate topics that belong to more than one category. Use them sparingly, when it is only necessary to make a few cross-linkages. They are much better used 'behind the scenes', for example in hyperlinking cross references at the topic level, rather than making them visible in the main taxonomy tree, as this tends to create ambiguity. The more cross linkages you make, the more confusing your overall structure will appear.	Having too many visible cross linkages will compromise your taxonomy's ability to map the knowledge domain for users and will reduce the predictability of your tree structure. It also makes your taxonomy more difficult to administer. If you need a lot of cross linkages, consider using matrices or facets instead of a tree structure.
Matrix	Use a matrix where you have a well-defined, cohesive body of content that can all be organised by the same two or three facets. This means that your content can consistently be described by the same two or three important attributes. In our examples we saw project documentation as one body and career-related information as another. Matrices are useful for checking completeness of a body of knowledge and can also function as powerful sense-making frameworks.	Diverse collections of content are not easily expressed by a matrix because the content does not possess the same common set of attributes and so is not easily placed into the matrix structure. Content that requires more than three organising facets is also difficult to represent in a matrix.
Facets	Use facets when you have a large, complex body of content or an area of content that is still emerging and not well-defined. Tree structures that have become large, complex and unwieldy are good candidates for facet analysis and reorganisation. Different facets represent important attribute types of the content – here 'important' attributes are defined as important for the manipulation or navigation of the content. Facets are also extremely useful if you plan to use metadata to manage and retrieve digital content. Typical facet types are: • people and groups • things and parts • activities and processes • location • time • subject discipline.	Facets rely on post-coordination of content, which means that they do not easily represent the overall structure of a knowledge domain in a single 'coup d'oeuil'. This makes it more important to have strategies for simplifying the facet structures and clarifying the terminology used. The same set of facets may have difficulty in serving user communities at different levels of knowledge – e.g. both novices and experts. The post-coordination feature means that faceted searches may result in many 'false drops' where no content matches the specified facet topics. This will also require compensation strategies to avoid user frustration.

Form	When to use	Issues to watch
System map	Use system maps when you have a coherent 'system' or knowledge domain that needs to be described. System maps can be descriptive (of physical systems) or conceptual (of abstract object systems). Their power lies in their ability to communicate the elements of a taxonomy in a rich context, so use them where you want to strengthen the mnemonic power of a taxonomy structure. They are much better than lists or trees in this regard. System maps are also good for checking completeness in your knowledge assets. In knowledge management, process maps are useful for building functional taxonomies. Other examples of system maps are: • analogue maps (follow physical forms and collocations); • mind maps; • concept maps.	The power of a system map is in its visual simplicity, so it should only be used where the domain can be represented in a vivid, expressive way. Overly complex maps, or maps of interacting domains do not serve this purpose well. System maps also tend not to deal well with depth of content – they are much better at representing list data than multi-level tree data, for example.

3

Taxonomies and infrastructure for organisational effectiveness

Given the distributed character of organisational knowledge, the key to achieving coordinated action does not so much depend on those 'higher up' collecting more and more knowledge, as on those 'lower down' finding more and more ways of getting connected and interrelating the knowledge each one has.

(Tsoukas, 2005: 112)

In the next two chapters we examine the broader role that taxonomies have to play in helping organisations to function effectively. In this chapter, we look at how organisations fail to be effective. It is failures, especially systemic failures, that teach us most about the infrastructures we need to maintain in order to sustain our effectiveness. As Star and Ruhleder put it, 'infrastructure becomes visible upon breakdown' (Star and Ruhleder, 1996). We will identify and describe the factors that, in an increasingly interconnected world, render organisations ineffective. This helps us to identify the important stabilising and enabling roles that taxonomies play as boundary objects in – and between – organisations.

In the following chapter, we look at the things that organisations need to do in order to be effective, using an interpretive framework called the strategic information alignment framework (Marchand, 2000). We will use this to identify a range of practical ways in which taxonomy work is done to support effectiveness in organisations. This will set the context for Chapter 5, where we will consider the different roles that taxonomies play within knowledge management more specifically.

Before we embark, however, we should define what we mean by *organisational effectiveness*. For our purposes in this book organisational effectiveness is evidenced by a combination of:

- the ability to set collective, realistic and achievable goals;

- the ability to make detailed plans, organise and manage resources and coordinate actions in pursuit of those goals;
- the achievement, partial or otherwise, of at least some of those goals;
- a degree of consistency in the extent to which goals are achieved;
- the ability to make appropriate changes to plans and actions in the light of changes in the environment;
- the ability to identify and respond appropriately to opportunities and risks in the environment.

By *ineffectiveness* we mean a systemic and consistent pattern of failing to demonstrate these abilities, in particular the achievement of agreed goals. Ineffectiveness can also be demonstrated by single instances of catastrophic failure.

Organisational ineffectiveness

On the night of 24 February 2000, a small, eight-year-old girl from the Ivory Coast was admitted to North Middlesex Hospital in London. She had been sleeping for days, the hospital staff were told, and wouldn't wake up. She was in a desperate condition. Her heart was barely beating, and her body temperature was so low that medical staff couldn't get a reading on the standard hospital thermometer. She was hunched in a foetal position and medical staff were unable to straighten her limbs. Despite their efforts, her condition continued to deteriorate, and the consultant paediatrician leading the team decided that the little girl required more specialised help. So at 2.30 a.m. she was transferred by ambulance to the paediatric intensive care unit at St Mary's Hospital, Paddington. There, a specialist team fought for over 12 hours to save her, as her vital systems all began to fail. Her heart and lungs stopped numerous times, and each time they brought her back. Her other vital organs, liver and kidneys, then began to fail. At 3 p.m., she suffered her last cardiac arrest. The team tried to resuscitate her for 15 minutes before she was finally declared dead. The little girl's name was Victoria Climbié.

In the post mortem examination carried out the next day, the pathologist, a Dr Nathaniel Carey, recorded 128 separate injuries on Victoria's body, caused by a range of blunt and sharp instruments. The injuries were in varying stages of repair, indicating that they were the product of a systematic and consistent pattern of abuse. Deep abrasions on her wrists and ankles showed that she had been kept tied up for extended periods of time. The immediate cause of death was hypothermia caused by malnourishment and being kept in a restricted, damp environment. Dr Carey reported that it was the worst case of child abuse he had ever seen.

In the investigation that followed, it emerged that Victoria had been systematically and savagely beaten, scalded and burnt by her great-aunt and guardian Marie-Therese Kouao and her guardian's boyfriend Carl Manning over at least the previous eight months; she had been kept tied up every night and for days at a time throughout the winter in an unheated bathroom, taped into a black plastic sack so that she would not soil the bath with her urine and excrement; she was forced to eat her food cold, and by pushing her face into the food, like a dog, because she could not use her hands. On 12 January 2001, Kouao and Manning were convicted of her murder.

The public outcry over Victoria's horrific fate, and the clamour for an independent public inquiry, was occasioned not merely by her terrible injuries. Child abuse is a difficult crime to detect, because it is often, as Climbié inquiry chairman Lord Laming observed, cloaked in secrecy and deceit. What shocked the public in Victoria's case was that her abuse had been carried out in full sight of the very agencies charged with a duty to protect children. She had been under child protection twice and was still under the supervision of an assigned social worker at the time of her death. These agencies, it turned out, had had numerous and obvious opportunities to intervene but had not done so.

> Victoria was not hidden away. It is deeply disturbing that during the days and months following her initial contact with Ealing Housing Department's Homeless Persons' Unit, Victoria was known to no less than two further housing authorities, four social services departments, two child protection teams of the Metropolitan Police Service (MPS), a specialist centre managed by the NSPCC, and she was admitted to two different hospitals because of suspected deliberate harm. (Laming 2003: 3)

It is a consistent feature of major disasters and tragic failures that multiple small causes conspire to bring about the tragedy. Despite our desire to identify simple causes – preferably people we can blame – terrible things most frequently come about because of complex combinations of failures: personal, cultural and systemic (Perrow, 1999;

Douglas, 1992). As Diane Vaughan puts it, 'mistakes ... are socially organised and systemically produced' (Vaughan, 1996: 394). The Victoria Climbié case is no different.

Among the contributing factors to Victoria's abandonment in full view of child protection agencies were (Laming, 2003):

- sloppy and unprofessional conduct by social services and healthcare professionals and managers;

- a culture of over-delegation and non-accountability among healthcare and social services managers;

- information access issues – the UK Data Protection Act forbids transfer of medical records between hospitals: Victoria had been treated for her injuries in two separate hospitals in the eight months prior to her death, and her case history was not available to the second hospital, missing an opportunity to demonstrate a pattern of abuse;

- over-worked and under-trained social services case workers;

- lack of holistic case-handling procedures resulting in no single person getting an overview of Victoria's situation or taking overall responsibility for it;

- procedural complexity and constant procedural change resulting in lack of clear guidance to social services staff;

- independent reorganisations of police, health and family services authorities, resulting in multiple mismatches of geographic coverage and asymmetric scales of operation, leading to poor coordination, few established, standardised or routine channels for communication and information transfer between agencies, and inability to gather relevant information from different sources to form a coherent picture;

- divergent perceptions and descriptions of Victoria's situation based on functional compartmentalised views, ranging from domestic difficulties (police), child-guardian tensions (social services – Victoria and Kouao were known to have fierce rows), medical condition (some doctors – Victoria suffered from the skin condition scabies), unsuitable housing (assigned social worker – sharing a one-room bedsit with boyfriend Manning), child abuse (hospital staff – catalogued Victoria's injuries in July–August 1999 and saw her involuntarily wet herself when Manning visited her in hospital), demonic possession (church pastor – based on Kouao's report of incontinence, bad temper and self-inflicted injuries).

While some of these problems are personal and cultural failures, it is the systemic ones that interest us here. Lord Laming concluded in his inquiry report that the two most significant failures were the professional failures of management in healthcare and social services agencies, and the information systems failures that prevented the various pieces of the Victoria Climbié jigsaw puzzle – obvious as those clues were – from being pieced together and acted upon.

To a knowledge management eye, these issues go beyond information systems and information management. Individuals and agencies *knew* what was happening to Victoria but were unable to transfer that knowledge to where it could be actioned or to act on it themselves. This was a knowledge management problem, not simply an information management problem.

The symptoms of this problem turn up all too frequently in other disastrous mistakes, from the *Challenger* space shuttle disaster in 1986 (Vaughan, 1996) to the poor emergency services coordination during the World Trade Center collapse after the 9/11 attacks (Dwyer, 2002), to the shambles of the crisis response to Hurricane Katrina in New Orleans in 2005. Typical symptoms include:

- a culture of not caring about the implications of knowledge held beyond a narrow task-fulfilment role;
- different ways of describing and naming the same problem;
- inability to integrate multiple perspectives on the same problem;
- lack of opportunity for routine information exchange between parties involved;
- incompatible information systems;
- lack of access to other parties' information systems;
- few shared attentional cues among the parties involved – warnings from external parties are not taken seriously because there are no mechanisms for recognising their authority or the experience upon which the warnings are based;
- few informal socialisation opportunities to build up a common language, shared categories, or trust mechanisms that underpin a group's shared attentional cues and sense of authoritative knowledge-based experience.

In natural human social groups, we have numerous strategies inside our groups to defeat these problems. We instinctively build a *shared language* which includes shared categories so that we can communicate quickly and effectively. We socialise informally, we share stories and build a common sense of identity and mutual responsibility. We have scripts and routines and collective habits. We know how to recognise and pay attention to the voice of experience. We agree on what's important, and we rehearse infrequent collective actions so that when the time to act comes, we are well prepared.

All of this we can call *knowledge articulation work* – it is the work we do in groups which allows us to articulate our knowledge collectively so that we can act. It is the work that enables us to coordinate our actions and remain effective as a group, without having to argue, discuss or plan every collective act in detail. Cognitive psychologist Gary Klein calls this phenomenon the 'team mind' (Klein, 1998: 233–57).

The problems we have listed surface when we need to coordinate our actions on a wider scale, involving many different groups. Without knowledge articulation infrastructure and mechanisms that help us connect to external groups, we fail. The very things that make us effective *within* our groups – our private languages, authority recognition mechanisms and shared routines – make us ineffective *between* groups. But increasingly, this kind of coordination is what we are being asked to do.

Knowledge articulation issues arise therefore in any situation where groups need to coordinate their actions or where it is necessary to 'tune into' a cohesive group's knowledge base very quickly. These situations are becoming more and more ubiquitous:

- in induction and orientation, where we need to speed up the learning curve of newcomers on a team;
- in outsourcing and offshoring of key business activities, especially where undocumented process knowledge and client knowledge needs to be transferred;
- in franchising and licensing of technology, including 'soft' brand management knowledge;
- in mergers and acquisitions;
- in joint ventures, especially in new overseas markets, where local knowledge needs to be acquired and technology transferred to joint venture partners;
- in virtual teams, particularly on large, distributed, international projects;

- in major organisational restructurings where normal patterns of information flow are broken up and need to be reconnected in new ways;
- in subcontracting of complex tasks;
- in 'joined-up government' initiatives, e-citizen services.

All of these scenarios are notoriously prone to failure or delay, and it is knowledge articulation dysfunctionality that renders them so. Even where an organisation has relatively good knowledge articulation capabilities, they are too often taken for granted, weakly managed and too easily disrupted. Nick Leeson's uninterrupted £830 million gambling run and the subsequent collapse of Barings Bank were at least partially facilitated by a number of what Stewart Hamilton (2000) calls 'dislocating events'.

The securities trading operation was new to Barings, and so not well integrated into the knowledge infrastructure of the bank. When profits fell, Barings fired its chief, who left with most of his team. A traditional banker was appointed in his place, which set the scene for supervision by management inexperienced in this business. (Experience makes attentional cues available to the group, the things that tell you whether things are going well or badly.) There had been three major reorganisations in Barings Securities in as many years. This produced confusion in reporting lines and information flows. The technical infrastructure was inadequate and error-prone, and it had weak governance. In Singapore, Leeson had responsibility for both front- and back-office systems, which meant he was able to fix 'errors' in the front office by playing with the back end (Hamilton, 2000: 199–202).

To those who believe therefore that good knowledge management and information management practices are a 'nice to have' rather than a 'necessary to have', these challenges and the symptoms of dysfunction we have described tell the opposite story. And as organisations increasingly have to coordinate their activities, information flows and knowledge use on a much wider scale, the coordination demands will amplify and the weight of the many, small contributions towards potential failure will cascade towards real failures, big and small. Knowledge management is not the only device for addressing this problem, but it is one of the primary ways of doing so, the more so as it consciously combines technical, social and organisational strategies.

Where do taxonomies sit inside this? One of the principal levers of effective information flow is a common language – by which we mean common vocabularies, common understanding of the terms in those vocabularies and categories that roughly match. This is what a taxonomy, formal or informal, provides.

While knowledge articulation difficulties arising from 'language' differences are to be expected between organisations, they exist inside organisations as well, especially large ones. They are present wherever we notice what we loosely term 'a silo culture'.

In the private sector, the many mistakes arising from silo cultures tend to remain invisible. The public sector is under much greater pressure to account for its internal mistakes. To give just one example, on 20 July 2001 Australian citizen Vivian Alvarez was removed by the Australian Department of Immigration (DIMIA) to the Philippines (her country of birth) as 'an unlawful non-citizen'. This was despite being present in DIMIA's databases as a citizen, despite being listed in the national fingerprints database and despite being officially listed during her detention and investigation as a missing person with the Australian police (McMillan, 2005).

The official inquiry into the matter found that many of the knowledge articulation problems we have identified existed internally within DIMIA as well as between DIMIA and other agencies. There are strong resonances with the Climbié case. Indeed, officers repeatedly failed to act on the belated realisation that Alvarez had been unlawfully removed to the Philippines, even while the missing persons campaign for Vivian gathered force and another major public inquiry into the unlawful detention by DIMIA of another Australian citizen in March 2004 in very similar circumstances was under way (Palmer, 2005). Only four years of persistent action by her former husband brought the mistake to the surface, resulting in her eventual location in 2005. One of the many reasons for the mistake was that DIMIA databases had eleven different variants of Vivian's name. A thesaurus to link all the alternate forms would have been a useful tool. Other typical symptoms were present.

> Although communication between DIMIA and external organisations such as the police appears to have been generally responsive and professional, this was not the case with intra-departmental communication. Information about Vivian passed between DIMIA units such as the compliance and investigations teams but was not adequately recorded or acted on. Respective roles and responsibilities were blurred, and it seems there were no clearly established mechanisms whereby information could be shared and disseminated. (McMillan, 2005: 34)

In Victoria's case, we have already seen that the different agencies that encountered her had widely varying classifications of her case. Both hospital consultants who had treated Victoria during a two-week hospitalisation in July–August 1999 told Lord Laming's inquiry that they believed the information they had given other agencies was misunderstood or misinterpreted – a clear signal of category systems that are not shared (Laming, 2003: 10–11).

> I cannot account for the way other people interpreted what I said. It was not the way I would have liked it to have been interpreted. (Dr Ruby Schwartz)

> I do not think it was until I had read and re-read this letter that I appreciated quite the depth of misunderstanding. (Dr Mary Rossiter)

The problem of Babel

So taxonomy work sits as a central cipher within this network of knowledge management issues and challenges. Ciphers conceal at the same time as they reveal, and so, curiously, do taxonomies. To understand why, we need to go back to an ancient story told by the Hebrews. It was told, probably, to explain the origins of Babylon and urban life, as well as the all-too-human contradiction in our simultaneous capacity for collaboration and discord.

> Now the whole earth had one language and few words. And as men migrated from the east, they found a plain in the land of Shinar and settled there. And they said to one another, 'Come, let us make bricks, and burn them thoroughly.' And they had brick for stone, and bitumen for mortar. Then they said, 'Come, let us build ourselves a city, and a tower with its top in the heavens, and let us make a name for ourselves, lest we be scattered abroad upon the face of the whole earth.' And the LORD came down to see the city and the tower, which the sons of men had built. And the LORD said, 'Behold, they are one people, and they have all one language; and this is only the beginning of what they will do; and nothing that they propose to do will now be impossible for them. Come, let

us go down, and there confuse their language, that they may not understand each other's speech.' So the LORD scattered them abroad from there over the face of all the earth, and they left off building the city. Therefore its name was called Babel, because there the LORD confused the language of all the earth. (Genesis 11: 1–9 RSV translation)

The problem of Babel is one that all organisations must face once they get above 20 or so people in size. This ancient story reminds us that while we as a species are extraordinarily good at large-scale coordinated action, we are also extraordinarily good at the opposite – at the same time. At the heart of both abilities is our drive to create a shared language and agree common categories and ways of organising. Tom McArthur calls this the 'taxonomic urge' (McArthur, 1986). But our taxonomies are double-edged instruments. They divide as much as they unite, they exclude as much as they include.

In the physical world, objects must be organised in one consistent way if they are to be organised for easy retrieval and management. You can't have several different organising principles operating at the same time in your music CD collection and still easily locate the music you want whenever you feel like it. (This is perfectly possible in the digital world, but psychologically we haven't yet got over a hundred thousand years of conditioning – we treat the digital world just like the physical one.) If we all agree on a common set of organising principles for our shared resources, all will be fine. The whole group can access and manipulate those resources in consistent and reliable ways.

At the local group level, and with shared resources, we tend to muddle our way through to reasonably functional common categories, labels and ways of organising. But our natural taxonomies are also designed to keep other people out. Beyond the local level, as well as with resources that we consider private, we have an astonishing capacity for variability in naming, categorising and organising. This means 'outsiders' find it very difficult to figure out how to use our resources, and conversely we don't easily understand 'their' organisation schemes.

We can see this every day in our organisations when we look at shared drive folder structures from department to department. Within my own department the structure makes sense and has broad predictive power. Another department's structure may be completely opaque and impossible to decipher without exhaustive investigation or a guide.

As an experiment sometimes I ask a workshop group to list the ways that they organise their music CD collections. Music CDs are relatively simple objects, but the last time we did this exercise after only five minutes we had almost as many ways of organising as we had people in the group:

- by artist's last name;
- by artist's first name;
- by music genre;
- by date;
- by mood inspired;
- by frequency of listening;
- by colour of spine;
- by who they were dating at the time they bought it;
- by composer;
- by country of composer;
- by record company;
- by degree of liking;
- by personal music appreciation history – the music they were 'into' at any given time.

From this we learn the very important lesson: *taxonomies are determined as much by their user's perceptions and worldview as they are by the attributes of the things classified*. Different worldviews and contexts mean different taxonomies – for the same objects. Taxonomy development is not just about analysis of entities according to a predefined scheme, it is also about interpretation of different perspectives and worldviews. And these are not minor differences. They include absolutely contradictory worldviews and everything in between.

In knowledge management, we are, of course, eager to break open the private taxonomies that keep other people out, but to do so, we must first understand and interpret the perspectives that created them. The private taxonomies we find become evidence for the negotiated common structures that we need to put into place for effective knowledge articulation to take place. And we are partially liberated by the fact that up to a point, using a faceted approach, we *can* now, in the digital domain, represent multiple perspectives on the same content. Diversity, to a degree, can be enshrined in our taxonomy work for the first time since Aristotle introduced us to the hierarchical tree based only on objectively observed attributes.

We can distinguish then two main kinds of taxonomy in our lives. The first kind is the private taxonomy. These are the informal, 'natural' taxonomies that we construct in our immediate environments, either for private use or local small-scale coordination. They might be more or less ad hoc, more or less well-structured, more or less consistent and predictable. The main thing to note about private taxonomies is that they are typically idiosyncratic, highly determined by local perspectives and frequently opaque to outsiders.

The second kind is that of the public taxonomy, whose main purpose is to enable broader social coordination. As Figure 3.1 shows, public taxonomies themselves fall into three types:

- The 'objective', publically observable taxonomy, usually of physical things, based on observable attributes. The objective taxonomy is not as objective as it appears from a distance, but once the principle of analysis is accepted, it is the easiest to implement.

- The 'negotiated' taxonomy, usually of social artefacts, based on stakeholder agreement and aimed at supporting collaboration. The negotiated taxonomy works very much like a standard for information exchange.

Figure 3.1 **Public and private taxonomies**

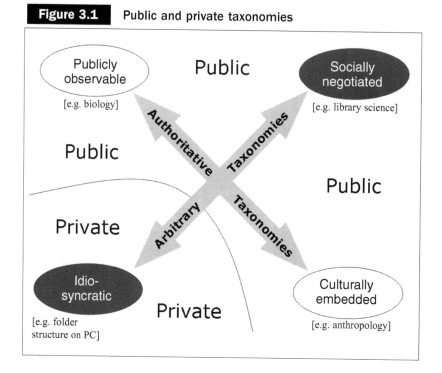

- The 'embedded' taxonomy, usually of inherited cultural artefacts such as military rank or social hierarchy, probably based on authoritative definition in the past, but now completely taken for granted. Embedded taxonomies represent 'the way we do things around here' and are extremely difficult to dislodge.

The knowledge management taxonomy, it is important to note, is neither objective nor embedded; it is a socially negotiated taxonomy which gives us immediate guidance on how to approach a taxonomy development exercise. Observation and analysis are not sufficient. Simply developing a taxonomy to describe our information, records and knowledge assets is not enough. We need to mine the languages and perceptions of our audience, and we need a strong framework for negotiating a common, well-structured set of categories. A socially negotiated taxonomy functions as a *standard* for communication and information exchange. As a standard, it can only be developed by investigation, consultation, drafting, testing and revision. It cannot simply be defined and imposed.

All of these taxonomy types, public and private, coexist in the same social space. They jostle to organise our semi-private, semi-overlapping worlds. Simply put, this means that the raw materials of our knowledge management taxonomies will be drawn from the other public and private taxonomies that we find being used in our organisations. Social negotiation of a taxonomy means:

- bringing into the foreground, making explicit and structuring
- the labels and categories and organising perspectives that already exist in the background environment
- for the purposes of enhancing coordinated social action
- in the pursuit of group objectives.

Taxonomies as boundary objects

A knowledge management taxonomy is an object that enables broader social coordination in an environment of multiple private and semi-private taxonomies (i.e. localised organising languages) that tend to disable collaboration. A knowledge management taxonomy is a *boundary object*.

Boundary objects were first described by Susan Leigh Star and James Griesemer in 1989. They were studying the role that museum exhibits of stuffed birds played in relation to 'amateur' communities of birdwatchers and 'professional' communities of zoologists. Each type of community interpreted the exhibits quite differently, and brought entirely different worlds of knowledge and perception to play. But the same exhibit was a meaningful point of contact for each – which meant that it afforded a point of contact and an opportunity for communication across the boundaries of very different groups. A boundary both divides and connects different groups. A boundary object makes differences explicit, but also provides an opportunity for contact and a basic structure for agreement (Star and Griesemer, 1989). Boundary objects turn out to be key instruments for enabling collaboration across social boundaries – from knowledge management to sectarian violence.

> Such objects have different meanings in different social worlds but their structure is common enough to more than one world to make them recognizable, a means of translation. The creation and management of boundary objects is a key process in developing and maintaining coherence across intersecting communities. (Bowker and Star, 1999: 297)

In linguistics an excellent example of a boundary object – and an illustration of its power – is the written Chinese language, which unites the many spoken dialects. Written Mandarin is ideographic, not phonetic – that is to say, the characters represent ideas and have no relationship to sound or pronunciation. People who speak different dialects will find it impossible to understand each other using spoken language, but can communicate using the same written system. It is not uncommon in a Chinese city to see non-locals tracing characters on their interlocutor's hands when they want to communicate. In fact, the linguistic distance between the twelve major Chinese language groups leads many experts to consider them distinct spoken languages. The written language as a boundary object is a powerful unifying force, binding many peoples and languages into a single cultural and historical tradition.

To see how a taxonomy can act as a boundary object to connect different groups, let's consider the case of a small industrial utilities company. In this company, whenever anything out of the ordinary happens within the plant, an incident report is generated. Incidents can be a wide variety of things. They can involve instrument malfunctions, equipment breakdown, major stoppages, contamination, accidents, injuries, human error, unexpected events. The diagram in Figure 3.2

Figure 3.2 Incident report – facet analysis

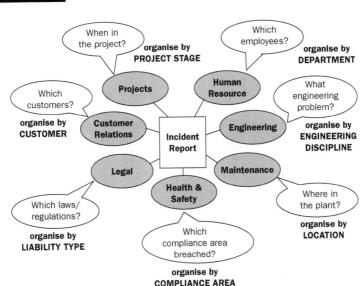

illustrates the different perspectives that different groups within this company take on incident reports – and by implication, the different ways that they need to organise and access incident reports.

> [W]ith so many different perspectives and activities to take into account in a typical organisation, how can one system for organising all information for all audiences in all contexts be created? We need multiple ways to look at things – multiple perspectives and contexts – to serve the needs of employees, customers, suppliers, investors, or any other user group. (Earley, 2005)

A single tree taxonomy structure will never accommodate everyone's needs, and therefore cannot function effectively as a boundary object – but a faceted taxonomy can. The anchor facet, the one that provides the structure that all parties agree on, is in this case the document type facet – the fact that it is an 'incident report'. In the museum studied by Star and Griesemer, the anchor facet would be the species of bird. This provides the boundary conditions.

As a boundary object, the faceted taxonomy provides the common point of contact and reference for all communities, but supports alternate perspectives residing in different groups' needs. By providing a standardised common structure it helps ensure that incident reports are not described differently by different departments, that alternate versions are not kept in different collections, that they are not scattered across different departments with no provision for a coherent, complete record, and so on. Oh, and it means that supported by an appropriate system, each group can retrieve and organise *the same* incident reports in the way that best reflects their work.

Information and knowledge infrastructure

Public taxonomies are also an integral part of our knowledge and information infrastructure. They do not stand alone, disengaged from other kinds of knowledge articulation work. This is another way of saying that taxonomies are not alone in helping an organisation articulate its knowledge effectively.

By knowledge and information infrastructure we mean all the things that combine to facilitate the flow of information and knowledge in support of the myriad tasks and actions and decisions that comprise organisational activity. Hence, information infrastructure does not just mean the technical IT infrastructure, although it includes that. It also encompasses human, social and organisational elements. Within your information infrastructure you will normally find information management policies, process and practice routines, standards, arrays of tools and resources that are visible to their users, conventions and assumptions, shared vocabulary and categories (see Figure 3.3).

Infrastructure is integrated and intertwined, which means that one component can never be disentangled from the rest. It has grown historically, which means that any changes are always done on an already installed base and will take time to 'grow in'. It has an overall maturity level, so that it will generally not easily accept elements that are discontinuous – 'too advanced' or 'too outdated' for its overall orientation. It is arranged for a wide variety of use, so is complex and complicated to manage. It is pragmatic, and since it balances many needs, it is always a product of negotiation.

Most of all, infrastructure is taken for granted, and remains invisible unless it fails (Bowker and Star, 1999: 33–7). This, together with its interconnectedness, makes it very easy to neglect, and makes it very difficult to implement conscious, radical or rapid changes in infrastructure.

Figure 3.3 The elements of information and knowledge infrastructure

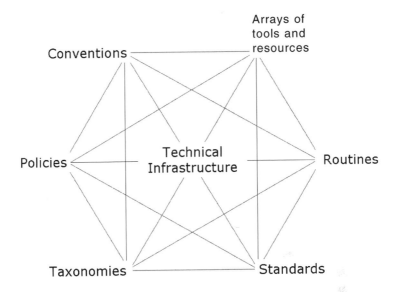

In consequence, when taxonomy work is aimed at improving the knowledge articulation capabilities of an organisation – as it frequently is – it can rarely be done apart from other infrastructural work. Taxonomy projects are frequently undertaken alongside knowledge audits, process redesign, collaboration mapping, information management policy reviews, standards development and implementation, training and change management projects. Because infrastructures are invisible and taken for granted, a good deal of the initial work in taxonomy development lies in attempting to identify and bring to the surface hidden things so that conscious decisions can be made about them.

Taxonomies do not therefore exist in isolation from other boundary-spanning mechanisms. They are a part of knowledge and information infrastructure, which comprises objects and practices that enable knowledge articulation across boundaries.

Would a taxonomy have saved Victoria Climbié? No, and it would trivialise her suffering to pretend that it might. But an information and knowledge infrastructure, shared by the agencies to which she was entrusted, might have improved her chances – and a good public taxonomy is an essential component in that infrastructure. With neither objects nor practices to bridge the institutional boundaries that she was jostled between, Victoria was lost in the gaps. If she had been saved during those fateful eight months leading to her death, it would have been more by accident than design.

4

Taxonomies and activities for organisational effectiveness

A wonderful harmony is created when we join together the seemingly unconnected.

(Heraclitus, quoted in von Oech, 2001)

It's time to move beyond a consideration of infrastructure (and taxonomies as part of infrastructure) to the role that taxonomy work can play in the basic activities of organisations as they pursue their goals. We will be guided in this task by another taxonomy of sorts, Donald Marchand's strategic information alignment (SIA) framework (see Figure 4.1).

Figure 4.1 Marchand's strategic information alignment framework

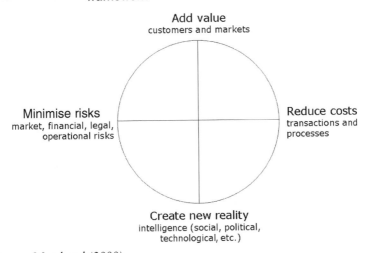

Add value
customers and markets

Minimise risks
market, financial, legal,
operational risks

Reduce costs
transactions and
processes

Create new reality
intelligence (social, political,
technological, etc.)

Source: Marchand (2000).

Marchand developed this framework to help organisations align their information management practices with their business objectives, so it is based on a simple taxonomy of four categories of business focus. In its original intended use, organisations assess how effectively they are using information to support each category.

The first and the most primal business focus (yes, this framework has an implicit hierarchy) is the management of risk. Risk comes from both internal sources as well as the external environment. After risk, organisations must worry about reducing costs – or, more accurately, increasing the productivity of their resources and assets in relation to their costs. This dimension is about margin and efficiency. Once they have set their internal house in order, organisations tend to focus on their income streams – outwardly, to their customers and markets, where they must add value in order to compete. They must understand customers (information gathering) as well as inform and educate them, so this involves a two-way information flow. The most mature focus is on innovation. If risk, costs and customers are all well served, then resources turn towards the creation of new reality (Marchand, 2000: 24–8).

Marchand's framework is useful because it is oriented towards information work and matches information needs to the primary types of activity that contribute towards effectiveness. Two important activities (for us) that he does not cover, strategic planning and talent management, can be accommodated when we look more closely at knowledge management applications of taxonomy work in our next chapter.

Risk

Categorisation is, of course, fundamental to the management of risk. Different kinds of risk must be identified and grouped together based on origin, severity or remedy. Risk intelligence systems need to identify the signals or clues that would indicate particular categories of risk and put in place monitoring mechanisms (strategic early warning systems) so that these signals are picked up whenever a risk is emerging (Gilad, 2001). Control, avoidance or remedial strategies need to be prepared for each category of risk.

In increasingly complex and uncertain environments, new and unexpected risks emerge with unsettling frequency. Here our established taxonomies of risk are of little help. The greatest contribution the organisation can make is in *early category creation.*

When unusual events occur of which we have no prior experience, this is the same as saying that they do not fit into our established categories for understanding and dealing with things. But it is a basic human coping mechanism to seek to place the unusual event into our taxonomies of response. This is because *we use taxonomies to identify unknown things.* Taxonomies are sense-making frameworks to the extent that they allow us to take an unknown thing and relate it to other similar things that we do know in our taxonomy. If it has feathers, wings and a beak, we know it's a bird, even if we don't know what type. This is closely related to the practice of *diagnosis.*

If we categorise an unknown thing ineptly, our response strategies may be inappropriate. When the disease SARS first launched itself into the world via the Hotel Metropole in Hong Kong, it looked – and was treated – like a type of viral pneumonia. In such diseases, the lungs gradually fill with fluid until the victim can no longer breathe. Standard procedure when this happens is to perform a tracheotomy – cut a hole into the victim's windpipe and allow the fluids to drain from the lungs.

What was unnerving about SARS was that it didn't behave 'normally' – i.e. according to the category of disease to which it had been assigned. Healthcare workers who were treating SARS patients started to get sick and die in alarming numbers. The strength of the categorisation actually hindered appropriate response – it couldn't be viral transmission the experts said, because *this type of virus can't survive for very long outside the body.*

The countries with the most highly developed healthcare systems often fared worse than those without. The first SARS infected country to come off the World Health Organisation's danger list was Vietnam. I'm told that when a senior Vietnamese official was asked how they had managed to control the SARS infection rates so effectively, he replied:

> We saw what was happening in other countries, so we did two things. First, we put troops round the hospitals – people could go in, but they couldn't come out. Second, we stopped doing tracheotomies – which the French had taught us as standard procedure. All that fluid coming out under pressure from the lungs had to be the transmission vector. We just pumped the patients full of antibiotics and hoped for the best.

Whether this anecdote is true or not, tracheotomies were highly risky procedures in the absence of very strict controls against infection via droplets, airborne transmission or direct contact (Ohara, 2004).

Now, of course, we know that the SARS corona virus does not behave like other respiratory tract viruses, and it does remain active and infectious for considerable periods outside the body. We now have a new category for it.

The SARS case illustrates one of the dangers of strong taxonomies. Human beings are dangerously prone to making first bets on scanty evidence – 'but it *looks* like viral pneumonia, it *must* behave the same way!' And once we are sure it's in the correct taxonomic slot, we'll ignore overwhelming evidence to the contrary.

HIV AIDS shows another aspect of the importance of category creation. When it was first noticed at the beginning of the 1980s, it was a deeply mysterious disease. It behaved like nothing else known to medical science. It was initially thought to be a skin cancer disease since that was how it became visible to doctors – the puzzling thing was this was previously an extremely rare condition limited to narrow racial groups. Gay men seemed particularly at risk, and so it was labelled a 'gay disease'. Its easy transmission through unprotected sex or reuse of needles by drug addicts made sure its early categorisation was not a scientific one at all. It entered our taxonomies of morality and blame faster than it entered our scientific taxonomies of treatment. For years, it was socially visible but invisible to taxonomies of treatment.

However crude or discriminatory the categorisations of those early years, and however much they slowed the establishment's efforts in addressing the disease, they still had some effect. Haemophiliacs also got the disease, so it could also be transmitted through the blood. Gay men and haemophiliacs getting sick in other ways began to reveal the many other symptomatic expressions of the disease and helped identify it as an immune disorder. Finally, other groups of sufferers also became visible.

The challenge for the medical community in respect to HIV AIDS was that they had to learn about it from zero. Nobody knows how long it took before it was even 'seen' as a disease, since nobody knows how many people's deaths before the 1980s were AIDS-related but classified on death certificates as due to other causes (death certificates must use the International Classification of Diseases) (Bowker and Star, 1999: 124–5). Frozen tissue samples from 1968 suggest that it was killing people at least since the 1960s (Osmond, 2003). If it doesn't exist in the taxonomy it is invisible. If it is invisible it is unknown. If it is unknown it is untreatable.

It's hard to study something that doesn't exist in a taxonomy. The virus itself was isolated in 1983 but not definitively linked with AIDS until the following year. It was not given a place in the International Committee on the Taxonomy of Viruses classification until 1986 (Osmond, 2003). Why did it take so long? Because it behaved like nothing else in our taxonomies of disease – we had no related categories to compare it with so that we could learn about it by proxy.

Indeed, the discipline of virology was just starting to emerge as a separate discipline in the 1980s – previously, the study of viruses was scattered across the taxonomy of research disciplines according to the virus hosts – plants, animals, human beings. So there was little reliable integrated knowledge of viruses at all. And viruses are notoriously resistant to classification by traditional scientific means. They mutate in their hosts, they cause wildly different effects, they trade genetic material with their hosts. In short, they refuse to remain in a neat biological box. There are still biologists who believe that viruses do not constitute a true taxonomic category at all because different viruses originate in different species and belong to those species (Bowker and Star, 1999: 96–8). Of course, if they are scattered across the taxonomy of living things, it is virtually impossible to study them in any depth. Gathering things together into a taxonomic class is the only true way to study, compare and learn. *Taxonomies determine by inclusion and creation of categories what you can see and know, but also by exclusion or scattering what you cannot see or know.*

Now, of course, by creating a medical category and building a body of questions and knowledge around that category we know considerably more about HIV AIDS and other viral diseases, and by extension have strategies and drugs to deal with other viral and auto-immune diseases.

Taxonomies are incredibly powerful for the recognition of risk, but taxonomy flexibility and new category creation are vitally important for the anticipation and management of new risk. Our only warning is that strong taxonomies can also inhibit the recognition of new risk. Flexibility is an important requirement.

Department of Homeland Security digital library

In 2002, in the wake of the 9/11 terrorist attacks, the United States government decided to formally recognise a new risk on a new scale and established the Department of Homeland Security. Soon afterwards, the Department's Office of Domestic Preparedness saw the need for a digital library that could be made available to a broad range of local, state and federal policy-makers.

This library would contain the latest information on homeland security strategy, policy and current research so as to ensure common awareness, consistent response and regulatory compliance. It would cover a broad swathe of risk areas that had been identified for the United States: border security, disaster management and response, epidemiology, inter-governmental relations, intelligence, law enforcement, money laundering, weapons and technology. In short, it would form part of the United States government's risk awareness and risk response framework.

Information would need to be distributed in a way that supported consistent and coordinated awareness and response across many different agencies. Moreover the content itself was collected from a wide range of agencies in different formats and styles of presentation. Officials very quickly identified the need for good metadata and categorisation to broker a common search across this diversity and enable effective and relevant retrievals from the system.

The original intention was to use auto-categorisation, where a programme indexes the materials automatically, and assigns categories based on the content of documents and defined semantic rules. However, this was difficult to apply in practice because the topics covered by the collection spanned many different disciplines, the terminology and format of documents varied widely, and the area of homeland security itself was a new creation, with fluid and evolving terminology and categories of its own.

The user community would need a common language of search spanning different disciplines and working contexts. It was decided that a taxonomy would have to be built from scratch, and only then could this be used to teach the auto-categorisation engine how to recognise the contents of documents and tag them in ways that diverse user communities would recognise in browsing and searching.

The taxonomy was built over two years, manually. It was built inductively from the content for the digital library as it was collected. This is a classic 'cluster and sort' technique in taxonomy building. Because it was such a new domain and contained many cross-disciplinary linkages, a large body of content was necessary to be able to define the overall shape and scope of the domain, discriminate the boundaries of useful clusters of content and label them appropriately. At the same time, the vocabulary of homeland security was itself emerging and changing, and required some time to stabilise into a common, widely understood vocabulary.

The taxonomy development process was emergent and iterative, mirroring the domain of homeland security itself. The first stage was a relatively simple tree structure taxonomy of topics and sub-topics. This was then expanded into a thesaurus by adding alternate terms and cross-relationships between topics in the taxonomy structure. Finally, the taxonomy was turned into a faceted scheme by adding schedules for geographic region and event type. It now had three facets: Topic, Geography and Events. A fourth facet covering Agencies was under development in late 2005.

In 2004 the taxonomy team acquired Teragram auto-categorisation software and settled down to train it. There are several different techniques for training auto-categorisation software – you can write semantic rules for it by specifying the semantic patterns within documents that indicate particular topics; you can give it training sets to analyse of typical documents for each topic; you can let the tool crawl your content and make suggestions and then correct the mistakes. Teragram uses a semantic rules-based approach.

Defining rules is a very labour-intensive, skilled process. The topics in the taxonomy must be described to accommodate the variety of ways that they are expressed in the documents themselves – another reason for having a good-sized representative collection of content to build from. Hard work though it is, the advantage of using this approach is that as topics, vocabularies and issues continue to change, the rules themselves can be edited and adjusted promptly and with relatively little effort. The rules for the taxonomy term 'Hurricanes' were revised in the wake of Hurricane Katrina, for example, to include rules that would capture documents describing levees and flooding.

The Homeland Security Digital Library project is a good exemplar of how taxonomies are critical to enabling coordination around risk. In this case the project was founded on the need to make a common resource base available to the various agencies involved in homeland security – and quickly evolved into the need to establish a common language and set of categories for that community. It also illustrates some of the difficulties of taxonomy development in new, cross-disciplinary, emergent or rapidly changing knowledge domains – and strategies that can be deployed to deal with those difficulties:

- Collect a lot of content.

- Work iteratively, from simplicity to depth.

- Wait for the vocabulary to stabilise.

- Define topics against their context of use.

- Use facets to expand your collection's openness to different perspectives.

- Design for flexibility and openness to change.

Source: Pitts (2005).

Costs

Managing costs usually requires an intimate knowledge of your internal processes and constant information flows to monitor and control them. In this way you can maximise the productivity of your resources, minimise waste and reduce mistakes, redundant effort and re-work.

The most obvious taxonomic work in support of this is systems mapping – or, more precisely, process mapping. Of course, not all process maps are taxonomies (because they don't always fulfil our three requirements for a taxonomy), but they are first cousins and have many family resemblances. Business process maps translate very easily into taxonomies.

Moreover the mapping process itself often uses taxonomic frameworks and establishes common vocabularies – as taxonomies do – to ensure that the mapping project team members are all viewing and describing the processes in the same way. For example, in Six Sigma process improvement methodology, teams develop an early, high-level process map called a SIPOC – an acronym for the categories to be analysed: Suppliers, Inputs, Process, Outputs, Customers (see Figure 4.2) (Rath & Strong, 2000: 11).

This activity bounds the process to be mapped and analysed, and establishes a common vocabulary for all the key elements in play. *Exactly the same framework* (under different names) can be used in knowledge mapping exercises to take a knowledge and information view of a business activity (see Figure 4.3). Here, for each business activity, you establish and name the key knowledge and information inputs (and their suppliers) and outputs (and their customers), which can then be used as a basis for:

Figure 4.2 SIPOC process map

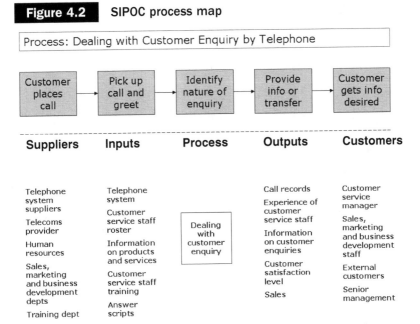

Process: Dealing with Customer Enquiry by Telephone

| Customer places call | Pick up call and greet | Identify nature of enquiry | Provide info or transfer | Customer gets info desired |

Suppliers	**Inputs**	**Process**	**Outputs**	**Customers**
Telephone system suppliers	Telephone system	Dealing with customer enquiry	Call records	Customer service manager
Telecoms provider	Customer service staff roster		Experience of customer service staff	Sales, marketing and business development staff
Human resources	Information on products and services		Information on customer enquiries	External customers
Sales, marketing and business development depts	Customer service staff training		Customer satisfaction level	Senior management
Training dept	Answer scripts		Sales	

- creating an information and knowledge inventory;
- making resource decisions;
- identifying gaps, redundancies and duplications;
- mapping coordination and collaboration opportunities;
- improving information flows;
- informing an 'Activity' facet in a taxonomy;
- informing a records management facet in a taxonomy.

In many respects, the *process of mapping* is as important as the product. Mapping exercises are best done with all the process's stakeholders and actors present in a room with a large whiteboard and lots of sticky notes. You ask the people present to map out the process in question, building out the detail into micro-steps indicating decision points and actions from the high-level map composed for the SIPOC exercise. Most important, they are asked to map the process *as is* – that is to say, not what the manual says the process should be, but how it actually works in the real world, warts and all. The reason for doing this as a collective exercise is that the exercise will uncover variations in understanding and variations in practice among the different actors. It will also uncover variations in how the processes are described – ripe ground for

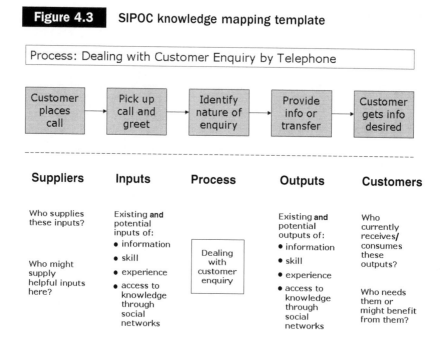

Figure 4.3 SIPOC knowledge mapping template

Process: Dealing with Customer Enquiry by Telephone

| Customer places call | Pick up call and greet | Identify nature of enquiry | Provide info or transfer | Customer gets info desired |

Suppliers	**Inputs**	**Process**	**Outputs**	**Customers**
Who supplies these inputs? Who might supply helpful inputs here?	Existing **and** potential inputs of: • information • skill • experience • access to knowledge through social networks	Dealing with customer enquiry	Existing **and** potential outputs of: • information • skill • experience • access to knowledge through social networks	Who currently receives/consumes these outputs? Who needs them or might benefit from them?

misunderstandings and rich material for taxonomy building later on. Many of these steps will have documents and information resources attached to them.

The mapping exercise stabilises a common standardised view of the current state among all the players, and it is this baseline view which can be analysed for loops, errors, dead-ends, and circumnavigations ripe for abbreviation.

If you have never done business process mapping, you will be surprised by the degree of variation in practice and understanding – among different practitioners as well as between practitioners and the official manual. Sometimes, where different grades of staff are involved, this variation may not come through in a group setting, so you will need to compare across several mapping interviews. The real illumination always comes when the whole group sees the variances, bad and good, and collectively resolves them.

In one consultancy I undertook for a non-profit organisation that also conducted commercial training programmes, the training unit manager was convinced that the front-office staff – who served the whole organisation – knew how to handle potential customer enquiries. According to the procedure, calls should be put through to him or his deputy immediately. He was convinced because it was a simple process, he had trained them himself and he was regularly receiving telephone calls as per plan.

Mapping interviews with the front-office staff unearthed at least three other pathways. Two of them were new hires and didn't know that the deputy manager could also receive enquiry calls so she was rarely disturbed. If the manager was out (which was frequently, because he also trained) they improvised – either forwarding the call to one of the trainers or attempting to answer the questions from the brochures to hand. Sometimes they took messages, but these were limited to name and number with no details of the enquiry and were passed to the department secretary. It might take some time before the unit manager got them.

Improvisation in the face of organisational dislocations or lack of specific guidance is one of the biggest causes of variation. It's not always a bad thing. When my local bank was acquired by another bank some years ago, it temporarily suspended international remittance services while the two operations were being integrated. Only the acquiring bank provided these services. As a customer, I didn't discover this until I tried to use the service. My teller didn't blink – she picked up the phone, called her colleague in the other bank (in a branch just across the road), gave her my details and asked her to prepare the documentation for me while I crossed the road. Impressed, I asked her if this was their standard procedure. She said, 'No, we are not really supposed to do this, but we arranged this privately because a lot of customers were getting upset.' This improvisation was an excellent indicator for a coordination opportunity that had been missed, but should really have been built into the standard process and scaled. Officially, it didn't exist.

As this example shows, collective or individual mapping interviews are not always enough. You have to go and see the process in action to uncover the issues that the players may be unaware of or think unimportant. In my non-profit organisation sometimes, it turned out, front-line staff made category mistakes – they interpreted the call as meant for a different department, resulting in customer frustration and multiple call backs. Sometimes, while trying to be helpful, they gave the wrong information based on outdated information, or mis-understanding, or partial information. Sometimes the call was put through without checking whether the manager was at his desk and it was left to ring until the potential customer gave up.

In my non-profit organisation the collectively constructed map allowed all the players in the process to identify improvement opportunities which included:

- a simple set of diagnostics to identify the enquiry type and customer type (two implicit taxonomies here!);

- standard information scripts for general enquiries, together with a call record log where calls were categorised by topic;

- checking that the manager or deputy were in before putting through calls;

- message forms containing more customer information and details of the enquiry for non-standard enquiries.

The discovery method for taxonomy building is very similar to the discovery method for business process mapping. This should not be surprising, since all but the most mechanised of processes rely on the supply, movement and application of information and knowledge. Taxonomy development fulfils the same stabilisation and standardisation role as process mapping, and is frequently an extension of process mapping. Taxonomies meant to support the internal activities of an organisation must do some form of process mapping.

Like process mapping, taxonomy work enhances visibility, control and improvement. It is based on current language in use and current real-world practice. The collective mapping approach allows for improvements that are mutually agreed, prioritised and owned by the actors involved, giving them significantly greater chances of adoption. Conversely there are few process improvement projects that do not rely on establishing new information flows and semantic standardisation to measure, monitor and assure consistency.

While mapping work and semantic standardisation is an important dimension of cost management in organisations, it's not the only way that taxonomies can have an impact. Taxonomy work is also fundamental to the management of resources and the planning work around resource deployment.

Let's take a planning taxonomy from the domain of agriculture as an example. Crop rotation is the discipline of changing the nature of crops grown on any given land every year to ensure its sustainable fertility. It is based on a simple classification of crops according to their interactions with the soil – the nutrients they take out, and the nutrients they leave behind. This forms the basis for a crop rotation *plan*, just as the BCG matrix forms the basis for a product development *plan* (see Figure 4.4). It's one of the most basic things to know as a farmer if you want to minimise your artificial fertilisation interventions and farm the same land sustainably into the future.

Figure 4.4 Crop rotation plan for a kitchen garden

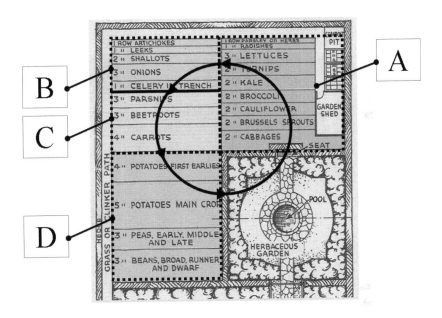

Planning and resource management always requires some form of organisation of resources according to a taxonomy, whether it is implicit or explicit.

Taxonomic strictness can vary of course. Companies tend to go through cycles of *growth* and capacity building, when taxonomic rigour is relaxed and cost management is placed second to opportunity building. They acquire based on opportunity, not exact fit with the traditional categories of their business. The other side of that cycle is *focus*, when simplification is the order of the day, and cost control and cost effectiveness become paramount. Here, the contribution of taxonomy work becomes much more apparent, because its primary purpose is to *consolidate* – i.e. reduce to agreed categories. After all, one of the primary goals of taxonomy work is to *simplify* – either access to, or management of, a knowledge domain.

Case study 4.2

Unilever's brand simplification exercise

In early 2000, Unilever announced that it was slashing its 1,600 portfolio of brands to the 400 'jewels' that already earned 90 per cent of its revenue.

It was a conscious exercise in simplification. In a June 2003 presentation in Chicago, Unilever executive John Ripley quoted a McKinsey report: 'A lot of our clients have been choking in their own complexity, resulting in little innovation or employee fulfillment' (Ripley, 2003).

The more brand labels you have to manipulate, resource and manage, the harder it is to navigate your landscape of brands and products effectively. Unilever expected their simplification strategy to double growth (optimistically, as it turned out), but also to save some $3 billion in four years, half from business process simplification and half from procurement simplification. In procurement for laundry products alone, they would eliminate more than two-thirds of Unilever's 152 sets of specifications for perfume ingredients.

When you look at the final stable of products that emerged from their simplification exercise, mapped into a tree structure in Figure 4.5 for the purposes of clarity, it's immediately obvious that their brand simplification exercise was also, in all respects except in name, a taxonomy exercise.

Unilever's brand management structure falls easily into a taxonomy tree structure: divided first into three industries, then into 13 categories, with the 400 or so brands behind those.

Like many other real-world taxonomies, it has some untidy features and polyhierarchical links inside it. Some brands appear in multiple categories (e.g. Dove, Slim.Fast, Lipton). Others have a family of sub-brands beneath them at the fourth layer (e.g. Surf, Heart), while others move immediately to a single product or cluster of products (e.g. Snuggle, Hellmann's).

Many brands are in transition – Carb Options is an aggregating meta-brand for the health conscious and is being stamped onto other Unilever brands (such as Hellmann's, Lipton and Skippy) in an attempt to give them a lateral (polyhierarchical) association. In 2004, Unilever adopted a new corporate mission centred on the theme 'Vitality'. This has now had a knock-on effect, as a selection of brands across the taxonomy become identified as 'Vitality' brands, creating new polyhierarchical linkages. As complexity grows after their simplification, the tree structure will become increasingly difficult to manage and will likely transform into a faceted structure in the longer term.

This exercise illustrates how powerfully taxonomies maintain the

Figure 4.5 Unilever's taxonomy of brands

organisation of resources, people and products in support of strategic or operational effectiveness, just as much as they can help organise knowledge and information content for retrieval. It also shows how simplification and complication coexist in a constant dynamic. Above all it should demonstrate that there is plenty of work for taxonomists beyond information retrieval.

Customers and markets

Customers are mysterious and difficult creatures, largely because, despite our best efforts, they insist on making their own decisions. And they change. Like viruses, they mutate and evolve, stubbornly evading predictable categorisation. They are a taxonomist's nightmare.

We might build taxonomies organised around our own internal worlds – for example, taxonomies of sales enquiry types for sales teams, or taxonomies of complaint types for call centres. Japanese cosmetics company KAO has a centralised customer service department to handle complaints, but it also has a policy that complaints are dealt with as close to the root of the complaint as quickly as possible. Their customer service staff have to categorise and despatch complaints to 150 different destinations as soon as they come in. That requires a very good taxonomy of complaints mapped to the organisation structure, and good, consistent, diagnostic mechanisms to ensure the complaint ends up in the most customer-friendly place (Marchand, 2000: 43).

But most of our customer taxonomies are determined less by our world and more by theirs. I have just watched a TV advertisement for Knorr packet soup (coincidentally, a survivor of the Unilever brand simplification exercise). We see a husband opening a packet of yummy tomato soup and preparing it while his tired wife unwinds after a hard day's work. The narrator describes the events in a tongue-in-cheek recipe format 'Allow wife to steam gently in bath'. The catchphrase, as our loving couple snuggle up with spicy tomato soup on the dangerously white sofa, is 'Knorr: Recipe for Living'. The ad is witty, heartwarming and relevant. It's not just about soup and its nutritional value any more – it's about stories and contexts. And those stories and contexts are determined by things that matter to us – or at least, what marketeers think matter to us.

Knowing what matters to our customers and being able to provide it is the key to successful competition. As futurist Rolf Jensen puts it:

> The English AGA stove has had no product development since 1922. The price is in the $10,000 to $15,000 range, installation not included. Yearly sales are at 7,000 units, but the stove has a clear future because of nonexistent product development. *Time* magazine quotes marketing manager Ian Heath as saying, 'What other kitchen appliance can promise family togetherness? They (the customers) want family life and AGA is at the center of that wish. They see the AGA in a very emotional sense.' This is not a status appliance, although the price tag would seem to indicate otherwise. It is a lifestyle appliance with a story of family togetherness, something that abounded in the old days, back when family values and gender roles were not up for discussion and before mass production robbed products of their spirit. (Jensen, 1999: 39)

How do we get to know what our customers think? In a large, noisy and confusing marketplace, how do we even know who our customers are? Which ones matter most? Or who we want to be our customers? Which of the opinions we unearth matter more, because they represent a whole category of customers and not just an individual voice? How do we know what a customer will respond to, and buy, even though they are not yet aware of this incipient desire? In a world of conglomerates, global markets, mass media and the Internet, where our customer population is so diverse and distant, how do we learn, organise and deliver – quickly? The answer is, at least partially, in taxonomy work. The role of taxonomies, after all, includes domain simplification, description and charting for reliable and speedy navigation.

In the management of risk the taxonomic traits that matter are category recognition and knowing when it's time to create new categories; in the management of cost the taxonomic traits that matter are standardised description, collaborative mapping and simplification. When it comes to customers, the taxonomic trick, the real competitive edge in adding value for customers, is in *discovering categories that work*. Our taxonomies of customers must reflect their worlds, not ours. The onus on *category discovery* is very high.

Customer segmentation is the traditional approach – and in its way is quite Aristotelian, insofar as it attempts to categorise on objective, observable attributes. Depending on your goals, you can segment by intrinsic properties or by behaviours – or both. If you want to know who buys what, you'll segment on demographic data like age, gender, marital status, as well as attributes of geography, socio-economic position, lifestyle. If you want to know why they buy, you'll segment on frequency of purchase, consumption patterns, price sensitivity, media exposure and so on. Add to this the formulas for customer lifetime value and cost of acquisition and you start to get categories that look actionable (Fleisher and Bensoussan, 2003: 162–79).

The Moor Hall Health Club in the UK felt that the so-called 'grey market' of seniors was under-exploited in a largely youth-oriented industry. In their area, seniors made up 38 per cent of the population. Against all expectations, the club was remarkably successful, doing better even than clubs that targeted the younger population.

A segmentation analysis of this market using a matrix taxonomy, comparing the three dimensions of financial assets, social support needs (loneliness factor) and whether seniors' motivation for staying fit was intrinsically or extrinsically driven, generated a typology of eight potential customer profiles. Moor Hall had effectively targeted facilities, events and marketing strategies towards the ones that made business sense – resulting in above average performance for a health club and a trailblazing model for health clubs in a greying population (Fleisher and Bensoussan, 2003: 177–8).

Moor Hall had some advantages: they were situated in a local community which they could get to know well and which had a fairly well defined population. What if we could do segmentation analysis on a very large scale? This is the stuff of which myths are made, particularly among those who sell data warehouses and OLAP systems. In a data warehouse you gather all of the segmentation data compiled from surveys, research and transaction records from multiple systems. OLAP stands for online analytical processing and is a data manipulation technique which allows you to examine your vast reservoir of data by any combination of attributes, e.g. 'show me the pre-Christmas spending patterns of married bald men over forty in Germany'. You can slice and dice your data in myriad ways, and what you are doing is looking for that combination of winning attributes – the winning categories in your million different taxonomic combinations – that will give you actionable customer profiles. It's essentially a matrix taxonomy with unlimited dimensions of comparison.

This is the stuff from which the fabled beer and nappies story comes from – which I have never been able to find an authoritative source for. The story goes that transaction data analysis applied in a supermarket chain discovered that nappies and beer had especially high sales on Friday evenings – when sliced and diced to perfection, it was discovered that husbands did the nappy shopping for the wife just before the weekend and were compensating for the shame by stocking up on beers for the weekend football on TV – hey presto, nappies and beer were thenceforth placed close to each other, just in case the husband was tempted to forget the nappies (upsetting most senses of proper categorisation along the way). The supermarket chain decided that the category of football-and-beer husbands with young children was one worth having.

There are also lots of more credible stories about business intelligence applications for customer segmentation and categorisation based on behaviours and demographic data (Vitt et al., 2002). But the approach is far from problem free.

The attributes you are using and comparing are not as objective nor as stable as they look. Data warehouses gather data from many, many different sources, and the data they collect has been input in many, many different contexts with varying standards and definitions for the attributes that are assigned. Remember that Vivian Alvarez had eleven variants of her name in the various Australian immigration department databases. And that was just her name. What about attributes that are more open to interpretation?

What, for example, puts someone in the category 'unemployed'? Is it somebody who is between jobs? Between graduation and first job? If I'm self-employed and don't currently have a job, am I unemployed? Do I have to be on social security? How long do I have to be unemployed before I'm unemployed? Your wife will probably have a different view on this compared to your local social security office. Such distinctions are important: one nameless government department took a conservative interpretation of the category 'unemployed' because they wanted to send a political message about their success in reducing unemployment. Then they realised that they were funded based on how many people were 'unemployed' and their interpretation became more liberal. Needless to say, long-term trend analysis was somewhat complicated by this switch. Historians might later become curious about why there was a sudden leap in unemployment in the year of the categorisation change.

Don't be fooled: *all categorisation is subjective and fluid*. The issue for taxonomy developers is: how much variance can you permit consistent with your goals and how can you improve consistency where you need it?

Different data collection processes may be gathering segmentation data inconsistently. In France I might check the '35–45' age range box, while in Singapore I check the '40–50' age range box. How can the segmentation data be compared?

The truth is, data warehouse and OLAP systems have enormous data normalisation problems arising from inconsistent standards and variant understandings of the meanings of the categories being used. It's rarely easy to figure out and correct for all these variances without going back to the contexts of data collection and original categorisation decisions. They are a model lesson for taxonomy developers: in the usefulness of scope notes to give context to the interpretation and selection of taxonomy terms, and in the importance of training and standardisation *if the purpose of your taxonomy will be compromised by lack of precision*.

For this reason, despite the alluring specificity of the data warehouse stories, segmentation is a crude instrument unless allied with a more intimate knowledge of your customers. It only gives very broad profiles and very general patterns, and really only works well as a very high-level pattern-identification technique. As Fleisher and Bensoussan point out, 'predictions based on customer characteristics may fail to materialize in sales due to the impact of more influential behavioral factors that were not identified during the segmentation analysis' (Fleisher and Bensoussan, 2003: 172).

It certainly does not get us inside the head of the customer with sufficient granularity to understand their dreams, desires, stories and resonant contexts. The increasing trend towards product and service mass customisation, personalisation and co-creation increases the demand to find better ways of discovering actionable customer categories. In fact, it turns out that the famous Moor Hall story was not a pure customer segmentation analysis story at all – the segmentation analysis was done *retrospectively* and then used to explain the decisions they had already made intuitively based on their local knowledge.

If we are not confident about how to categorise our customers then the logical next step is to allow them to categorise themselves. The trouble here is that we have to give them something to select. One of the ways we do this – usually badly – is in automated voicemail menu systems. Here we construct 'if-then' decision trees – essentially a taxonomy of choices, guiding our callers into the taxonomy of ways that we are organised to deal with them.

Voicemail has a huge disadvantage as a tree structure. Visually, we can navigate 12–15 categories in a single list, and we can take time to interpret the less obvious terms in the list before we make our choice. Aurally, we are easily confused above four categories in a list, and we have to rely on our memory to compare the choices and figure out which category belongs to us or promises something in the right direction (Byrne, 2001).

Limiting the breadth of the top level of a tree means that the taxonomy has to be deeper – which means that the 'real' topics will be pushed deeper under more intermediate generalities, multiplying the number of choices we have to make to get to them. Remember (from Chapter 2) that cognitively human beings start in the middle of a taxonomy with base level categories somewhere between extreme specificity and extreme generality. We know what we want – we may not necessarily know how this company sorts it and generalises it.

No wonder the aural taxonomies of voicemail have such a reputation for being confusing and frustrating. The generic topics at the top are too generic to be meaningful, and we may not discover our error until we get three or four levels down and then find we have to start again. Unfortunately, the people who design these trees break one of the primary rules of taxonomy building (use the language and categories of your audience), because they almost invariably build the choices around the organisation's categories and not the customer's categories. The study of usability may have become respectable in website design but has not yet penetrated telephone voicemail. (It's improving only now because voice user interface design for computers is developing fast.) In 1996 a Reuters study found that voicemail menu navigation was taking an average of 20 per cent of the call time (Reuters, 1996). Things don't seem much better a decade later.

About a year ago I spent some time in London and rented a house from friends who were travelling. I was taking over the telephone bills in my name, but wanted to keep the old number for my friends' return. I called the British Telecom helpline and chose the option 'Customer Service' and then 'Moving House'. However, the options here were requesting the telephone number of my old house in the UK which, being resident in Singapore, I didn't have. Not being able to navigate backwards (no option for that) I called again, but couldn't find any other category at the top level that matched what I wanted. Finally I pressed zero to speak to an operator (a long wait), who put me through to sales. The sales person wasn't able to deal with my enquiry and passed me back to someone in the depths of customer service who passed me to somebody else. I wasn't able to find out which category I should have chosen or ended up in because the person I was speaking to didn't know. I was saved only by social networks among the telephone support staff. I got what I wanted in the end, but I'm sure there must have been a way through the voicemail tree. This teaches us a few further lessons about taxonomies:

- We should never underestimate the capacity of human beings to misunderstand our labels.

- We can never assume our staff will know what our categories mean any more than our customers will.

- Aural taxonomies are particularly prone to errors because of the lack of immediate 'checking' context – designers need to anticipate mistakes and provide navigation out of them.

- Social networks compensate for taxonomy mistakes, but the more effective they are, the more they conceal taxonomy faults.

There are more positive developments. In recent years, work on the development of *personas and archetypes* has gone some way towards developing categories that more truly reflect our customers and our customers' world (Pruitt and Rudin, 2003; Goodwin, 2001). We are getting closer to rich category discovery from our audiences, and the tools for doing so come from anthropology.

Case study 4.3

Club Med, storytelling and archetypes

In the 1990s, Club Med discovered that it was getting a lot of customer complaints. Over 40 per cent of customer dissatisfaction was linked to miscategorisation – customers were choosing or being recommended the wrong type of resort for their needs. For example, adventurous singles would end up in resorts oriented towards families with kids, sports enthusiasts in party-oriented resorts, party-goers on lush, deserted islands, and so on.

When they looked closely at their customer profiles, they identified the following persona-types among their customers:

- Tubes – family types oriented towards comfort.
- Celebrators – young people oriented towards partying.
- Epicureans – oriented towards luxury and comfort.
- Cultivated – independently minded, oriented towards exploring the local culture.
- Activists – oriented towards adventure and sport.

They used this small taxonomy as the basis of their 'Key to Happiness' programme, which is a self-completed diagnostic questionnaire available to prospective customers in all Club Med retail outlets. It is designed to identify the characteristics that match customers to their closest persona. The resorts themselves are styled according to the preferences of each category. The taxonomy was being used to allow customers to self-select into resorts that were most appropriate to their preferences (Horovitz, 2000: 63).

Building customer personas in this way is often no more than imaginatively extended customer segmentation. The original segmentation analysis can be enriched through focus groups and customer observation. By marrying this with customer self-categorisation, Club Med had created a categorisation process that was much less likely to result in category mistakes.

But these personas are still a long way from getting us inside customer's heads. We cannot guarantee that they are uncontaminated by our own internal categories and concerns. Dave Snowden of the Cognitive Edge network (formerly Cynefin Centre), building on work done in the 1990s with the IBM Institute for Knowledge Management, has developed interesting new techniques for generating personas (and the implicit taxonomies that lie behind them) that come directly out of customer self-perceptions.

The key to the technique is the use of storytelling. Instead of bringing customers in for focus groups and leading them with questions structured by our internal concerns, you bring them in to tell stories – about their experience with your product, your brand or the particular lifestyle area you are interested in. The stories are written down as they are told. The same customers then work with their stories to identify stereotype characters appearing in their stories and the attributes associated with them. In a two-stage process drawn from cultural anthropology techniques, the attributes of these stereotype characters are removed from the original stories and clustered according to how customers see the relationships between them. Each cluster becomes the basis for a new fictional character that expresses all those attributes. These characters are called *archetypes*, because they are grounded in the collective experience of that customer group and express general sets of values, behaviours and attitudes across the group (Snowden, 2000a). Archetypes are extremely interesting persona-sets from a marketing standpoint, because they are drawn directly from the customer experience by customers themselves. The biases of corporate category systems have not been imposed on them.

Collections of archetypes derived in this way form a special kind of taxonomy called a *typology*. They are different from the matrix typologies we discussed earlier in Chapter 2 and the segmentation typologies discussed earlier in this chapter because they are arbitrary clusters of attributes – they have not been constructed along set dimensions of comparison. They basically exist as a list of characters. But they do represent subliminal types of personality or 'customer identities' that exist within the perceptions of the customer community that has produced them, and have very high resonance when 'played back' to those customers. They fulfil the 'mapping' criterion for taxonomies if the process has covered a sufficiently representative cross section of your target population. The full archetype set represents a map of the cultural perceptions of your population in regard to your target topic – lifestyle perceptions, customer experience, life aspirations.

These archetypes, and the story-collections that underpin them, form a powerful resource for understanding the category worlds of customers. They can be used, as in the Club Med example, to drive self-categorisation initiatives that attract customers towards categories that are natural to them. They can be used to organise products and services in ways that make more sense to customers. They can be used as proxy customer types to interrogate for value adding ideas or to test innovations.

Innovation

Taxonomies can be as dangerous for innovators as they are for risk managers. Complexity guru Dave Snowden is fond of saying at conferences, 'If you want to focus on the future, don't start with a taxonomy project, because a taxonomy represents your past.' After all, if innovation is about getting out of the box, taxonomy work is mostly about putting things into boxes. Strong taxonomies can blind managers to innovation opportunities just as much as to risk, because true innovation, by definition, is as yet uncategorised. Extreme risk and extreme opportunity are both extreme because they come at us unforeseen and unrecognised.

There's a noteworthy degree of truth in this, but taxonomy work can also support innovation in two major ways:

- Innovation can sometimes be stimulated by taking existing categories and breaking them apart or combining them in unusual ways – we see this in lateral leaps of the imagination where new connections between categories are made that are not naturally resident in the taxonomy as it stands.

- Existing taxonomy categories can provide a foundation for disciplined ways of exploring innovation opportunities – they give a structured foundation for exploring the unstructured. We see this in technology mapping activities of research and development teams.

In both cases, a taxonomy can form a lever against which innovation work can be done, *by using the taxonomy against itself*. Innovation almost always puts stress on a taxonomy, but the taxonomy itself is a tool in that process, a stable counterbalance against which innovation work is defined. Furthermore, innovations must always end up being incorporated into our taxonomies, because without this integration into our infrastructure and basic operations, we cannot make our innovations productive.

Innovation's relationship to taxonomy work is therefore strained: taxonomy work enables innovation, but innovation challenges taxonomies, and taxonomies must grow to accommodate innovations.

The relationship is not entirely dialectical, however. The taxonomy work we have labelled *category discovery* together with the use of taxonomies for *sense-making* are two aspects of taxonomy work that are particularly supportive of innovation work.

Category-busting activity is a classic innovation generation strategy – but to do this, you need a firm base of categories to challenge or recombine. Without the old categories as reference points it's hard to recognise and place the innovation when it arrives. One of the five key attributes of innovation success, according to Everett Rogers, is *compatibility* – by which he means that the innovation can be matched to existing categories and understood sufficiently to support adoption, even if this is by comparison or contrast (Rogers, 1995: 224–34).

Cirque du Soleil is a classic example of innovation by category-busting. It advertises itself as circus, but circus reinvented. Despite its title, it lacks many of the traditional features of circus – the ring format, the animals, the big name acts. 'It is not quite a circus and not quite opera or theater either, but takes elements from them all' (Williamson, 2002: 3). In some respects, it differs from all three – in the anonymity of its performers, for example. It is successful not simply because it breaks traditional categories, but by self-consciously displaying its category-busting as innovation. The resonances of circus, street performance, theatre, opera and ballet are all superbly put on show to be appreciated *as a sophisticated blend*.

R&D departments in large corporates must make a discipline of continually breaking down categories and making new blends. Many use science and technology mapping techniques that embody clear features of taxonomy work. Science and technology mapping relies on the assumption that primary scientific research holds the key to downstream commercial innovations, so it tries to identify indicators of promising categories of research. Mappers track investments in particular areas of technology by industry players and research scientists to identify promising new technologies; they map the citations in scientific primary research papers, to look for clusters of disciplines interacting with each other in novel ways, and they map patents, categorised by the basic science areas behind them. Such activities indicate promising combinations of scientific categories – sometimes in unpredictable areas.

In the late 1990s a global consumer products company had determined to make a significant innovation in its soap products. They would do this by moving beyond the traditional knowledge domains in soap research: dermatology, physical chemistry and clinical medicine. They created basic science maps of research being invested in by their competitors as well as in the public research sector, across the whole science universe. They were looking primarily for 'high-performing' research areas – areas that promised commercially viable technologies, determined partly by the intensity of citations and size of the research clusters, partly by competitor investment in those areas, partly by the nature of the research itself.

Once they had identified promising areas, they mapped these in greater detail, looking for patterns or weak linkages with dermatology that might show promise. Their mapping activity picked up interesting work being done by a group of geophysicists who were working on mathematical modelling of the cracking of the earth's surface in times of drought. 'Cracking' was also a category of interest in dermatology, so they contacted the geophysicists and initiated a collaboration. They were eventually able to incorporate the geophysical modelling of cracking into a new soap product that had superior anti-cracking capabilities (Pauker and Whitaker, 2000: 21).

This entire project simultaneously relied on established categories and strong taxonomies (to be able to map the interaction of scientific disciplines), and undermined them (by looking for opportunities in weak linkages across widely separated categories). And it used the taxonomic work of semantic mapping to be able to achieve the job.

Case study 4.4

Unilever Research and disposable taxonomies

Innovators don't always like rigid taxonomies, but they usually appreciate taxonomy work. Here's how Unilever's former head of knowledge management Adrian Dale described the approach of research teams at Unilever in 2001.

Unilever operates in a diverse range of fast-moving consumer goods markets. Its products span ice cream to tomato sauces and shampoo to washing powder. Its scientists work in diverse fields from anthropology to mathematics with every physical and life science in between. Building durable company taxonomies across these ranges has been impossible and will probably always be so. Instead, Unilever Research has taken a pragmatic 'just-in-time' approach – creating taxonomies quickly and dynamically for a specific task and then throwing them away. To do this, mind mapping and creativity tools have been deployed in facilitated sessions to develop a shared language for the worlds in which research teams operate. (Dale, 2001)

For the research manager seeking innovations, it appears a waste of time to focus on big taxonomies representing all of the disciplines at play. He or she won't bother with taxonomies of their own discipline, because they already know the structure of their discipline backwards. They don't want to know the deep dark recesses of every other discipline, either. They want to be able to pull together an interdisciplinary domain map of the relevant areas in the relevant disciplines at a sufficiently high level to be able to make investment decisions. The research teams want to be able to pull together topic oriented maps at a more granular, very specific level, as they work on issues within the research programme.

The approach to solve this problem is not external expert-driven taxonomy development at all. The members of the team build their instant taxonomies themselves, using whiteboards and sticky notes.

Each mapping session lasts 2–3 hours and involves dialogue and arguments between the participants. In this process a shared context and language is developed, building on the combined knowledge and experience of the team. Between each session, time is required for the facilitators to tidy the documentation and for participants to reflect on their experience. The number of mapping sessions required depends upon the scale of the field but a minimum of 3 is recommended. (Dale, 2001)

The results of the sessions are transferred into durable documents using mind-mapping software and are used in:

- *patenting* – to identify patent infringements and opportunities: the maps indicate the science areas that need to be checked for possible prior art;
- *environment scanning* – to programme search agents to crawl external repositories for intelligence in the identified fields;

- *intranet* – to structure specialist intranet sites.

Dale is obviously aware in his account that his approach may not sit easily with traditional taxonomists.

> We cannot claim any rigor for the taxonomies we build using this methodology and make no apology for this. They are fit for purpose, just-in-time and throw away by design. However, their leverage is enormous. We are easily able to engage teams in the exercise and get them thinking in great depth about their fields. (Dale, 2001)

His account gives three important insights about good taxonomy development practice, however. First, the flexible, needs-driven taxonomy activity he describes is a great model for how to build any taxonomy:

- Know why you are doing it.
- Involve the taxonomy users.
- Negotiate a common understanding.
- Have a clear idea of how it will be implemented.
- Don't get too attached to it.

Second, it demonstrates that, as Jean Graef puts it in her commentary on this case, taxonomy work goes far beyond the stereotyped view of a tree structure and a thesaurus for a content management system: 'The bottom line is that taxonomies can take different forms depending on the applications they are designed to support' (Dale, 2001).

Third, despite Dale's protests, his account *assumes* a strong taxonomy infrastructure in the background. Interdisciplinary maps of the depth and complexity he describes cannot be drawn out of thin air. Every specialist in the room during a mapping session is bringing detailed, strong, *public* taxonomies to bear. It's just that they are not on paper. They are in their heads.

Unilever has cropped up a lot in this chapter. They appeared in our discussions of managing costs, customers and innovation. Taxonomies are supposed to promote serendipitous discovery, and it so happens that serendipity brought three useful, documented examples from Unilever which were hard to refuse. For that we have to thank them, because taxonomy work, in common with other infrastructure work, is not widely documented and not easily made visible. The contexts and the issues this organisation faces, together with our other examples, are generic enough. The basic taxonomy work of categorisation, category creation, semantic standardisation, collaborative mapping, domain simplification, category discovery and category mixing pervades the basic work of organisations.

This should not be taken as a landgrab attempt for taxonomists, but an invitation to see the value of conscious taxonomy disciplines and approaches for all the core aspects of what makes an organisation effective. In Chapter 3 we described how important taxonomy work was within the information infrastructure of organisations, and we made the point that without strong infrastructure, coordination on a large scale becomes difficult and failure prone. In this chapter we traced the many ways in which taxonomy work either consciously or unconsciously informs our basic business activities. Taken together, it becomes very clear that taxonomy work holds a wider range of application and use than simply as a tool for information retrieval.

5

Taxonomies and knowledge management

Organise your content; there may be a need for librarians.

(O'Dell and Grayson, 1998)

The label 'taxonomy' is a relatively recent arrival in the world of the knowledge manager. The early classics of knowledge management do not mention taxonomies and refer only fleetingly to issues of categorising content. You won't find them in Verna Allee's *The Knowledge Evolution* (1997), neither will you find them in Davenport and Prusak's *Working Knowledge* (1998) although they do discuss knowledge mapping and the desirability of standardised vocabularies. Davenport and Prusak's earlier *Information Ecology* (1997) devotes a page and a half to the need to categorise information but never mentions taxonomies and clearly favours a thesaurus of subject terms over a classification scheme. 'If information is to be captured and leveraged, it must first be categorised' (Davenport and Prusak, 1997: 173).

Nancy Dixon's *Common Knowledge* (2000) is explicitly focused on knowledge transfer but makes only fleeting reference to categorisation and the need to use the common language of the organisation in describing that knowledge. O'Dell and Grayson's *If Only We Knew What We Knew* (1998) spends less than half a page on taxonomies and the need to classify knowledge. They prescribe briefly: 'Organise your content; there may be a need for librarians.'

Apart from the fact that not all librarians know how to *build* taxonomies (as distinct from *applying* them), there is a startling lack of sophistication in how these eminent authors see the issue of information or knowledge organisation.

We might forgive them by pointing out that these early writers were largely concerned with the big picture of knowledge management – how to identify and drive forward an agenda for the better management of knowledge in organisations. Yet even the more pragmatic and applied writers, such as Amrit Tiwana in his *Knowledge Management Toolkit* (2002), fail to deal with taxonomy development – although Tiwana deals with almost everything else. In his fairly sophisticated discussion of how to use metadata to make information and knowledge assets more findable, he actually discusses (briefly) taxonomy development without even realising he is doing so (Tiwana, 2002: 151–4).

It wasn't that taxonomy work wasn't being done. Some of today's leading taxonomy experts have up to 15 years' experience in the field. Even before the explosion of content on the Internet, consultants were helping companies to categorise content in repositories like Lotus Notes. In fact, the taxonomy problem becomes obvious wherever (a) you have a lot of content in one or more repositories and need to improve its accessibility; (b) you need to coordinate more effectively as an organisation. If the corporate lawyers in a firm refer to a 'deed' as a 'deed' and the real estate lawyers in the same firm refer to it as an 'agreement' then neither party will be able to pull together a complete picture of the work that that firm has done for a particular client (Rusanow, 2003: 244).

There are documented taxonomy case studies in knowledge management efforts as far back as 1994 and probably earlier, though the word 'taxonomy' is not used to describe them. Denham Grey traces the current tradition of taxonomy work in knowledge management back to the late 1980s (TaxoCoP, 2005).

Taxonomies and findability

In 1994 the Chevron oil company launched a project to share best practices across its business units. They had multiple existing networks, communities and projects to bridge. Their solution was to build a Best Practices Resources Map pointing to this content. They structured the map according to the main categories in the Baldridge Award framework, and the sub-categories according to the International Benchmarking Clearinghouse's Process Classification Scheme, both of which were already in use at Chevron to structure work practices. While this map was initially in a paper format, it was so popular (and difficult to keep current) that it was quickly used to structure the content on

Chevron's intranet via navigation links. In the final stage of the project, best practice teams would tag their content according to the categories in the map as they published it to the intranet, and the search engine was configured to enable keyword searching with the categories in the map (Bukowitz and Williams, 1999: 43–4).

Also in 1994, Ford Motor Company became concerned that its product development teams could typically find only half of the information they needed to do their jobs. They also took an intranet route, and developed a search/browse system similar to Yahoo!. Here content was tagged with topic keywords drawn from controlled vocabularies. It took two years to implement, but teams reported a jump in findability to 90 per cent as a result (Bukowitz and Williams, 1999: 51–2).

In information management and records management, classification schemes have been an important element of practice for many decades, although here, the temptation has always been to follow the example of librarianship – adopt/develop a classification scheme and then let it roll, with minimal adaptation along the way. This has two consequences: first, schemes gradually become unwieldy and disconnected from the work patterns of the organisation – you get *relevance drift*. Second, subsequent generations of information or records managers have no experience in taxonomy creation or design, which means that they do not notice relevance drift. This is probably one of the reasons why knowledge management projects like the Ford and Chevron examples rarely think of calling on their records or information managers for help, or of adopting the existing information classification schemes in use.

Taxonomy practice preceded the taxonomy label. Behind the glitz of knowledge management, taxonomy work quietly followed. It was not until around 2000 that the word 'taxonomy' suddenly became a much more visible label, and as with HIV AIDS (see Chapter 4) making the category created the opportunity for organised effort on a larger scale. The lonely taxonomist suddenly had companions, the availability of rapidly developing tools and a flurry of projects as organisations became aware that they needed to 'buy' taxonomies along with their intranet and content management projects.

The core connotations of the 'taxonomy' label in knowledge management have been mostly around the *findability* of content. For this we partly thank Yahoo!. In a post-Google world, it's hard to recall how revolutionary their simple topic categorisations seemed in the mid-1990s, and how radical an improvement in search results the Yahoo!

engine produced (compared to before). Crude and inconsistent as their taxonomy may now appear in relation to the universe of content it attempts to describe, it achieved two things: it improved precision of retrievals in the wash of synonyms, homonyms and contranyms that confuses word-based search, and it popularised categorisation. (Contranyms are especially nasty, being words that can have opposing senses: e.g. cleave (to cut in two, to join), buckle (to bend and break, to fasten together), clip (to attach, to cut off), fast (not moving, moving rapidly).)

By 2000, there were already several sophisticated categorisation tools on the market (e.g. Verity, Autonomy), and 'taxonomy' was the *mot du jour* (TaxoCoP, 2005; Graef, 2005). Taxonomies were suddenly 'chic' (Edols, 2001).

Taxonomies and content management

In practice, taxonomies can be expressed in many different ways: in paper filing systems, in shared drive folder structures, in file numbering systems, in site structures, in metadata, and so on. In the wave of taxonomy awareness we have just described, taxonomies were associated primarily with improving the findability of content in large repositories and this focused attention on the use of metadata.

Initially taxonomies, like Yahoo!, were quite simple, using drop-down topic lists of keywords. They might be extended into thesauruses. As the technology developed, however, the wider role that metadata plays in the control and management of content began to influence and broaden the perceptions of the role that taxonomies can play. We first defined metadata in Chapter 2. Now we look in a bit more detail at how it can be applied.

Metadata is used for a number of purposes:

- It *identifies* content – e.g. descriptive metadata captures author and title fields and distinguishes each document from all others.

- It helps systems *manage* content – e.g. administrative and structural metadata capture things like version numbers, archiving date, security and access permissions, links to multiple components in a document, file type.

- It aids *retrieval* of content – e.g. descriptive metadata captures things like taxonomy topics, subject keywords, document description.

- Increasingly, it is now being used to *connect* content to other content – behavioural metadata is being captured about the transactions that users have with each document and this is used to infer relationships or connections about the other things the same people transact with. The best known example of this is on Amazon.com, where if you buy a book, you can see the legend 'other people who bought this book also bought ...' These instant taxonomies, generated on the fly, give a marvellous serendipity to complement the formal topic categorisations in the 'real' taxonomy structure.

The close association of taxonomies with metadata has meant that the attention of the taxonomy community has shifted from an initial overly narrow focus on search and retrieval towards the *content management* implications of taxonomy development. When a taxonomy project is also a metadata project, the real implications of taxonomy as a part of information infrastructure start to become obvious.

Large volumes of content going into repositories can no longer be handled by limited numbers of 'professional' classifiers. The bottlenecks are too narrow and the flow of content too large. So content needs to be metatagged at the point of creation. That means users have to decide what categories to use. That means changes in work practices and training effort, and trying to ensure standardised interpretations of the taxonomy. It means education about the wider potential use of content, because if the document creator tags it just according to its local use in his department, it may not be tagged appropriately enough to be found by others. Automated metatagging only addresses a few of these questions – we'll discuss that in a later chapter.

The implementation of metadata to manage the document's life-cycle (its status as a business record or not, when it is archived, when deleted, who should be able to access it) involves the development of new workflows and quality assurance, and it frequently exposes weaknesses in information management and records management policies which need to be addressed.

If, in the period from 1995 to 2000, taxonomy was seen as primarily an aid to *findability*, the period from 2000 to 2006 has broadened perceptions to an awareness of taxonomy as a *content management tool* – meaning findability plus a whole host of other organising activities. The two perceptions, narrow and broad, often coexist. This can cause disconcerting disconnects when organisations try to commission taxonomy work on the narrower assumption that they are simply trying to improve the findability of content, and they find themselves enmeshed in a more complex project than they had anticipated, involving all those infrastructure issues of policy, process, workflow, roles and change management. No wonder some prefer the magic wands promised by Google-like search engines.

If the arguments in this book stand, then the perceived role of taxonomies still has some further maturing to do. The current content management and metadata focus – while it represents a more mature awareness of taxonomies – frequently threatens to isolate taxonomy work as primarily a technology-assisted (or technology-assisting) activity.

It also confuses taxonomies with metadata, which has its own destiny to work out. Jean Graef points to the need for metadata standardisation across the enterprise (Graef, 2004), while Denham Grey points to the democratic impact of social tagging (TaxoCoP, 2005), and Peter Morville suggests that the role of semantic metadata might be overtaken by automated pattern-sensing devices (Morville, 2005: 88–90). To the extent that metadata is an important instrument of taxonomy work, all of these potential changes will be relevant. But they will not affect the core of what taxonomy work is about.

Our earlier chapters strongly imply that there are areas of taxonomy work that are independent of technological applications but which require skill, professional attention and collective development. These include basic skills of vocabulary identification, list-making, facet identification, tree design and knowledge-mapping and process-mapping skills. More advanced skills would include consultation, observation, facilitation and interview skills, user experience design, subject analysis, category discovery, knowledge representation skills, standards development, designing knowledge and information governance frameworks, policy development, knowledge of sense-making techniques, change management.

In particular, within knowledge management, taxonomy work needs to play a more conscious role beyond the content management space. In the rest of this chapter, we'll explore a number of different ways that we can do this. As in our previous chapter, we'll use a framework to guide us.

Taxonomies and knowledge management

The knowledge lens framework was developed by my firm Straits Knowledge to categorise the different ways in which knowledge management can operate within organisations (see Figure 5.1). It is a matrix framework on two dimensions, the vertical one representing two categories of event-based knowledge transactions compared with knowledge built over time. The horizontal dimension compares individual knowledge transactions with social knowledge transactions.

Figure 5.1 Knowledge lens framework

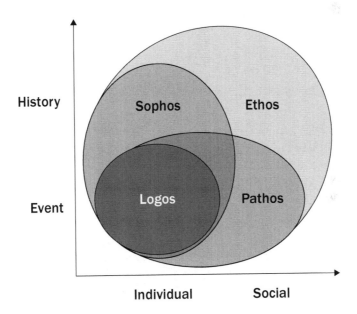

The framework is derived from four domains of ancient Greek rhetoric, representing four different levels at which you need to communicate if you want to communicate effectively. While we also interpret this framework using a variety of English terms, the master framework is best introduced through the Greek terms, because they provide a much richer reading and allow more flexible interpretations.

- *Logos* represents the word, the language used in communication. For our purposes, it represents information. This is the domain of information management, of supplying the right information at the time it is needed.

- *Sophos* represents wisdom, knowledge that can only be acquired over time by virtue of experience. For our purposes in knowledge management it represents experience, expertise and learning. The comparison between the domains of *Logos* and *Sophos* might roughly correspond to the distinction between explicit and tacit knowledge.

- *Pathos* represents fellow-feeling, the ability to connect and engage with other people on a personal level. For our purposes, it represents collaboration and socially distributed knowledge.

- *Ethos* is a complex concept representing character, identity, style of behaviour, values, reputation and practice. It contains both a sense of origins as well as a sense of where one is going. *Ethos* provides the personal context that determines the way in which any knowledge will be enacted. For our purposes in knowledge management, Ethos represents the character of an organisation, its culture, its history and its sense of direction.

The framework is portrayed as a series of lenses, because in fact, all of these layers are always in operation, to varying degrees, at the same time. The framework simply refracts these different categories out, for conceptual clarity and to support the different types of management action that are appropriate to each domain.

Notice that *Logos* is the foundation domain and that *Ethos* encompasses all of the domains. *Logos*, the domain of information management, is the anchor domain – it's hard to do knowledge management to any great extent without having reasonable information management discipline. *Logos, Sophos* and *Pathos* combined will make up what is required for information and knowledge infrastructure. *Ethos* is the hardest domain of all to influence, and it usually cannot be influenced at all without structured interventions in the other three domains.

Overall, the framework seems to capture the full range of knowledge management concerns, from information management, to collaboration and communities, to experience and expertise, to culture and purpose.

Figure 5.2 displays the same framework, this time with explicit knowledge management labels, and in each domain we have mapped a range of taxonomy activities and taxonomy goals.

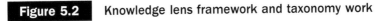

Figure 5.2 Knowledge lens framework and taxonomy work

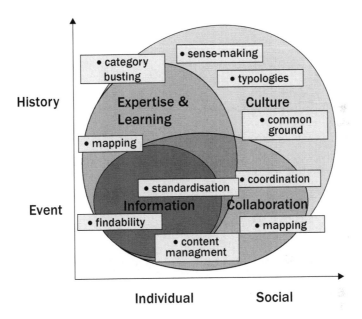

Logos/Information

One of the immediate insights this framework produces is that the current perception of taxonomy work (as enhancing findability and content management) is heavily oriented to the *Logos/Information* domain. For those knowledge management projects that are primarily focused on information management, taxonomy projects will take a strong semantic standardisation approach, and will focus on making relevant content easily retrievable to meet user needs *at the point of need*. 'Taxonomy as content management' straddles the needs of information management and collaboration, and so does semantic standardisation. Both of them support individual users in retrieving useful content whenever they need it, but they also support the availability of relevant and timely content across a wide population.

But taxonomy work can also support knowledge management work in additional ways. Remembering that the *Logos* domain is the anchor domain and that taxonomy work will always standardise, will always enhance findability and will always support content management, we now need to explore in a little more detail how taxonomy work can contribute to broader knowledge management goals while also serving those basic information management needs.

In the rest of this chapter we'll look at each of the other three domains in turn, and in each we'll give an example of how taxonomy work has been used to pursue broader knowledge management goals.

Sophos/Expertise and learning

Knowledge management cannot limit itself to the information and knowledge embedded in documents, databases and tools. It must also attempt, depending on local need, to harness, nurture, propagate or activate the knowledge that resides in people – and especially the knowledge of people who know a lot.

The knowledge in people is not like knowledge in a document. It is typically very difficult to communicate in any rich or substantial way. At one level it's similar, to the degree that in both cases you might be concerned to find and get access to it. Here you might want to build experts into your knowledge maps, identify who they are and how they can be contacted. You might build special expertise directories, which themselves are a form of map and, if classified by subject, form a taxonomy that leads to people.

However, the knowledge in people is fundamentally different from the knowledge in documents and other artefacts, in the sense that it is a living thing. Knowledge in people is *reflexive*, it changes and deepens (we hope) as it is used, as the knower interacts with other knowledgeable people and in the light of experience. Simply to focus on findability is of limited value in this domain. The knowledge manager needs to be asking, 'How do we grow this kind of experience and knowledge?' 'How do we acquire it and make sure it flourishes?' 'How do we position our experienced people so that they get the right kind of exposure and build their expertise further?' 'How do we foster the growth of knowledge through sharing and dialogue?' 'Given our corporate direction, what kinds of knowledge and expertise will we need in the future?'

Knowledge maps, social network maps and taxonomies can be used to identify where this people-based knowledge resides, but the real work lies in fostering things like communities of practice and undertaking human capital development initiatives – which are organisational knowledge initiatives even if they don't always fly under a knowledge management flag.

Mapping and taxonomy work can help here too. Social network mapping is a way of mapping information and knowledge flows across an organisation. A typical exercise would survey the members of a social group, and ask everyone to name, for example, the people they would turn to for help or advice in knowledge domain X. The resulting names are entered into social network mapping software, which shows who is communicating with whom and which people are the central nodes in this network of knowledge. It can be used to identify socially active experts, potential knowledge champions, knowledge silos and gaps, or incipient communities of practice (Cross and Parker, 2004). In Case study 5.1 below we'll look at how *competency mapping* addresses the human capital development need.

In areas of advanced knowledge, we may want to draw down what our experts and our expert communities know and turn it into something that *can* be communicated, such as information assets, new processes and tools, methods or recipes. For example, we are currently working for an organisation whose senior management team founded and grew the business thirty years ago, and who are all nearing retirement about the same time. It's important that the business does not suffer from the loss of their experienced eye and steady judgment. It's important to try and figure out what they know that matters to the business, and try to codify what can be codified and arrange for the transfer of what can be transferred, whether by training, attachment, mentoring or shadowing.

Storytelling is a useful technique to use, but the stories need to be indexed to be helpful, and patterns of themes and issues need to be identified, working preferably with the story owners. The task is to turn a largely tacit understanding of the business into a collection of context-rich stories, and then generate a knowledge map to be laid over the top. The knowledge map then helps the knowledge management team decide which domains need further work and exploration, and how the knowledge identified can be exposed and communicated.

Where you have identified the domains of knowledge you want to expose and describe, *concept mapping* is an extremely useful tool for sketching the structure of the domain. While stories carry the subtleties and ambiguities in a knowledge domain, concept maps are powerful ways of checking for coherence and completeness. Concept mapping can be conducted in group settings, as in our Unilever Research case study (Chapter 4), or it can be based on individual interviews.

It is also in the *Sophos* domain of expertise and learning that you will find the kind of innovation work we described in Chapter 4 – category busting and blending work, where teams are looking for new or hybrid knowledge domains.

Case study 5.1

The British Council maps its competencies

The British Council is a non-profit organisation which is partially funded by the British government to be the UK's cultural and educational agency abroad. Among their many activities are UK education promotion and counselling, English language teaching, teacher training, promotion of UK arts, science and technology, administration of aid projects, libraries and information services, and organising exchange visits and seminars.

The Council works in over a hundred countries worldwide and its approach is to try to foster mutually beneficial relationships between the host country and the UK. This means the organisation must tune itself to the agendas and needs of its host countries, and in turn this implies a very diverse range of activities, contexts and work profiles across the British Council network. While there is a core group of common services and activities across the network, no two offices will be the same in how they combine and deliver their programmes and services.

There is a talent management cost to this variability. If British Council staff are to be developed consistently, and if they are to be transferable across the network to build and apply their experience, then the organisation needs a common language for describing and managing competencies and skills. The British Council reviews its strategy every five years, and in 2000 it explicitly set out a 'strategy for staff' to address this need. Among other initiatives it launched a project to build an 'organisational skills profile' for the British Council.

The goal of this project was to achieve greater consistency in how skills and competencies were described across the organisation. John Mackenzie, project leader, described the issues thus (Mackenzie, 2005):

- It was hard to be consistent in what people were asked to do in their jobs.
- It was difficult to compare jobs and roles across the network.
- Recruitment decisions were intrinsically mysterious.
- It was difficult to be confident about the consistency and quality of performance management across the organisation.

'Our objective in this project was to codify in a consistent way across the organisation some of the basic planks of good people management' (Mackenzie, 2005). As the project evolved, it focused on two main strands:

1. Performance management processes would be reviewed and improved, using a standard vocabulary for core competencies and skills and the behaviours that demonstrated them.

2. Professional development could be more systematically and positively managed with a vocabulary of competencies and skills and a framework that would help identify gaps and opportunities.

The skills profile project was divided into three areas:

- *Behavioural competencies* – to identify the working and management styles exhibited in behaviours that best reflect the values of the organisation and promote its work.

- *Job families* – comprising the technical skills, knowledge, qualifications and experience that would attach to the range of jobs within the Council, matched to professional standards in the wider employment market.

- *Generic skills* – to identify the skills, knowledge and experience that should be available throughout the organisation.

When fully developed, each of these three elements would come into play in combination. For example, a job description would indicate the specific requirements of its place in a job family, the behavioural competencies relevant to the post and the generic skills required.

When the project got under way in 2001–2, organisational culture was a strong focus of senior management, so the first area to be developed was the range of behavioural competencies. This was not necessarily the easiest area to start with. Behavioural competencies are difficult to pin down, often seem abstract and are difficult to make concrete. It is also not always easy to distinguish competencies from skills and behaviours.

Here the goal was to build a 'competency dictionary' which would provide a vocabulary to describe the desired competencies in a way that could pragmatically be matched to concrete behaviours. It would provide descriptors for the behaviours that indicated the presence of the competency.

It was a highly consultative exercise. Taking a large dataset of several hundred typical competency statements provided by a human resources consulting firm, the project team involved 250 staff members from around the world in a series of workshops. Staff came from a wide range of functions and levels. Their task in the workshops was to identify and tailor the competencies that made most sense to their work – using card sorting for the competencies and drawing up typical role profiles with tasks and activities to which competencies would be attached.

The two outcomes of this stage were a draft competency dictionary, and a set of global role profiles. John Mackenzie noted wryly the impact of this exercise:

> For the first time people were able to talk to each other about their work. It really took off. We had intended the global role profiles only to be a stepping stone to the competencies, but people actually started using the documents when they were writing job descriptions – we had to rein them in a bit, because they were not intended for that purpose. (Mackenzie, 2005)

When balanced for consistency across the organisation, the process produced twelve core competencies:

- Achievement
- Analytical thinking
- Customer service orientation
- Entrepreneurship
- Flexibility
- Holding people accountable
- Leading and developing others
- Professional self-confidence
- Relationship building for influence
- Self-awareness
- Teamworking
- Working strategically.

'The consultative part of the process was very important,' says John Mackenzie, 'because it was the only way we could get these abstract competencies to relate to real jobs. We had a few surprises: leadership didn't end up as a separate competency, for example. It's actually made up of two or three other competencies' (Mackenzie, 2005).

Another surprising gap was that intercultural competencies didn't emerge as a distinct entity. The British Council felt that, given their global role, it could not be considered as a composite of several other competencies but needed its own category, so created a set of descriptors for it using an external diagnostic tool. The lesson here is that *taxonomies often need to function as boundary objects between operational use and strategic direction*. Organisational agendas need to be negotiated against operational agendas. For example, the competencies identified by the Council are now consciously mapped against the organisation's values and inform those values, although they were not originally derived from them.

Having created a taxonomy, you must then validate it in practice. The first roll-out of the new framework for the British Council was through their annual performance management cycle. The competencies were integrated into job descriptions, evaluations and job plans. Mackenzie notes the difficulty in working with competencies.

> We had a hard time getting consistency in how the competencies were being used in evaluations. In a very large organisation, it's difficult to roll out a very consistent process, because of the availability of trainers. If you just do lots of highly scripted training with less experienced trainers then the trainers are not prepared for the difficult questions and ambiguities. Very experienced trainers are in short supply.

Moreover, closer to the ground, Council staff were more interested in getting guidance on specific skill sets than on competencies. They would have preferred the work on job families to have come first.

Any taxonomy, before it is implemented, is a theory. It is normal for it to meet variable interpretations. The first implementation of a taxonomy is the most important opportunity you will have to correct errors and tune the language to its population. Despite the initial teething problems, Mackenzie already feels there has been significant progress. Annual surveys show improvements in staff perceptions of how the organisation practises its espoused values. Inconsistencies in interpretation and overlaps in meaning are gradually getting ironed out with every performance management cycle. John Mackenzie does not interpret this as migration to a common standard, however – he interprets this process as an important negotiation of meaning in relation to performance management across the Council, reinforcing its role as a boundary object that successfully mediates different contexts and understandings (Mackenzie, 2006).

The project on skills for job families is well under way, followed by work on the generic skills project. The Council's network of English teaching centres is launching its own project, so that specialist teaching skills and competencies can be brought into the framework.

When the project is finally complete, Mackenzie is confident that the organisation's goal for improvements in culture, more effective global coordination and consistent people development will be achieved. But it requires patience and persistence. 'It takes time to work such changes into an organisation and see the benefits,' Mackenzie says. 'The real payoffs from this project will only become widely visible in the next 4–5 years' (Mackenzie, 2005).

Competency mapping is a tricky business. The rigour with which it is undertaken, combined with a previous poverty of language, can mislead staff into over-enthusiasm and over-rigid application. But competency frameworks do not capture everything that is necessary in making recruitment decisions, or evaluating performance, or making self-development plans. Human beings and human behaviours are infinitely subtle, and only a portion of what we do is susceptible to the standardised descriptions of a taxonomy. Boundary objects are just that: they enable communications across *boundaries*, but they cannot simultaneously be both boundary objects and central scripture.

It's a hard balance to maintain: on the one hand, a competency framework and the standardisation processes through which it is enacted provide a common language and stabilise common perceptions. They enable conscious, intelligent management of human capital resources, and the development of needed skills, knowledge and experience. On the other hand, they can easily become a bureaucratic trap if not combined with pragmatism and a recognition that they sketch only common outlines and do not tell the whole story. Any taxonomy that attempts to describe what people know will meet this challenge.

Pathos/Collaboration

Social groups make it possible for individuals not to have to know everything. Knowledge is typically distributed across a social group, and so long as I have a way to access other people's knowledge (e.g. by asking questions) the burden on my own memory and expertise is lessened. I simply need to know roughly who knows what. Communities of practice pioneer Etienne Wenger studied a group of insurance claims processors and noted that it 'supports a communal memory that allows individuals to do their work without having to know everything' (Wenger, 1998:

46). It is much more efficient to distribute memory and processing capacity over numerous individuals than to expect everyone to know everything that needs to be known.

Furthermore, in knowledge work, as in other kinds of work, humans divide up their work into a web of interconnecting and interdependent tasks and sub-tasks, with different members of the group being assigned different functions, expectations and roles. 'Assigned' can mean explicitly allocated, implicitly indicated or simply a result of volunteering because somebody saw a gap that needed to be filled. This weblike nature of work is why coordination and communication are so important in organisations.

This system of distributed knowledge and distributed knowledge work also assures the sustainability of the work into the future. People can come and go, but the work of the group continues. Groups implicitly understand this: they assign different roles and set different expectations for newcomers and juniors, as compared with old hands and experts. When Jean Lave and Etienne Wenger first identified the phenomenon of communities of practice, they were studying 'legitimate peripheral participation' which is a means by which newcomers can learn how to participate in the knowledge work of the group simply by hanging around and observing how the experienced practitioners operate. Social groups allow, expect and facilitate this process because it is an important way of transmitting the knowledge of the group into the next generation (Lave and Wenger, 1991).

Mapping work – whether social network mapping or knowledge mapping – can obviously enhance the effectiveness of our normal mechanisms for leveraging social knowledge. Our individual private knowledge maps of 'who knows what' are limited to the social networks we have been able to build for ourselves. Knowledge maps such as the one developed by Chevron can make the distributed knowledge of the group more accessible to everyone. Social network maps can locate the authoritative and helpful 'old-timers' and verify that group knowledge is indeed protected by having a viable mix of knowers, from the experienced to those who are learning the ropes. Process mapping can make many of the undocumented aspects of our distributed work networks more explicit. This renders work easier to manage, simplify and resource.

The knowledge articulation work we do to enable large-scale coordination is also an important set of activities belonging to the *Pathos/Collaboration* domain. Here straightforward taxonomy building exercises can play a significant role, not just in making content findable, but in enabling different parts of the same organisation to act together in a consistent and articulated way.

Cabot Corporation builds a taxonomy to coordinate global quality

Cabot Corporation is a chemical company operating in 21 countries with over 4,000 employees. Until recently it was structured according to regions and businesses, but in the late 1990s it was restructured into seven global businesses. The knowledge and information systems that supported its work were all built to coordinate work within the local businesses and the regions. Now they had to reconfigure to operate globally.

In particular, quality management and the documentation that goes with it, vital to chemical manufacturing, had evolved in parallel among the regions. Standardisation to ISO 9001 which requires intensive documentation in itself encouraged the businesses to look at tighter coordination to simplify that arduous process and share the burden.

An audit of quality systems revealed that Cabot had 'seven different systems in six languages, mainly stored on shared-network drives and delivered on paper. Each system was fit for purpose in its own right, but without structural consistency across each site, regional business needs would be difficult to anticipate' (Lambermont-Ford, 2005). A document management system and a tree structure taxonomy with some polyhierarchies would deliver the solution.

The ISO 9001 process provided some ready-made standards – the documentation types are always consistent. However, there was wide variation in how the main classification structures had been developed. 'Each quality manager had developed their own system with its own classification structure, and was understandably reluctant to abandon it – after all, it had worked well at their site' (Lambermont-Ford, 2005). In particular there was a strong division between those who organised their systems by function and those who organised by process.

Negotiations resulted in a compromise. Some categories such as policies and procedures would be organised by function, while others such as controlled documents and work instructions would be organised by process. This matched the orientation of the principal users of each of these types of documents. Polyhierarchies were used to give functional views into process documents and vice versa. While facets were not used here, this would have been a classic opportunity, if their document management system had accommodated them.

Cabot also took a semi-devolved approach. The taxonomy core was controlled centrally, but individual sites were allowed to define local terms beyond the common core set of categories.

In the roll-out, some effort had to be given to help local sites use the taxonomy. Categorisation decisions were not always straightforward, and the team decided to give each site a 'sandbox' database to practise with before going live onto the real system. Training was important. Lambermont-Ford notes that it also provided opportunities for staff to get more insight into information availability at other sites.

The federated structure of this project was clearly right for the history of this company. Building a shared core but allowing local control beyond a certain level has probably meant that potential resistance to an imposed standard has been avoided – even if it has had a cost in 'taxonomy creep' and parallel taxonomies being developed as different sites are tempted to migrate their categories back to what they are comfortable with. Quality director for Europe Alain Benoist reflects that, in retrospect, he would have delayed giving the local sites autonomy over local terms until they had had some time to get used to using the common taxonomy core.

Overall, Cabot is very happy. They claim that they see more information awareness across sites, more openness to sharing and significant savings in the cost of documenting quality. Most important, Cabot has much greater confidence in its ability to coordinate globally, share good practice and benchmark quality performance.

Source: Lambermont-Ford (2005).

Ethos/Culture

Culture is as mysterious as personality, if not more so. Indeed, we can say it is the aggregate personality of a social group. Culture has been defined as the shared practices, values and beliefs of a group of people (Schein, 1985). It can exist at a local level, an organisational level or at a national or ethnic level. Many of the mechanisms for knowledge articulation we have already discussed (e.g. shared routines, resources, relationships) will have an impact on a group's culture, and a group's culture will in turn affect how those mechanisms operate.

In our knowledge lens framework, culture also embodies a strong sense of *identity* – and this is not just how a group defines itself in its present context, but also how it defines its past and the future it aspires to. This composite sense of common history, common context and common goals influences how people behave, what motivates them, what they take for granted and what common actions they agree on.

A culture, whether at local or organisational level, forms a shared lens for how the worldview of the group can be interpreted by its members. It determines acceptable and unacceptable behaviours, enforces group norms, promotes specific ways of communicating and sharing, and transmits shared values through its stories and the daily visible behaviours of its members.

Culture is a very important vehicle for establishing the common identity and shared language that allows us to transmit our knowledge in shorthand without having to explain all our assumptions in detail. It also helps individuals interpret what is happening to them in their daily lives, and therefore shapes the way that knowledge is codified, transmitted and shared. 'Knowledge Management (KM) projects ignore culture at their peril' (McDermott and O'Dell, 2001).

Etienne Wenger notes that a big part of what a group knows becomes embedded in a repertoire of routines and ways of doing things that anybody inducted into the group becomes familiar with. 'This is the way we do things around here' (Wenger, 1998: 83).

This has a couple of benefits. First, individual thinking costs are reduced (and the risk of errors), because the group's knowledge is embedded in a semi-automatic routine. Individuals do not have to think through every task from scratch, but rely on heuristics, shortcuts, tips and habits, built up by the group over time and observable in action around them every day.

Second, the cost of transmission is low: once the routine has been observed a few times by a newcomer, it is often very easy to pick up without extensive explanation. More effective or improved ways of doing things that people have learned through experience can be transmitted or inherited by becoming a routine or a habit with minimal effort.

This feature is such a powerful characteristic of human social behaviour that it largely explains why change management is such a difficult endeavour – difficult, because managing change is not simply a matter of persuading individuals of the merits of the change. Persuasion is a relatively easy task compared to unpicking all of the routines and habits that are socially reinforced but which are inconsistent with the change you want to introduce. Because they are socially constructed, because they are not consciously practised and because they are ingrained habits that you see around you every day, changing routines and habits is a very difficult task indeed. The group's knowledge can slow down innovation as well as empower it.

This aggregate of shared things – history, language and categories, goals, routines – together make up what knowledge management theorists call *common ground*. Common ground establishes the possibility for collaboration and acting as a single unit. It does not just entail a shared language and shared categories, but a whole intricate weave of common purpose and common habit. The day-to-day expression of this in communication, collaboration and trust is often referred to as *social capital* – that is, the value the group can create for itself simply by behaving socially (Portes, 1998; Baker, 2000).

So culture is diffuse and complex, made up of many interacting parts. In some respects we can characterise it as the 'soft' counterpart of knowledge and information infrastructure. Knowledge management initiatives that need to change a culture cannot avoid getting involved in infrastructure work. Dysfunctional cultures that do not support effective knowledge articulation always require work in the area of establishing or strengthening common ground. Cultures that are unsure of their way forward always require sense-making interventions – which if not consciously managed will emerge in the more primitive sense-making activities of rumour, gossip, faith in magic bullets and dictatorial behaviours.

These complex characteristics of the *Ethos* domain expose us not merely to how and why we organise knowledge in the ways we do, but also to the enormous knowledge creation capacity of groups (Nonaka and Takeuchi, 1995). This 'latent' knowledge or 'knowledge potential' of the group is an inherent strength of social groups (Cross and Parker, 2004). It is demonstrated by (Thomas et al., 2001):

- the group's ability to answer questions when they arise from individual members;
- the problem-solving and sense-making ability of the group when members collaborate;
- the different perspectives (and disagreements) that members bring to bear on any issue;
- new knowledge creation when the group uses dialogue and co-discovery techniques.

The point, of course, is that this latent knowledge does not exist in any specific form before the members of the group apply themselves to an issue. Nor can it be said that the new knowledge is the sum of the collected knowledge of its individual members. It is a product of synergy and interaction between group members, a kind of collective thinking process.

To the extent that infrastructure influences culture then straight-forward taxonomy work will support a knowledge management agenda in the domain of *Ethos*, particularly in helping to build and sustain common ground. But the contribution of taxonomy work can go beyond the technical issues of shared vocabularies and categories, and this is illustrated in our next case study.

Case study 5.3

The Civil Aviation Authority of Singapore uses a typology to structure and communicate its knowledge management strategy

The Civil Aviation Authority of Singapore (CAAS) regulates civil aviation in Singapore and operates Changi Airport. Its 1,600 staff are distributed across 14 divisions, spanning air safety, security, engineering, air traffic control, airport services, commercial operations, aviation training and flight operations among others.

In 2005 CAAS had decided to develop a knowledge management strategy to help it deliver its business objectives. As operators of an iconic airport with a history of excellence and in the midst of a turbulent industry, the authority was simultaneously building a third passenger terminal to accommodate planned growth, building a low-cost carriers terminal for the burgeoning regional budget airline industry, and re-fitting its runways and gates as the first airport to receive the new Airbus 380.

CAAS was also concerned to ensure that its knowledge management strategy was appropriately tuned to the organisational culture. This was particularly important because it has a very strong and stable culture – in an organisation which had had few major disruptions or shocks, and with a strong track record of success over several decades. Such cultures are difficult to change, and are better assessed carefully before major changes are introduced.

As part of its preparation for the knowledge management strategy work, CAAS undertook a cultural archetypes exercise to derive a typology of personas that characterised its own knowledge-sharing culture. The exercise was conducted through a series of focus groups and workshops involving about 70 employees from across the organisation and representing differing levels of staff. The methodology for archetypes extraction was the same basic methodology for deriving customer personas described in Chapter 4, except that our focus question invited stories about employees' experiences of knowledge and information either being shared or not shared within the organisation.

Quite apart from the archetypes, anecdotes and stories that are grounded in the daily experience of our target audience (in this case CAAS employees) are also useful in themselves because they carry with them many of the perceptions, attitudes and experiences of their owners. They are less likely to be biased by the form of the enquiry as in surveys, and they communicate a lot of useful contextual information that sometimes surprises and often helps to clarify the 'hard' information that is collected by other means. This approach is particularly useful for gaining novel and unanticipated understandings of employee issues, where more traditional research methods have failed because they were not framed to capture them.

The archetypes extracted from the workshops were the main target to help characterise the organisation's culture in relation to knowledge use and sharing. The methodology used ensures that these personas are generalised, archetypal personalities that reflect the core shared values, perceptions and behaviours of the group being studied.

The set of ten archetypes that emerged from this process forms a typology that represents the collective culture of the organisation – in relation to the focus area of knowledge use. Together they characterise the strengths, challenges and opportunities resident in the culture for a knowledge management strategy. As it turned out, this exercise produced such resonant archetypes that after close analysis of business and knowledge needs, CAAS decided to structure its knowledge management strategy and initiatives around the key insights in this typology. We can see how they did this by looking at just two of the salient archetypes in the typology (Figure 5.3).

The first of our examples is an archetype named The Sage. He is a positive archetype, associated with leadership in CAAS.

The Sage is a gem cut from many years of serving the organisation. He is experienced, wise, and a visionary. His subordinates look to him for guidance and advice, of which he dispenses freely. He gives advice by telling you stories from his vast experience. He is able to illustrate a point clearly with a specific instance from the past. In a way, he is a walking history book. He manages his subordinates gently but firmly, acting like a father figure to them. However, he does have his quirks, which instills nervousness in those in awe of his seniority and reputation, sending them scrambling to find out about his likes and dislikes to avoid incurring his displeasure. Yet, long after he is gone, he will still be remembered for his wisdom and genuine care. (Ng, 2005)

Figure 5.3   **Example archetypes from CAAS**

Our second example is an archetype named Charlie New. Charlie is a new hire, and comes across as a very vulnerable character.

Charlie New is a newbie to the organisation, and possibly new to the working world as well. His youth and inexperience mean that he needs close supervision, but he may not get that upon joining the organisation. The person he is taking over from may have already moved on, and he is left to find things out from file records or from other colleagues. You can find him snoozing over volumes of such files. But there are all sorts of things that he needs to know that are not in the files, and so he has lots of bumps along the way. If his Buddy is helpful, the induction into the organisation will be smooth. If not, Charlie is in for a rough ride. Sometimes, Charlie is thrown into the deep end of the

> pool almost immediately upon joining the organisation. For instance, he may be tasked to lead a project. Depending on his luck and tenacity, he either swims or sinks. (Ng, 2005)

The two poles of interest represented by the Sage and Charlie New are the issues of knowledge that is resident in long-experienced staff who may be approaching retirement compared to the knowledge acquisition challenges of very new staff. CAAS had previously identified possible knowledge management issues around their large pool of long-serving staff, and the rapidly growing population of younger staff as CAAS grew and changed. The archetypes exercise sharpened these issues and gave them context; their resonant presence in the culture suggested that these would be profitable and helpful avenues to pursue, and that they would align with the needs that the culture itself was acknowledging.

CAAS's knowledge management strategy was drawn up through a formal analytical and balancing process, in which the archetypes study was one of several inputs. However the typology allowed them to structure and characterise the plans that emerged – both for planning purposes as well as for communications purposes.

Two initiatives in CAAS's knowledge management plans relate specifically to issues raised by the Sage and Charlie New archetypes. The plans call for CAAS to develop techniques for eliciting the knowledge of very experienced staff through storytelling and concept mapping interviews among other things. Knowledge maps, repositories and mechanisms for transferring softer aspects of their knowledge will follow to help the release of this knowledge back into the organisation in useful ways.

Another project focuses on Charlie New, and aims to establish a new hires portal on the CAAS intranet, designed by recent hires (while the memory of being new is still fresh), using the input of operational managers for the formal knowledge that is required and structuring resources in ways that make sense to an incomer who needs to tune quickly into the culture and working routines. This will also involve knowledge mapping and traditional taxonomy work.

After the knowledge management strategy had been developed, CAAS wanted to explain the strategy to its staff, and to elicit their support for the various projects and initiatives that would come their way. It used the annual staff conference as a platform. The staff conference was combined with a mini-knowledge management fair in the foyer outside – with demonstrations of a staff portal, competitions to build up a collective history of Changi Airport, and life-size cutouts of the archetypes to prime their curiosity – some took photographs with them.

Inside, the knowledge management agenda was introduced first in the themes of the Director General's keynote speech. Then the archetypes were introduced in detail, and the audience was asked to indicate by the strength of their applause how common each archetype was in the organisation. This was followed by a drama skit performed by a theatre company following Charlie New's first day at work and his interactions with the various archetypes in CAAS. By this time, the staff – from front-line staff to senior managers – were rolling in the aisles with laughter. The skit finished and the knowledge management team presented the strategy – each thrust of the strategy linked to specific archetypes and the issues associated with them.

Knowledge management goals are often difficult to communicate to employees at large. By developing a typology of characters that resonated with the organisational culture, CAAS was able to plan and communicate in an unusually effective way to a broad range of staff.

Does this qualify as taxonomy work? If we stick to our description of taxonomy work as categorising, describing and mapping, then it does. The typology developed by CAAS structured their self-awareness in relation to their own culture; it created categories, descriptions and relationships that could be used to make sense, plan and organise.

In this chapter we have explored a number of ways that taxonomy work can contribute to knowledge management goals beyond its more limited application to information retrieval and content management. In truth, the traditional concept of the tree or facet taxonomy is never far away. Information management activities will almost always accompany interventions in other knowledge domains. In some of our examples, such as the Cabot Corporation case, the connections have been explicit; in others, such as the CAAS case, they have been implied as a consequence of the typology and sense-making work.

We have seen how taxonomy projects help us create categories that work, use categories for sense-making and focus on the goals of coordination. This directs our attention away from one of the dangers of taxonomy work: a tendency to be pedantic about *form and structure* at the cost of a productive focus on the taxonomy's *purpose* and the *processes* that produce it. With this final insight, we are now ready to look at how a taxonomy development project can be shaped to meet particular needs.

6

What do we want our taxonomies to do?

*[In South Africa] race classification and reclassification provided the
bureaucratic underpinnings for a vicious racism ... classification systems are
often sites of political and social struggles.*

(Bowker and Star, 1999: 232)

One of the main objectives of the first five chapters of this book has been
to break down the limited traditional view of what taxonomies are and
of what comprises taxonomy work. In this chapter we briefly review the
diverse ways in which taxonomy work contributes towards organisation
effectiveness, and structure this understanding in a way that will allow
us to plan effectively for our own taxonomy projects in practice. We look
at an organising framework for what taxonomies actually enable us to
do, and this will help us to make better decisions about how to align our
taxonomy work to our organisational and business objectives.

Taxonomies are tools for effectiveness, and as such they can be
developed and used badly, or they can be developed and used well.
Judging which taxonomy development strategy is appropriate to take
depends on circumstances, environment and objectives. By the end of
this chapter we should have a better idea of how to set our pragmatic
taxonomy goals and define the approach we should take in any
particular project.

In Chapter 3 we looked at the critical role that information and
knowledge infrastructure plays in supporting organisation effectiveness,
and the important contribution that taxonomy work makes towards
enhancing large-scale coordination across and between organisational
boundaries.

In Chapter 4 we looked at the way that taxonomy work underpins
effectiveness in four major areas of business activity:

- *risk* – supporting risk recognition and response;

- *cost* – giving visibility into process and control over variance, redundancy and error;

- *customers and markets* – discovering customer categories and organising communications, prices, products and services appropriately;

- *innovation* – discovering emergent domains through category busting or blending.

In Chapter 5 we focused on the roles that taxonomies and taxonomy work can play in knowledge and information management. While the professional taxonomy community is gradually evolving from an overly simple 'findability' approach to taxonomy work, it has still not moved beyond a technology-assisting role focused on managing 'content' or information.

We looked at a variety of ways in which taxonomy work can underpin other important dimensions of knowledge management, including different kinds of knowledge mapping, supporting collaborative work and knowledge transfer, supporting decision-making, organising strategy and establishing or enhancing common ground in support of collective identity and commitment.

What taxonomies do

In the range of examples given in the chapters so far, we can see that taxonomies can play five distinct roles. We'll unpack each of these in turn.

- Taxonomies structure and organise.
- Taxonomies help establish common ground.
- Taxonomies can help span boundaries between groups.
- Taxonomies can help in sense-making.
- Taxonomies can aid in the discovery of risk and opportunity.

Taxonomies structure and organise

This is probably the most common understanding of what taxonomies do. In biology, taxonomies organise *things* – organisms – placing them into relationship with each other by means of superordinate concepts such as family, genus and species. In sociology and anthropology, taxonomies organise ideas about *people*, using the attributes of particular interest at the time of study. In library and information science and knowledge management, taxonomies organise *knowledge and information*, embedded in books, documents and databases. This much is pretty uncontroversial.

We may be less aware of the fact that taxonomies also organise *work* and *resources* in organisational settings. We saw in Case study 4.2 on brand simplification at Unilever in Chapter 4 that their new taxonomy of brands helped Unilever to allocate resources and effort in a more effective way to achieve their objectives.

There is another well-established way of using taxonomies to organise work, and that is through organisational structure. We might organise our work by type of work, concentrating together our specialist functions such as finance, engineering, sales and so on in a functional organisation structure. Large multinationals often organise themselves around customer groups, such as on a geographic divisional basis; banks organise themselves into divisions for consumer banking, corporate banking and private banking.

Organisation structures are typically represented like taxonomies, usually as trees. They also suffer from the shortcomings of tree structures: if you collect like things together on one basis (e.g. specialist work function) you separate them from each other on another basis (e.g. type of customer served). In fact, what knowledge managers call organisational knowledge silos are the products of taxonomic separation of work.

Organisations have their strategies for overcoming this problem, just as taxonomists do. They create polyhierarchies and matrix structures to build cross-linkages between the separated work areas, and just the same as in taxonomy work, too many cross linkages disrupt the predictability of the tree structure and create reporting confusions and degraded information transfer.

There are other ways in which taxonomies organise work. Consider the case of Linda X who is responsible for coordinating customer feedback at a busy international airport. All customer feedback comes to her, whether it is spontaneous customer complaints or structured feedback gathered by her market researchers. Because this is a progressive organisation, feedback is not merely reviewed and responded to but the organisation actively seeks to change the way it works to prevent such complaints arising again.

When it renovates its terminals and facilities or builds new ones, it must incorporate this knowledge about customer preferences and perceptions into its design and implementation.

> If the architects for our new terminal propose graduated floor levels using low, semi-concealed steps, this might open up the space visually in an aesthetic sense, but we know from experience that passengers who don't notice the steps might fall, not to mention the difficulty for passengers in wheelchairs or with heavy bags. We have to make sure our experience of customers is fed back into the designs. If we don't catch it and happen to build it that way, we then have to fix it.

The feedback involves a tremendous variety of topics: from toilet cleanliness, friendliness of duty free sales assistants, slowness of immigration procedures, availability of Internet access or the smell in the movie theatre. Linda therefore has a taxonomy of topics which she uses to route feedback issues to respective subject officers across and beyond the entire organisation, whether it be Engineering, Planning, Maintenance, Facilities, IT, commercial tenants, Department of Immigration, and so on. She also uses this taxonomy to monitor responses and manage communications with customers where appropriate.

This is more than a simple feedback routing system. Her taxonomy leverages the organisational structure taxonomy to locate responsible parties, but is organised around feedback topics and action officers and feeds directly into the organisation of work at micro and macro levels.

We call taxonomies that organise work *operational taxonomies*, and they are important source taxonomies when we are engaged in organisation-wide taxonomy development – simply because they carry deeply embedded and daily reinforced vocabularies and ways of organising information. Despite our ever increasing rate of organisation restructuring, organisation structure is one of the few taxonomic structures that we invest a lot of time in educating our people about: at inductions and orientations, in organisation charts, telephone directories, intranets, and so on. Information structures follow work structures as well as feeding them.

The function of structuring and organising (whether it be things, people, work, resources or information) results in a number of benefits. As we've seen, it enhances findability – we know where to go to find what we need for a specific thing. But to stop at simple findability would be to under-exploit the value of taxonomies.

Taxonomies also play the role of an explicit, public memory structure. They help us remember things, as we saw in Chapter 2 in the example of Matteo Ricci's memory palace. Since taxonomies embody associations or relationships between concepts, coming across one item can stimulate our memory of others by association. They also provide structures into which items can be lodged, and therefore preserved for future reference, as opposed to being 'forgotten' in a mess of irretrievable noise (Bowker and Star, 1999: ch. 8).

By virtue of structuring and organising content, taxonomies can also help us distribute content or work to appropriate parties, or select items fit for particular purposes, as designers of supermarkets, department stores and catalogues well know. Conversely, they can also help us prescribe appropriate items based on different types of needs, as doctors and pharmacists well know.

It's worth noticing that the distribution, selection and prescription functions enabled by taxonomies involve the articulation of multiple taxonomies, all at the same time: for example, in Linda's case, customer feedback topics mapped to a taxonomy of operational areas; in the supermarket, customer needs taxonomies mapped to taxonomies of suppliers and products; in the doctor's surgery, taxonomies of symptoms mapped to disease taxonomies, mapped to treatments, mapped to medicines. This is why faceted approaches to taxonomy building are much more powerful if you are intending to resource more than simple findability in your taxonomy project and want to gear your taxonomies much more closely to the support of work.

Taxonomies help establish common ground

We spent some time in the previous chapter looking at the workings and benefits of common ground. Common ground counterbalances the fragmentation effect of the 'Babel Instinct' which drives us to build highly localised private languages and taxonomies. Where the Babel Instinct creates information opacity and coordination difficulties, common ground promotes transparency, information efficiency and coordination effectiveness.

Common ground goes beyond taxonomies, of course. It entails a common sense of shared history and identity, a sense of 'us-ness', stories that are held in common, well understood principles for access to resources, shared routines and habits and a sense of common purpose. So taxonomies alone will not build common ground – other factors such as trust, leadership, culture and socialisation opportunities will also have a substantial influence on the quality of common ground.

However, taxonomies do play an important role in enhancing common ground because they provide standardised vocabularies and public, consistent ways of organising information. They are a necessary, but not sufficient, condition for effective common ground. Case study 5.2 on the Cabot Corporation in Chapter 5 is a good example of a 'common-ground' taxonomy project – in this case building common ground among their global quality management teams so that they could gain information and operational efficiencies.

Taxonomies can help span boundaries between groups

We looked at the role of taxonomies as boundary objects in Chapter 3. Taxonomies act as boundary objects if they form a common frame of reference for two or more distinct communities. In terms of their effect, boundary objects perform very much the same function that common ground provides for a single community of relatively homogeneous workgroups: that is, they enable information and communication efficiencies across heterogeneous community boundaries, supporting coordination effectiveness. The pharmaceutical company's drug catalogue acts as a boundary object linking hospital administrators, doctors, insurance companies, pharmacists, regulatory agencies and researchers.

However, while taxonomies acting as boundary objects look very similar in their role to taxonomies that act to enhance common ground within communities, they actually perform a much more critical role, *because they enable coordination even in the absence of common ground.*

Consider the make-up of a medical team in an operating theatre. You'll have the surgeons, some assisting doctors, nurses, instrument technicians and an anaesthesiologist at the very least. Professionally and socially, in their different areas of domain knowledge and expertise, and in the detail of their everyday working lives, this group of people has very little overlap in terms of common ground.

Yet in the areas of their intersecting work, such as in the operating theatre, they have numerous boundary objects that enable them to articulate their knowledge and work as an effective, cohesive team for the duration of their team task: shared vocabularies and categories, shared scripts and routines, common frames of reference and mental models, authority structures to direct attention and work, and so on.

Boundary objects are also very important enablers for information transfer and transactions between different organisations, or as a kind of transactional 'glue' between a network of interconnected organisations. Geoffrey Bowker and Susan Leigh Star paint a graphic picture of the role of the International Classification of Diseases (ICD) in multiple interdependent domains: its categories guide the classification of cause of death on death certificates worldwide and structure official mortality statistics; these in turn influence the allocation of resources to health programmes at national and international levels; insurance companies use it to structure their policies, and pharmaceutical companies use it to guide research. This is even before we get into the medical profession proper (Bowker and Star, 1999). The ICD is not alone. If you are in a procurement role, standards such as the North American Industry Classification Scheme (NAICS) underpin the way you locate and transact with service and product providers.

The distinction between taxonomies as supporters of common ground and as boundary objects is an important one, because it will have implications for how you go about building your taxonomy.

In a common ground project, your task will be one of negotiating a common standard out of numerous semi-private (informal) categorisation schemes, and you can assume other preconditions for common ground will aid you. You may even be able to leverage them.

In a boundary object exercise, the negotiation will be much more formal: it will likely be between diverse public (often well-formed) taxonomy structures representing the different group perspectives, and you will have to navigate political inter-group issues including differences between experts (insiders) using 'deep' language and non-experts (outsiders) using 'shallow' language.

Case study 4.1 on the Department of Homeland Security in Chapter 4 is an example of a boundary-spanning taxonomy project, and we can see how these issues emerged in the provisionality and careful evolution of that taxonomy over time. We also see how a faceted taxonomy approach is an important bridging instrument to use in such cases.

Taxonomies can help in sense-making

We first looked at taxonomies as sense-making frameworks in Chapter 2. Frameworks as diverse as Mendeleev's periodic table and the BCG matrix can help organisations structure their thinking and make effective and appropriate decisions.

Sense-making happens in all kinds of environments, but in an organisational setting, it becomes especially important in fluid, unpredictable environments, where actionable understandings of the risks and opportunities can be formed so that strategic decisions can be taken. Matrices are very common in sense-making applications of taxonomy work, because they simplify multiple inputs in a confusing information environment into a few key dimensions, and therefore simplify the cognitive load in balancing different types and sources of information in pursuit of effective decisions.

The trick, of course, is in finding the few key dimensions that count for your particular need and the environment: in Mendeleev's case it was atomic mass and periodicity of behaviour, and they turned out to be pretty good predictors of chemical behaviours, even though the underlying science was not yet understood. So sense-making applications of taxonomy work tend to be experimental and often provisional. Often it is necessary to experiment with a number of key dimensions along which to organise and compare your information until you hit upon what look like productive combinations.

Sense-making frameworks and taxonomies are effective because they provide *salience*. This means that they draw our attention to important, actionable and relevant things, pulling them into the foreground, leaving the mass of less relevant information as noise in the background. Salience can only be achieved if we can identify the key dimensions or aspects of the environment that matter to us at that time, and which are robust enough to filter out non-salient noise reliably and consistently. In Mendeleev's case his dimensions of atomic mass and periodicity survived the test of time and advancements in science. In the BCG matrix case, relative market share and market growth turn out to be very robust predictors of a product's future performance.

Because matrices and other sense-making frameworks are very simple, they are also risky. They filter out a lot of possibly relevant information. Hence in sense-making it's important to deploy a wide range of sense-making frameworks and devices so that multiple perspectives on the domain can be tried and tested.

But even more complex taxonomies such as hierarchies and tree structures can also play a sense-making role. Because a taxonomy also maps the structure of a domain as well as describing it, it cannot avoid helping to make sense of novel circumstances or items by providing a context against which to examine and interpret those new things.

The way in which Linnaeus and other scientists of his time built their taxonomies of species is instructive. They started by collecting organisms, either physically in their collections or virtually in their notebooks which they filled with detailed descriptions and drawings.

Then, when they had a critical mass of material, they started structuring their collection according to organising principles that often appeared quite arbitrary. In Linnaeus's case, his decision to organise flower species according to their (male) sexual characteristics caused social uproar, not least because he channelled his evidently repressed sexuality through florid, romantic descriptions of the reproductive process of flowers, inadvertently spawning a whole genre of semi-pornographic fiction allegorising human sexual activity in botanical guise (Blunt, 2001).

Pornographic side effects apart, Linnaeus's organising principle based on anatomical distinctions also turned out to provide useful salience. The science behind his taxonomy work has moved from physical differentiation to genetic differentiation, but his taxonomies, like Mendeleev's, have proven remarkably robust.

More to the point, having a reliable structure based on robust principles for differentiation and similarity then meant that the botanists had a sense-making framework to interpret and classify any new species that came along – even though the initial catalogue of species from which they originated their structure was woefully partial and incomplete.

Comparing new things or situations to existing, known, classified things allows us to make sense of new things, make reliable predictions about them, describe their characteristics based on very little information and deal with them appropriately, so long as our organising principles are robust and hospitable over time.

Customer categorisations such as the Club Med customer typology covered in Chapter 4 and the CAAS organisational culture typology described in Chapter 5 are both good examples of sense-making applications of taxonomy work. They helped organisations make sense of the challenges facing them and helped them develop effective engagement strategies.

This type of taxonomy work is quite different from taxonomy work directed at organising things, work, information or knowledge. In sense-making work, the primary objective is to identify a powerful and productive *form* for the taxonomy – i.e. the major part of the work is in identifying and testing the salient organising principles for the taxonomy. In organising or standardising taxonomies, *population and maintenance* of the taxonomy are the ultimate objectives. There is a big difference between continual construction and testing of relatively simple taxonomies for sense-making and systematic building of a large-scale taxonomy for organising knowledge and information or mediating coordination of work between and within groups. Though there is some overlap in function between them, sense-making taxonomy projects tend to be more strategic, fluid and provisional. Organisational taxonomy projects aimed at supporting collaboration and standardisation tend to be more operationally focused, structured and long term.

Taxonomies can help in the discovery of risk and opportunity

We discussed the use of taxonomies in the management of risk and opportunity in Chapter 4. Radical innovations are initiated by 'seeing' an opportunity that others cannot. Innovation success, it is true, is driven by the ability to integrate the innovative product into existing public categories and ways of seeing things (so that the target audience understands how to adopt it and use it), but at its outset, the magic work of innovation is in seeing the invisible.

Similarly, risk appears most perilous when it comes out of nowhere, and it is for this reason that we invest heavily in various combinations of early warning systems, rampant speculation and nervous circumspection. These strategies at least reassure us that we are watching our environment closely for dangerous turns: but what is the shape of the things we are watching for? How would we know them if they are truly novel?

Our strategy in this uncertain world is guided by the knowledge that very little is truly invisible: all information is connected to other information. Our ability to recognise opportunity and risk alike is compromised by concealing noise and confusion, not by true invisibility. Our difficulty with novel risk is that we have no priming categories against which to match the alien thing and recognise its benevolent or malevolent nature. And this is where taxonomy work comes in.

When we looked at Unilever Research in Case study 4.2 we saw how strongly the *process* of taxonomy work dominated over the *products* of the taxonomy work – the domain maps – which Adrian Dale described as 'disposable'. In our analysis of Cirque du Soleil and the skin-products team using geophysical research we saw how constant loosening, interplay, fracturing, recombination and reconfiguration of categories was key to the ability to generate truly innovative approaches.

It's when we see the role of taxonomy work in the discovery of opportunity and risk that we begin to see the way that these different modes of taxonomy work (organising, common-ground, boundary-spanning, sense-making, discovery) connect to each other, graduating into each other on a broad continuum rather than being mutually exclusive categories each in their own domain. Taxonomies always structure and organise, and they always provide sense-making support, to a lesser or greater degree. The five different functions of taxonomies that we have discriminated and described separately actually overlap. The balance between them can change, however, according to the need and context of the organisation that needs taxonomy work.

Sometimes over time the focus of taxonomy work shifts gradually from the open provisional modes into the more highly structured modes. When we look at both innovation and risk, successful response involves being able to perceive something salient in a confusing and ambiguous environment, and ultimately to make sense by forming stable categories that allow us to explain it in relation to other things. Only then can we respond systematically and consistently in social groups.

So discovery connects and overlaps with sense-making, and thence to bridging boundaries between different knowledge domains that will need to collaborate to exploit the opportunity or evade the risk. If this turns out to be a large-scale opportunity or risk, then we need to develop large-scale, organised responsiveness, and so we must build this new category into our common-ground taxonomies, and start creating durable and stable vocabularies so that we can structure our knowledge and actions appropriately.

Hence, when we discussed the emergence and solidification of HIV AIDS as a medical category in Chapter 4, we saw how important it was that it became a stable, actionable category with a detailed nomenclature beneath it, co-evolving with the increasingly structured research and treatment actions that are needed to respond effectively to its threat. 'Seeing' the threat was only the first challenge; it had then to be integrated into existing knowledge structures, and then it needed its own knowledge domain to be built around it.

To see how this works we'll make use of a sense-making framework developed by Dave Snowden of the Cognitive Edge network to place our insights into some form of actionable structure and get a better understanding of the benefits and limitations of different taxonomy development approaches in different contexts. Snowden's Cynefin framework is particularly good at helping to identify appropriate strategies to adopt in different organisational environments.

Making sense of taxonomy work

The Cynefin framework differentiates the various kinds of environment that organisations typically have to manage and respond to (see Figure 6.1). In the lower-right domain, which Snowden labels the *Known*, we have predictable, stable, slow-moving, well-understood environments, where simple well-known rules hold sway. In this domain, if we need to make a decision or take an action, we simply look at the rule book or consult our standard categories and immediately the answer becomes obvious.

Above it, we have the *Knowable* domain. Here, life is more complicated and relies on specialist or technical knowledge, not simple rules. But the laws of cause and effect still hold sway, and if unsure of what to do, you can consult an expert, apply an advanced methodology, conduct some research or analyse what's going on at some depth and come up with a suitable answer.

Figure 6.1   The Cynefin framework

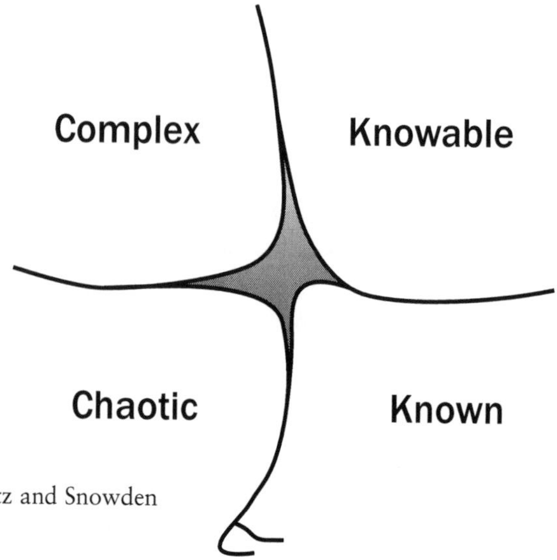

Complex

Knowable

Chaotic

Known

Source: Kurtz and Snowden (2003).

The left-hand side of the Cynefin framework is (for tidy minds) the zone of high organisational uncertainty and anxiety, because here the observable laws of cause and effect do not hold sway. No matter how much you categorise, look up rules, analyse or study, you will still not be able to make accurate predictions about outcomes. It's not obvious what you should do or how you should respond, because there are too many confusing, ambiguous signals and interacting influences. This is also a zone of high opportunity and innovation potential: risk and opportunity are often two sides of the same coin.

The *Chaotic* domain is the most dangerous (or opportunistic) because here the environment is so giddy with confusion and danger that you haven't the slightest idea of what's going on or how to respond. To pause to reflect here is even more dangerous: the only thing you can do is *do something*, anything at all, because by acting in this environment you can begin to observe the consequences of your actions, start to perceive relationships between inputs and consequences, and start to make sense.

If you're lucky, taking action in a *Chaotic* domain will move you into the top left, the *Complex* domain. This is the sense-making domain. Here, confusion and uncertainty still reign, but you can start figuring out appropriate responses by trying out multiple small interventions and looking for broad patterns in the consequences that will give you clues towards more successful strategies. Weather systems, ecologies, stock markets, organisational cultures and terrorism are all examples of complex systems (Kurtz and Snowden, 2003).

One of the key messages of Snowden's framework is that generating an inappropriate response by failing to recognise the type of domain you're in can be extremely dangerous. The impact of SARS, already previewed in Chapter 4, provides a graphic example. The first, dangerous response was to treat SARS as a 'Known' category. While Singapore (and Vietnam) were relatively quick to recognise that this was not 'normal' viral pneumonia where 'normal' rules of hygiene, treatment and social management held sway, other countries such as Taiwan and Canada were not so quick to acknowledge that standard category responses were inappropriate. Barely submerged panic among the general population and the healthcare staff in those countries was a direct consequence. Treating complex events as belonging to the *Known* domain generates a threatening pull towards the *Chaotic* domain.

Once they had recognised that SARS was not 'normal', Singapore's second response was to move the SARS epidemic into the *Knowable* domain. They set up a lab to study the virus and invited in a team of World Health Organisation (WHO) experts. But healthcare workers were still getting sick and dying, and they very quickly realised that the *Knowable* domain held no immediate answers.

So the government set up an inter-ministerial team and started treating SARS like a *Complex* problem. They generated numerous small- and large-scale initiatives and interventions: tightening hygiene and quarantine controls in hospitals for SARS patients; imposing legally enforceable Home Quarantine Orders on contacts of SARS patients; installing infrared fever detectors at airports and public buildings; imposing health declaration forms for travellers coming into Singapore; installing temperature checks at the entrances of shopping malls, hotels, public buildings and government offices; taking daily temperature checks in schools and offices; issuing free thermometers to every household; enforcing the separation of workforces in critical industries by migrating portions of those workforces to other locations or encouraging home-working; requiring taxi drivers to issue receipts to passengers with their licence number and time of journey – the list goes on. The initiatives that seemed to work best were resourced more (daily temperature checks), the ones that worked not so well (separation of workforces) were quietly dropped.

The message is simple: highly structured, stable, historically validated responses do not work in complex environments containing hazy, emergent threats and opportunities. Conversely, experimental, fluid and inconsistent responses are simply uncompetitive in stable, well-understood environments. Understanding which environment you're in will help you determine the appropriate response to make.

If you've followed the argument so far, it should now start becoming obvious that the continuum of taxonomy activity that we have just described – from structuring and organising through to sense-making and discovery – forms a chain of response across the three Cynefin domains that require a knowledge-based response: the *Known*, the *Knowable* and the *Complex* (see Figure 6.2). (Recall that the *Chaotic* domain is too confusing to wait for a knowledge-based response. Action – *any* action – is the first and only way to respond appropriately.)

In the *Known* domain, the primary role of taxonomy work is to structure and organise content and information according to the demands of the environment. Because the environment is stable and well understood, taxonomy work is often simply a matter of using and integrating existing standardised taxonomies.

In this domain, particularly at the level of homogeneous workgroups such as departments or project teams, you will often see a preference for monohierarchical tree structures – which maximise findability and

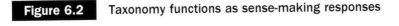

Figure 6.2 Taxonomy functions as sense-making responses

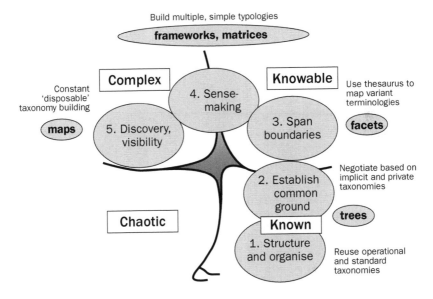

predictability of content in well-understood knowledge domains. These may be manifested in shared folder structures, filing systems or project management documentation templates. Taxonomy development tasks become primarily about finding existing operational taxonomies, tidying them up and integrating, publishing and maintaining them.

As we move into taxonomy projects that add a 'common-ground' purpose to the structuring and organising work, we are most likely looking at taxonomies that connect a pool of shared content and information across distributed same-functional groups. Examples might be quality management, IT projects, engineering projects, sales forces or distinct roles such as accountants, legal officers and technicians.

Distributed groups, especially geographically/culturally distributed groups, increase the likelihood of local variations in vocabulary and organisation, and therefore the need to negotiate differences into a standardised framework starts to become an important part of the taxonomy development process. Different localised needs and perspectives will start to encourage the use of polyhierarchical links in your tree structures, and as these needs grow, you'll increasingly start to see the benefits of faceted taxonomies.

Faceted schemes really come into their own when you need to develop a taxonomy to act as a boundary object to connect diverse functional groups and different knowledge domains that need to coordinate and interact.

By this time we are working in the *Knowable* domain, the domain of areas of specialist knowledge and expertise that need to interconnect. In the simpler focus on taxonomies as organising and structuring devices for well-bounded, well-understood content, and to an extent as common-ground enhancers, we are really looking at taxonomies as primarily supporting *information management*.

In the *Knowable* domain we start to rely on taxonomies as important enablers for knowledge sharing, knowledge transfer and information transfer across diverse community boundaries – here is where *knowledge management* applications of taxonomies start to kick in. Our taxonomies may be bridging boundaries within the organisation (e.g. an enterprise-wide taxonomy), or it may be boundaries between different knowledge areas (such as in the Department of Homeland Security taxonomy), or our intention may be to support the kind of inter-agency coordination that was so sadly lacking in the case of Victoria Climbié.

As we move away from the *Known* domain, through the *Knowable* domain towards the boundary with the *Complex* domain, the ability of our taxonomy structure to accurately represent standard accepted terminologies and approaches starts to break down. Not even a system of taxonomy facets will be able to comprehensively represent radical differences in view, vocabulary or organising principles. There are three possible causes for this:

- *The expert–novice gap.* In some cases, our knowledge management goal might be to make areas of expertise or specialist knowledge more accessible and usable by non-specialists. Our challenge is how to successfully bridge specialist and common working languages without alienating the specialists who may resent a 'dumbed down' taxonomy, or the general users who will be confused by a structure and vocabulary that appears to require four years of university education or twenty years of experience to navigate properly

- *The gaps between strong specialist domains.* In some areas the distinctions and the distance between different knowledge domains become more acute and it is increasingly difficult to find comprehensive bridging languages and structures (consider the challenge of building a taxonomy to bridge police, medical and social services aspects of child abuse information and knowledge). In each of the constituent knowledge domains the vocabularies and the organising principles may be strong and well defined, but looked at collectively, the connecting languages are simply not available

- *Emergent knowledge domains.* As we approach much less well-defined knowledge areas (e.g. emergent fields such as virology, biotechnology, knowledge management, complexity science) the vocabularies and relationships between concepts are much less stable, as we saw in the Department of Homeland Security case. It becomes hard to make these domains accessible through stable taxonomy structures.

Hence, as we approach the *Complex* domain, the *structure* of the taxonomy recedes in importance and *semantic* concerns begin to take centre stage. We will rely much more on a strong thesaurus behind the taxonomy to map multiple alternate terms to key taxonomy concepts. Our analysis and communication and 'translation' activity will become much more intense. We may present different instances of the same taxonomy to different user communities in simpler, or more complex, formats. Serendipity starts to become more important, and 'messy' parallel strategies such as folksonomies (see Chapter 10) start to become valuable alongside 'tidying' activities of taxonomy work (Snowden, 2005). And taxonomy work itself will recede in importance relative to other strategies, such as accessing relevant experience, creating the right kind of social interactions, and so on (Snowden, 2006).

Our crossover into the *Complex* domain proper marks a fundamental shift in how we do our taxonomy work. Or rather, as we have already argued, the boundary between *Knowable* and *Complex* also marks the point at which *the processes of taxonomy work become more important than the structures and contents of the taxonomies themselves.*

For this reason, when in Chapters 6 to 9 we describe systematic methodologies for the practice of building taxonomies, we'll focus on approaches to the *Known* and *Knowable* domains, where structure, validation and maintenance are key concerns. In the *Complex* domain, while good taxonomy discipline provides a useful toolkit of resources to work with, provisionality and not sustainability is the key. We are mapping and remapping and seeking to identify productive patterns that will help us build simple but powerful frameworks and matrices to filter out meaning from noise. An element of art also enters the fray: the ability to identify salient organising principles quickly is the mysterious additional skill we need to acquire.

It's worth pointing out that although we've separated out and numbered the primary purposes of taxonomy work in an implicitly hierarchical form, graduating from 'Structure and organise' in the *Known* domain to 'Discovery and visibility' in the *Complex* domain, these different purposes can combine and support each other in different ways. For example, the 'common-ground' purpose for taxonomy work can be a pre-condition for successful 'discovery' activity in the *Complex* domain. Several of these purposes can coexist in the same taxonomy initiative.

When taxonomies go bad

All tools can be used for ill as well as for good. Universal, pervasive tools such as taxonomies can have pervasive effects whether they are used well or used badly. Taxonomies can be vicious as much as they can be virtuous. Figure 6.3 summarises this.

Figure 6.3   Where taxonomies go wrong

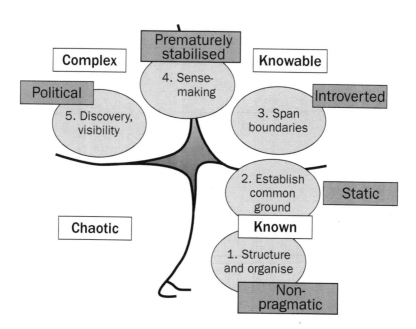

As much as taxonomies can be powerful enablers of sharing, coordination and common identity, so they can also fragment, sow discord, alienate, enforce violence and even destroy. Sometimes, such as in race classification used for racist purposes, this is intentional. Sometimes it is the result of using a strategy that is inappropriate to the need or the environment – which is why an instrument such as the Cynefin framework is such a powerful planning tool.

There are five major ways in which we can apply taxonomies badly, and they all relate to either not recognising, or deliberately subverting, the nature of the environment we are operating in:

- simple taxonomies in the complex domain;
- premature stabilisation;
- reinforcing boundaries and silos;
- failing to accommodate the future;
- failing to reflect pragmatic needs.

Simple taxonomies in the complex domain

Taxonomies can simplify a domain too much and produce highly dysfunctional results. This is frequently associated with the abusive use of power.

In his study of how human beings categorise themselves and others, David Berreby tells a harrowing tale from the Rwandan war crimes tribunal held in Belgium in 2000. In May 1994, as the Rwandan massacres gathered momentum, a group of Tutsi refugees from the town of Sovu sought refuge from the murderous Hutu gangs in Sovu's Catholic convent. The superior, Sister Gertrude, a Hutu herself, called in the Hutu militia. But she had a condition: the militia were not to take her nuns, some of whom were also Tutsis. As the militia began their grim work of dragging out the Tutsis for slaughter, one of the refugees, a girl named Aline, the niece of a Tutsi nun, begged to be given a veil to disguise her as a nun. Sister Gertrude refused. Aline was murdered along with hundreds of others who were shot, hacked or burned to death that day (Berreby, 2005: 18).

In the Rwanda massacres we have an awful but distressingly frequent example of what Amartya Sen calls the fallacy of 'singular affiliation', the simplification of multiple human identities to a single overriding identity, disregarding with horrible consequences the multiple categories to which we, as human beings, belong.

> There are a great variety of categories to which we can simultaneously belong. I can be, at the same time, an Asian, an Indian citizen, a Bengali with Bangladeshi ancestry, an American or British resident, an economist, a dabbler in philosophy, an author, a Sanskritist, a strong believer in secularism and democracy, a man, a feminist, a heterosexual, a defender of gay and lesbian rights, with a nonreligious lifestyle, from a Hindu background, a non-Brahmin, and a nonbeliever in an afterlife … This is just a small sample of diverse categories to each of which I may simultaneously belong – there are of course many other membership categories too which, depending on circumstances, can move and engage me. (Sen, 2006: 19)

Sectarian violence often involves suppressing other categorisations that would promote common cause and invalidate the violent impulse. In describing the Hindu–Muslim riots of the 1940s, whose consequences he witnessed as a child, Sen points out that both Muslim and Hindu victims often shared the same socio-economic status: poor, marginalised workers, driven by poverty into the dangerous streets to find work.

> Even though the community identities of the two groups of brutalized prey were quite different, their class identities (as poor labourers with little economic means) were much the same. But no identity other than religious ethnicity was allowed to count in those days of polarized vision focused on a singular categorisation. The illusion of a uniquely confrontational reality had thoroughly reduced human beings and eclipsed the protagonists' freedom to think. (Sen, 2006: 174)

Back in Sovu, we cannot say that Sister Gertrude was absolutely without the ability to think. She too had multiple affiliations, most of which she shared with her Tutsi victims. She was a Catholic (which should have precluded assisting in murder) and so were many of the Tutsis; she was a nun (which should have strengthened the prohibition to kill); she spoke the same language and had the same ethnic and cultural history as the terrified refugees; she shared the same genetic profile, though she may not have known this – the Tutsi–Hutu distinction was an administrative fiction invented by Rwanda's colonial masters less than a century before; she was a native of the same town; her nuns were related to the Tutsi townspeople by blood and family ties.

Sister Gertrude's case is unusual because it doesn't demonstrate the simple case of one category suppressing all others: in her case she developed a more elaborate categorisation strategy where one categorisation (members of her convent) 'trumped' the ethnic hatred category ('Tutsis who must be killed'), which 'trumped' all others (fellow-Rwandans, fellow-townsfolk, fellow-Catholics, relatives of her nuns).

The mother superior's subordination of ethically relevant taxonomic categorisations into a finely judged hierarchy of choice was just as deadly as the outright suppression of competing categorisation principles and, some might say, even more evil. In taking on the power to decide who should live and who should die, hers was a taxonomy of power. In technical terms, while facets might have enabled the peaceful coexistence of alternate identities, her hierarchy of categories simplified choices starkly and functioned as an all too useful instrument of domination and imagined revenge. And in general terms, in an overly simplified taxonomic frame on the world, the people who get to categorise, the people who get to choose which category you are in, are those who get to exert power.

In Cynefin terms, pretty much anything to do with human affairs resides in the *Complex* domain. Hierarchies and trees, with their rules for subordination and dominant, singular principles of organisation, cannot faithfully represent the multivalent, emergent, shifting, ambiguous shapes of meaning and knowledge in this domain. This is not a new insight, nor is it confined to the pantheon of complexity thinkers. The eighteenth-century Scottish philosopher David Hume was a confirmed empiricist but, finding it hard to pin down a rigorous and stable classification of 'national characters', threw up his hands with the uncharacteristic admission that any categorisation he might devise could be subverted 'by that inconstancy, to which all human affairs are subject' (Berreby, 2005: 34). Complexity might frustrate him, but he had to acknowledge it.

This is why, in the *Complex* domain, we insist on the provisionality of the taxonomies and typologies that we devise. They give and reflect useful insights, but are invariably partial. If we attempt to universalise their application or subordinate alternative views to a singular view we will only have bad results.

Genocide, terrorism, war, persecution and systemic violence are all in their own ways products of taxonomic over-simplification: the reduction of complex human perspectives to a single set of categories that must be rigidly enforced. Taxonomies can be evil too.

While few organisations are likely to enforce taxonomic simplifications in such horrific ways, they remind us of the importance of matching our taxonomy approach to the environment and problems we need to respond to. If our environment is complex, a taxonomic approach that is overly simple is always going to run foul of hidden risks, and must always be driven through power structures rather than organically through an alert and responsive awareness. Overly simple approaches in a *Complex* domain are almost always politically driven, since neither logic nor common sense offer them any warrant. And the more we try to persevere in an approach that is dislocated from our environment, the more we must use extreme measures to account for the differences. Bad things always happen when taxonomies become political.

At a much more mundane level, consider this report from a knowledge manager of a public sector agency, reflecting on his lessons learned.

> We spent almost three million on a portal, but after three years we only have 3,000 documents inside. One of our problems is the taxonomy. When we designed it, it was dictated top down, and we discovered that our users found it very difficult to understand. It's just not related to the way they work. Now it's troublesome for them to decide how to categorise, and they have difficulty in finding things.

Premature stabilisation

When we talk about premature stabilisation we are still in the *Complex* domain, but we are recognising the all too human impulse when faced with uncertainty, and that is to grasp at straws as if they were lifeboats. It's related to over-simplification, except that in this case, the choice of the simplification principle is not arbitrary but has some validity.

Premature stabilisation happens when, for example, you discover a framework that has promising results in interpreting your environment and you immediately assume that this framework must rule and guide all your actions from thenceforth on.

That is to say, you've forgotten the golden rule of the *Complex* domain, which is to test the limits of the perspectives you have rendered visible and keep prospecting for alternative ways of looking at your information and knowledge. The recent history of management 'thinking' is full of fads that prematurely stabilise and structure businesses around one overly simple framework, from business process re-engineering (BPR) to balanced scorecard to knowledge management in its early days. It's as if an empire were to identify and defeat one band of marauding barbarians and, on the strength of that victory, immediately abandon its garrisons and border posts.

Just as with over-simplification in the *Complex* domain the contours of power can also shape the drive to stabilise a framework or a taxonomic principle too quickly, and a key consequence is that these power principles may render critical areas of work invisible.

If we recall, one of the functions of a taxonomy is to render work and information visible in consistent ways over time. In Bowker and Star's terms, taxonomies function as an organisational memory: they preserve information over time in consistently structured ways for repeated access (Bowker and Star, 1999: ch. 8). This is related to the idea that taxonomies lift key features of our environment into salience, into the foreground of our attention. The obvious counterpoint of this is that other features of our environment are pushed into the background, out of our attentional range. Taxonomies filter into invisibility as much as they make visible.

The danger of premature stabilisation is that power structures authorise a singular, if partially valid and valuable, perspective on organising information, while neglecting other critical areas and rendering them invisible by default. The classic example, examined at length by Bowker and Star, is the invisibility of nursing work and nursing knowledge in the taxonomies that organise healthcare and medical work. 'Nursing work has traditionally been invisible, and its traces removed at the earliest opportunity from the medical record' (Bowker and Star, 1999: 258). The consequence of this is that while medical knowledge of doctors, surgeons and specialists can be netted and recycled systematically in the information and knowledge systems supported by their taxonomies, nursing knowledge must rely, bizarrely, on self-renewal and informal transfer, and accidental or anecdotal recycling through nursing practitioners who become teachers and trainers.

Clearly, this is dangerous in a complex and fast-evolving field such as healthcare, where numerous disciplines need to remain synchronised so as to coordinate effectively. If nursing knowledge cannot grow apace with medical knowledge, then failures and breakdowns will occur. For this reason among others, a group of nursing educators has been working on a Nursing Interventions Classification since the late 1980s (Bowker and Star, 1999: chs 7–8).

Ingunn Moser makes a similar point about the information and knowledge articulation work of administrative and secretarial staff in enabling information flows within a busy medical practice. Much of the flow of information is achieved *outside of* the electronic information systems that the clinic has invested in, via post-it notes, telephone reminders, routines and allocated responsibilities, verbal reminders as doctors pass reception and so on: 'The work of secretaries and administrative staff in particular tends to disappear from view and become invisible. It is the kind of work that only becomes visible and palpable once it is not done ... and that creates the conditions for flow that appears to be smooth and effortless' (Moser, 2004).

If prematurely fixed taxonomic principles can edit out important areas of work, they can also edit into invisibility important functions that we need to perform with our information and knowledge assets. An all too frequent example is the adoption of a taxonomy that suits the purchaser of a content management system and not other stakeholders in the information that the system is meant to handle. In a public sector agency, if the content system is an electronic records management system, the records management function may impose a taxonomy which is geared towards records management and archiving needs, neglecting the natural work patterns of the creators and users of the documents in day-to-day work.

Conversely, if the business user of a new system is in a narrow functional area like finance or sales, their taxonomy may be perfectly customised to the workflow within their departments, but may be all but inaccessible to others who need access to their information assets according to different organising principles and priorities – to draw up budgets, assess trends, manage the documents as records, and so on.

The lesson we taxonomists must learn from this is that structures of power and principal ownership may not be the best place to start when building taxonomies to support work, though they must always be acknowledged. It is not enough to consult senior management and subject matter experts; it's also necessary to examine the natural patterns of work among the 'invisible' articulators of work – if, that is, our intention is to support that work – as well as the range of stakeholders who have a claim on, or role to play with, our information and knowledge assets.

Reinforcing boundaries and silos

In the wrong circumstances, all good things can be turned to bad. If one of the opportunities afforded by a taxonomy is that it can reinforce common ground within a community, it can also strengthen an introspective view and isolate a community from its surroundings. The tremendous explosion in information access afforded by the Internet and its associated technology ironically strengthens this tendency. Now, more than ever before, it is easy to surround ourselves with information and knowledge that supports our point of view, whatever it may be, and there is more than enough of it to drown out alternate points of view. Worldviews both sane and insane can find content to bolster them and protect them from alternative perspectives. Paul Saffo, of the Institute for the Future, calls this danger posed by the Internet an 'erosion of the intellectual commons holding society together' (Saffo, 2005: 6; Sunstein, 2002).

Building information 'nests' that reinforce closed worldviews and protect them from challenge is a characteristic activity of extremists, sects and cults. Social networks expert Ronald Burt likens these closed networks to an echo chamber, which 'amplifies predispositions, creating a structural arthritis in which people cannot learn what they do not already know' and where unwarranted trust in 'insiders' (fellow community members) is matched by unwarranted mistrust of 'outsiders' (non-community members) (Burt, 2001).

But 'information nesting' happens in less extreme areas as well. From 2003 to 2004, before and after the US Presidential election, the social networking practitioner Valdis Krebs charted the extraordinary lack of common ground between people in the United States who were buying Democrat-oriented political books on Amazon.com, and those who were buying Republican-oriented political books. At one point, close to the Presidential election, the two communities had only one boundary object in common, a book aptly titled *America: What Went Wrong?* (Krebs, 2003, 2004).

And information nesting happens within organisations too, especially in environments where the infrastructure for information and knowledge flow and reuse has been weak and nesting becomes a compensating response. Nesting, combined with the Babel Instinct, produces silos.

There may be very clear organising principles and a consistently understood set of categories within a user community, and so taxonomy development may appear, at face value, to be straightforward – say, for example, within a research and development department. If, however, the information and knowledge assets of that community need to be exchanged and reused on a broader scale, then a strong 'common-ground' approach within that department will very likely undermine wider use, isolate the user community from alternate vocabularies and category systems and subvert broader coordination opportunities. The R&D taxonomy will be geared for experts and specialists and employ their specialist languages and deep categories, where instead perhaps it needs to be alerting marketing and operations people to new products and services in the pipeline, or attuning business leaders to productivity improvement possibilities, and so on.

When assessing the objectives of a taxonomy exercise, it is extremely important to be able to distinguish between a 'common-ground' need (typically where common ground is weak) and a 'boundary-object' need (typically where common ground within distinct communities is strong and there is a need to trade information or coordinate work across community boundaries). Simply interviewing the sponsors of a project will not tell you this. Only looking at the broader knowledge and information management needs of the organisation will inform you of the possibilities that sponsors might not themselves see.

Failing to accommodate the future

Taxonomy development on any large scale, especially across organisational boundaries, involves significant resources and effort. It is tempting, particularly where the domains covered by the taxonomy appear relatively stable, to heave a sigh of relief once it is completed, disband the team, implement the taxonomy in your content system and move on to another project. In some ways this is a more pernicious problem than premature stabilisation, because at least there we have plenty of clues about the instability of the domain to remind us that this is a rash act.

Stability in any domain is an illusion. Take geography and country names post-1989, with the breakup of the Soviet Union and the fragmentation of nation states across Europe. Knowledge itself is always fluid and provisional, but it sometimes deceives us by moving at different rates of change, some very fast and some very slow.

In any organisation that must respond to its environment, and uses information to help it do so (and which organisation does not need to do this?), then its taxonomies must also reflect the changing needs for information and knowledge flows arising from changes in its environment.

This means that taxonomies are fluid constructs, never permanent, not even semi-permanent. All taxonomy work whether geared towards *Known*, *Knowable* or *Complex* domains, must provide for maintenance and change, and this requires mechanisms for checking the taxonomy's alignment with current needs and a governance structure to ensure regular review.

Taxonomies in both the *Known* and *Knowable* domains can give a false illusion of certainty, particularly if they are combined with taxonomic dogmatism drawn from the use of taxonomies in science, where faith in the *form and structure* of a taxonomy and the maturity of a body of knowledge distract practitioners from the importance of *process and purpose* in taxonomy work.

In the *Known* domain, stability may be stronger but it is not absolute, and the need for maintenance will be less frequent but not absent. In the absence of organised maintenance and alignment checking mechanisms, taxonomies can drift away from current business and organisational needs. Information that is critical to the business will not be described and managed in ways the business requires, rendering newly important knowledge and information assets effectively invisible, and disabling or slowing the organisation's response.

In Chapter 9 we will describe the maintenance and governance structures that need to be put in place around taxonomies to keep them hospitable to future changes in environmental and informational needs.

Failing to reflect pragmatic needs

The last major mistake in taxonomy work is related to the mistake of premature stabilisation, where important actors and functions are not taken into account when developing a taxonomy. This is a failure to take the contexts in which the taxonomy must be applied into account. As we saw, such actors and functions are often 'invisible' from the point of view of authority structures, even though they play an important role in the articulation of work and information resources.

In the case of failing to recognise pragmatic needs, the mistake occurs most frequently in the *Known* domain, where knowledge and information needs are supposedly well understood and documented, and there is a strong temptation to develop or adapt taxonomies based on 'official' needs rather than real ones. This is why some elements of taxonomy work that are relevant to the *Complex* domain are useful in any taxonomy project, because they are more likely to uncover patterns that have been suppressed by the 'official' version of reality.

The failure to take pragmatic working needs into account happens most frequently where managerial insecurity pushes you towards a supposed 'best practices' approach, or system vendors offer you a pre-built taxonomy promising an easy answer to the troublesome work of figuring a taxonomy out for yourself.

These solutions are in themselves not necessarily bad things, but they should never be accepted at face value without looking inwards to the pragmatic needs of your internal taxonomy customers and the contexts in which the taxonomy is supposed to serve.

What, for example, should you do if your organisation needs a taxonomy for its human resources department? Should you build or buy? Should you adopt a taxonomy structure that reflects 'best practice' such as an APQC or professional HR association taxonomy? Should you buy a pre-built taxonomy containing 10,000 terms and four levels of detail?

The answer, unfortunately, is it depends. The first question goes to why you need an HR taxonomy in the first place. If you are a large networked organisation with dispersed HR departments and practitioners, then your objective may be about creating common ground and focusing on the concepts and terminology of the profession. Moreover, if your HR community needs to network with other HR communities outside the organisation and gain access to professional resources, then standardisation to a common vocabulary such as a profession-specific classification scheme makes a lot of sense. You will still need to check whether the current vocabularies and organising principles of your internal HR groups have a significant degree of diversity and whether they can be mapped easily to the proposed external standard. And you will need to decide whether the scale of information content you will be managing with this taxonomy matches the scale of the taxonomy. There's no point having a deep, detailed taxonomy if you only have a hundred pieces of content to manage.

If, however, your need is to make HR resources accessible to employees throughout the organisation, then the specialist HR vocabulary provided by the external taxonomy is completely inappropriate. You'll need instead a taxonomy that matches the needs of people who access HR resources, usually in the context of the employee's journey through an organisation from recruitment to departure. They are not going to be interested in the buzzwords and jargon of the HR community. Who is going to be helped by categories for Shared Services,

E-HR or Personal IP when they simply want to find out how their leave is allocated and processed? You might be lucky enough to find an external taxonomy around the employee journey that meets or can be adapted to meet your needs, but oftentimes you'll have to build it yourself, mainly because the task vocabularies around being an employee are often highly localised and vary greatly in simplicity or complexity relative to the size of the organisation. Pre-built taxonomies are often devoid of contextual relevance and cues.

Nothing ever excuses us from visiting our stakeholders and taxonomy customers, mapping their working vocabularies and implicit category systems, and prioritising the needs that our taxonomy will serve. This set of processes will be the focus of Chapters 7 and 8.

In this chapter we have surveyed the different roles that taxonomies can play in an organisation, and emphasised the importance of understanding the needs of any given situation when defining the purpose and intent of a taxonomy development project. A taxonomy that is inappropriate to the needs of its host organisation and to its principal customers (whether visible or invisible) is not merely superfluous. It can actively damage an organisation, cripple its responses, alienate its stakeholders and conceal important information and knowledge assets. All taxonomy work requires a careful review of the knowledge and information needs of an organisation, and careful preparation. It is to this process that we now turn.

7

Preparing for a
taxonomy project

The universe, real or intelligible, can be represented from an infinite variety of perspectives, & the number of possible systems of human knowledge is as large as the number of these perspectives.

(Diderot, 1755, quoted in Blom, 2005: 152)

Building a taxonomy is more a journey of discovery than a piece of analysis. The Babel Instinct requires that a successful taxonomist be more a diplomat than a scientist. In a knowledge management context, pragmatism will always trump tidiness, and the connection with organisational effectiveness must never be lost. This is why the people we assume might make good taxonomy 'specialists' (records managers, librarians, information scientists) may not necessarily be the best equipped to develop your taxonomy for you – unless they understand what drives your organisation's performance and effectiveness. Tidy minds make bad corporate taxonomies, for the simple reason that few corporate environments are, or can be, tidy (Norman, 2006).

In this chapter we look at the steps involved in preparing for a taxonomy project and the processes that will help ensure the pragmatism, relevance and usability of your taxonomy. As you'll see from Figure 7.1, arriving at a clear understanding of your purpose may be an iterative process and doesn't simply stop at finding out what the project sponsor wants. In fact, the entire taxonomy-building process is an iterative one, because competing needs and perspectives may need to be resolved and underlying needs may not always be immediately obvious.

Iterative development is based on the idea of continual refinement through trial and error ... [It] hones in on the target, refining its focus and perfecting the product until it has reached its goal. Each cycle consists of the same basic steps, and each cycle infuses the process with richer information. Solutions are created, examined, and re-created until the business and user needs are met in a consistent, regular and predictable way. (Kuniavsky, 2003: 28–9)

The first six key steps in preparing for a taxonomy project are:

Step 1: *Meet project sponsor* and get initial sense of purpose and rationale; map the scope of the project including knowledge domains and both visible and potentially 'invisible' stakeholders in those domains.

Step 2: *Engage stakeholders*, validate your map of the scope and understand their needs.

Step 3: *Refine the project purpose* and get sponsor's agreement.

Step 4: *Design your approach*.

Step 5: *Build your communication plan*, identifying benefits.

Step 6: *Start the process for taxonomy governance*.

Figure 7.1   **Preparing for a taxonomy project**

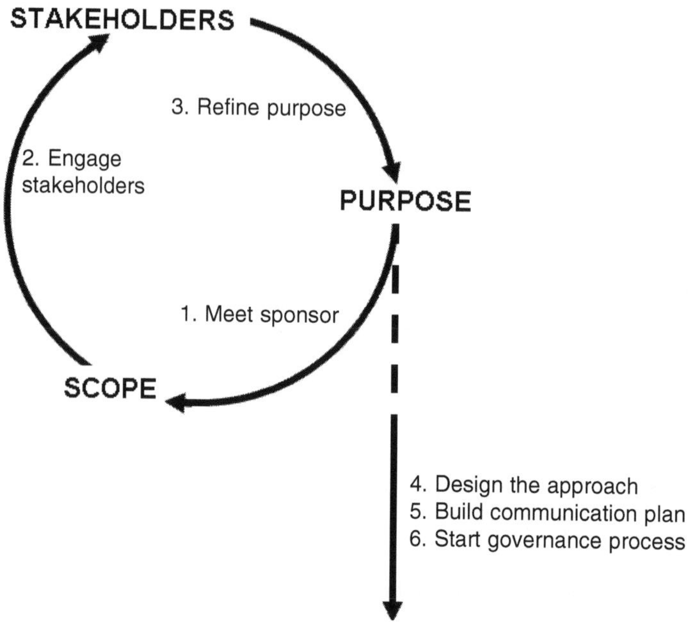

Step 1: Meet project sponsor

Because taxonomy projects are really information and knowledge infrastructure projects (and because infrastructure is rarely well understood) taxonomy project sponsors are often unaware of the ramifications of a taxonomy project. 'I just need a taxonomy' seems like a straightforward thing to ask. So project sponsors often need to be helped to see the potential opportunities and pitfalls – and the effort involved – before embarking on a project. However, you do not want to terrify them before you have a better sense of what the true scope and scale of your project is and the potential benefits.

Your first meeting therefore should be exploratory, examining their sense of the need and getting their help to map out the potential stakeholders involved. As we saw in our last chapter, missing critical stakeholders or activity areas can seriously prejudice the success of a taxonomy project.

Your initial scoping meeting should cover four main areas:

- mapping key stakeholders and activities;
- picking up cues on the purpose and intent of the project;
- determining the technology environment;
- assessing the knowledge and information management context.

Mapping key stakeholders and activities

In our taxonomy consulting engagements, we frequently use concept mapping as a technique for ensuring we capture all major activities and stakeholders in our initial scoping exercise. The basic technique is described in Chapter 2, and at greater length in Crandall et al. (2006: ch. 4). Other kinds of information mapping and knowledge mapping techniques will also work (e.g. Orna, 2004; Henczel, 2001), but we have found that for well-defined work domains, concept maps provide the greatest simplicity and clarity for discussing the scope of the project with project sponsors and stakeholders alike.

In a project scoping exercise, we will typically build the concept map on large sheets of flipchart paper, with sticky notes, pencil and eraser. We will agree a colour code for the concepts of three types, e.g. green may represent business activities, pink may represent agents and blue may represent resources that are produced or used in the activities.

In the first stage, we ask the project sponsor to brainstorm a number of key stakeholders who will benefit from the taxonomy and the activities that the taxonomy will support. Each stakeholder/agent is listed on one sticky note, each activity on one sticky note and so on.

Once we have a critical mass of sticky notes (usually when the project sponsor has to stop to think), we start organising the notes on the flipchart, pencilling in the relationships (e.g. by asking the sponsor 'how does this relate to that?') and adding sticky notes for resources.

The technique is powerful, because laying out activities, agents and resources in this way starts to identify interrelationships and dependencies between agents and activities, and to identify critical activities and agents affected by the taxonomy and ways in which the same resources may be used by numerous agents (we start to get early indications of resources that act as boundary objects). The identification of stakeholders is no longer purely dependent on the sponsor's memory or awareness: the map itself starts to indicate gaps and missing stakeholders.

Moreover, the map can subsequently be used with the stakeholders identified within it to complete it, to identify differences in language or perceptions, or natural boundaries or handover points. The map becomes a device for making the boundaries of the project scope explicit for everybody involved.

Figure 7.2 shows part of the detail from a human resource concept map, covering the learning and development function. We can already see potential stakeholders who might not have been immediately obvious (IT department, internal trainers, division heads) and we can see the activities that will likely require and produce information assets that may need to be managed within the activities. Even if it turns out that the scope of the project will eventually exclude some of these agents, your concept map will ensure that they are excluded for clear, stated reasons (e.g. they will not have access to the system that the taxonomy is being developed for), and not excluded simply because they were not thought of. It helps to have a rationale and clear criteria for inclusion and exclusion when it comes to communicating your purpose later on.

Figure 7.2   Detail from a human resource concept map

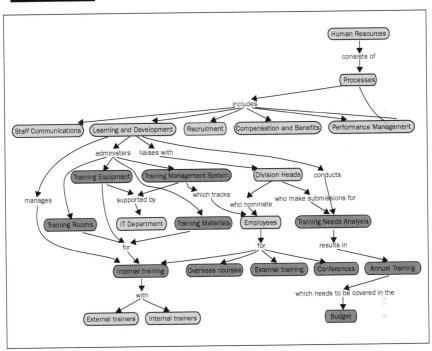

Picking up cues on the purpose and intent of the project

Getting your initial map of stakeholders and activities is probably the most important part of your initial meeting with the project sponsor. However, obviously he or she will also share the reasons for the project and whatever outcomes are expected. At this stage, this should be carefully recorded, but it is too early for detailed planning on this basis because you have not yet seen the needs and issues from the perspectives of the other stakeholders.

You do, however, want to start categorising the issues and drivers discussed by the project sponsor because they will give you important cues about the kind of taxonomy that is required and how it should be constructed (see Table 7.1). These cues will structure your discussions later on with the stakeholders.

It is very likely in the case of an enterprise-wide taxonomy project that you will receive mixed cues, suggesting a combination approach (usually

| Table 7.1 | Examples of important cues to taxonomy types and construction approaches |

Cues	Indicate
'We have a very clear workflow that everyone follows. Now we want to move it online and make all the information assets created along the way more accessible, easier to find.'	Structure-and-organise taxonomy – reuse standard vocabularies to support routine work
'Our shared folders are a mess. Everybody does their own thing, so it's very hard even at the department level, to locate the information we need. It's faster simply to ask the person responsible. If we can find them.'	Common-ground taxonomy – negotiate and resolve inconsistent vocabularies and organising principles
'Lots of divisions are replicating the same information over and over again. They don't know what information exists in other parts of the organisation. We should be getting much more value out of the information and knowledge assets we create. If we shared information with our key suppliers and partners, we could be much more effective.'	Boundary-spanning taxonomy – focus on reusable knowledge assets across organisational boundaries (internal and external); find or negotiate common vocabulary and organising principles for those assets
'This is a new area for us. We know we need a taxonomy, but the domain is changing too quickly. Is there a standard taxonomy we can just subscribe to? Our specialists can never agree, their approaches are too different. Our generic taxonomy just won't do. We need something much more specialised to support this function.'	Sense-making or discovery taxonomy – focus on processes for creating and using multiple frameworks, cross-disciplinary knowledge mapping, multiple 'disposable' taxonomies fit for very specialised purposes

some combination of structure-and-organise, common-ground and boundary-spanning). So you'll need to try to get a sense of where the greatest pain points are in the organisation to safely assess the relative importance of each cue.

Determining the technology environment

One important constraint that you will need to cover in your initial scoping meeting is the technology environment where your taxonomy is likely to be expressed. In many cases, the technology environment is going to be a given; in some cases, the organisation is planning a new technology initiative and wants the taxonomy project to inform the requirements-gathering for that project.

Typical technology environment types include:

Level I environments

- Collections of physical paper files
- Shared folder structure on shared drives/Lotus Notes databases

Level II environments

- Intranet web pages
- Portal with document libraries
- Content management system

Level III environments

- Document/records/digital asset management system

The implications for taxonomy development are given for each type of environment below.

Level I environments (*e.g. physical files/shared folders/Lotus Notes*)

Level I environments share the characteristic that documents should be found in only one location to avoid confusion over different versions; the primary role of the taxonomy structure is to facilitate browsing and navigation to get to that single instance of a document.

Manually compiled indexes to topics can also be used as supplementary finding aids, though they are rarely exploited outside the paper environment.

The taxonomy structure needs to be simple and shallow and the tolerance for ambiguity in taxonomy terms is very low.

These environments tend to support structure-and-organise and common-ground taxonomies better than others, because it is easier to represent the routine work of departments where there is low tolerance for ambiguity and no compensating mechanism for navigation mistakes. People are, after all, inducted into routine work patterns and so can compensate for navigation ambiguity.

Level I technology environments are pre-coordinated environments (see Chapter 2), in that content is arranged in advance in a particular, stable configuration, and finding the content is all about understanding the structure of that environment. This environment really only supports one taxonomy form well – the tree structure. *In Level I environments, the principal function of the taxonomy is to support navigation.*

Level II environments (*e.g. Intranet/portal with document libraries/content management system*)

Level I and II environments are similar in that they will use the taxonomy primarily to support navigation. If there is a search engine in use it is likely to be limited to indexing the contents of documents, which will mean a keyword search often returns low-precision materials – i.e. all documents that contain an instance of the keyword anywhere, including words that have multiple meanings.

The use of metadata to apply the controlled vocabularies within the taxonomy and improve the precision of search varies widely in such applications, from non-existent to moderate. Even where metadata is added, little of it can be picked up automatically, so tagging content with taxonomy terms is a laborious task, reducing the effectiveness of metadata use.

Such environments do not usually support large or deep taxonomies very well, because even if the navigation structure theoretically supports deep taxonomies, it is rarely easy (in the way many of these applications have been designed) to navigate the taxonomy and select the correct taxonomy terms when applying the metadata.

Since they tend to span the whole enterprise and are intended to make organisation-wide content available, they tend to support boundary-spanning and generic common-ground taxonomies better than localised (workgroup level) common-ground or structure-and-organise taxonomies.

Because of this, the structure of the taxonomy will usually be determined by very generic functional areas or organisation-wide activities rather than specialised work at departmental level.

Within portals, document libraries can be used as multiple virtual folder structures just like shared departmental folders, but the natural contours of work within a particular department will not be easily interpreted at an organisation-wide level, so there is often a gap between what is comprehensible at an organisation-wide level and how navigation is understood at a local workgroup level.

In content management systems and portals, predesigned page

templates will define what content is pulled onto which pages, so they have an advantage over shared drives in that the same content can appear on multiple pages depending on the activity areas they are linked to.

Level II environments are similar to Level I in that they support navigation and are also largely pre-coordinated environments. However, they can also support multiple ways of presenting or arranging the same content, and so in addition to *navigation*, taxonomies in Level II environments also support *arrangement* of content for specific uses. In this sense they can simulate post-coordination (e.g. templates can dynamically pull predefined content types together into one location/page whenever a specific task is called for). Tree structures are the easiest taxonomy forms to use, but portals and content management systems may also support polyhierarchies.

Level III environments (*e.g. document/records/ digital asset management system*)

Systems in Level III environments shift the information management effort onto sophisticated use of metadata to govern the way that documents are retrieved and organised.

They frequently use visual metaphors such as virtual folder structures to provide an element of browse and navigation like the environments above. However, they also use the controlled vocabularies of the taxonomy to enable very precise searches (usually buried, however, in the little-used 'Advanced Search' feature).

This means that taxonomies can be larger and more complex, and matrices or faceted schemes can be supported.

Adding extensive metadata is troublesome for users, however, so the better systems reduce the burden of manually adding metadata by a number of workarounds or tools, such as: (1) 'inherited' metadata elements that are picked up if you 'drop' a document into a particular virtual folder; (2) picking up metadata such as author, title, date from the applications or systems producing the document; or (3) 'autocategorisation' which is where the application analyses the content of documents according to rules that you have defined for it and decides which taxonomy categories it probably belongs to.

A good implementation of such a system should be able to support a range of taxonomy work, from structure-and-organise to common-ground to boundary-spanning. And once you are able to exploit metadata in sophisticated ways, the taxonomy may be represented through a combination of tree structures, polyhierarchies, matrices and facets.

The use of metadata effectively creates a post-coordination opportunity. Content can be pulled together at any point of need simply by calling on specific metadata elements. Level III environments therefore support both pre-coordinated taxonomies as well as post-coordinated ones. In consequence your taxonomy needs to be more versatile, because it supports three possible functions: *navigation* of content domains, *arrangements* of content for specific activities and *precision searching* for content based on a subject vocabulary.

Frequently you will need to make judgements about which of these functions is going to take precedence in your design, because navigation taxonomies tend to be very broad and shallow, arrangement taxonomies tend to be narrow and specialised, and search taxonomies can support complexity, depth and higher degrees of ambiguity. *It is very, very difficult to serve all three needs effectively without the use of a faceted taxonomy to reflect different perspectives on the same content.* Faceted taxonomies can easily generate trees for navigation and sub-taxonomies for localised arrangements of content.

In practice, no technology environment is entirely pure. You will almost certainly be aiming to build your taxonomy for a hybrid environment combining elements of all three levels.

In addition there will be other business applications that organise content for retrieval and arrange it for task support, where navigation, arrangement and search have differing priorities depending on the application – e.g. call centre management and information systems; medical records systems; facilities booking systems; customer relationship management systems; transactional systems; decision support and business analytics applications.

Such systems are almost certainly going to rely heavily on metadata and so belong most appropriately to a Level III environment. If you have a substantial Level III bias and multiple information repositories in your environment, then it's worth thinking about getting an enterprise search engine.

An enterprise search engine is one that should be able to search the content of multiple repositories, ranging from shared drives to intranet content, Lotus Notes databases, and content and document management systems. It will search based on document contents as well as document metadata, and can be configured to privilege some elements over others (such as metadata).

Clearly, if you have a hybrid environment with some repositories that have virtually no metadata (shared folders), some that have limited metadata (e.g. content management systems) and some that have extensive metadata, your searches will have very mixed results in terms of precision.

This is why all good enterprise search engines have the capacity to be taught how to search effectively (such as giving the engine a list of 'best bets' where you know that searches on particular keywords are usually aimed at certain types of documents) (Robertson, 2006).

Very sophisticated (and expensive) search engines will crawl the content of documents and infer the probable taxonomy categories through an 'autocategorisation' engine. This is not magic, however; it needs to be told how your taxonomy works, usually in one of three ways:

1. You give the search engine a typical set of documents for each topic in your taxonomy and it categorises new content based on similarity to that pattern of concepts.

2. You get subject matter experts to write down business rules for each taxonomy topic, including things like words that appear in the title, typical combinations of words in close proximity to each other, etc.

3. The search engine crawls the content and 'guesses' the topics, then subject matter experts correct the mistakes, over several iterations.

Not investing in rigorous quality control in the third option can result in embarrassing mistakes. In January 2006 Wal-Mart got into serious trouble when their algorithm suggesting related DVD titles to their Internet customers started linking titles such as *Charlie and the Chocolate Factory* and *Planet of the Apes* to movies with African-American themes. Autocategorisation engines can be racist too (Mui, 2006).

Related to enterprise search is 'federated search'. This differs from enterprise search in that a federated search engine does not itself crawl the other repositories. Instead, it passes a search query to the search engine (if any) that is resident in each repository, and then it passes back and compiles all the results from the various repository search engines. Federated search is useful only where your repositories have very strong internal search capability and/or cannot be crawled directly by your enterprise search engine, for whatever reason (e.g. third-party subscription databases). Because you often cannot influence the quality of search in those repositories, again your results will be very mixed, and it may not always be possible to differentiate in your results the true taxonomy category hits based on matching metadata from the hits based on accidental incidence of your search term within the content of a document.

Information residing in multiple business applications poses additional challenges (to the extent that your sponsor wants their enterprise search engine to be able to access it). Here you will probably need to inform your project sponsor of the need to develop an organisation-wide metadata policy, using a common metadata framework to express an enterprise-wide taxonomy. This means that all new business applications that use metadata to tag information resources should use the common elements in the metadata framework and the taxonomy controlled vocabularies to the extent that those information resources need to be accessed from outside the immediate business application itself.

Enterprise search comes with lofty promises of a 'one-stop shop' for information retrieval, so if this is the picture your taxonomy project sponsor is painting, this is an opportunity for some early expectation-setting on three common blind spots:

- Too often the spotlight on enabling search means that the needs for navigation at generic as well as localised levels, and for arrangements of content to suit frequently repeated tasks, are forgotten (Norman, 2006).

- The work involved in teaching a search engine how to be smart and in getting value from existing metadata is substantial and often underestimated.

- Organisation-wide policy development is often necessary to liberate information resources locked in multiple repositories and business applications, and this also complicates the taxonomy development task because more contexts need to be surveyed and negotiated.

Assessing the knowledge and information management context

Taxonomy work is only one part of information and knowledge infrastructure work. The same issues that drive the need for a taxonomy initiative often also generate other types of initiative aimed at improving management of information and knowledge to increase effectiveness and reduce risk. Taxonomists cannot productively remain aloof from larger-scale knowledge and information infrastructure work lest they find themselves competing with it; in fact, by taking account of it early, they can positively influence or leverage some of those other initiatives in a common direction.

At a very basic level, your initial discussions with the sponsor should include questions about whether the organisation has a knowledge management strategy. If so, its strategic focus (e.g. on fostering cross-boundary collaboration, leveraging knowledge assets, mapping expertise) will immediately give you additional cues as to the ways that taxonomy work in general and this taxonomy project in particular can help the organisation (see Chapter 5 for detailed examples).

Even if there is no explicit knowledge management strategy, there are at any given time likely to be numerous initiatives going on that touch on the information and knowledge infrastructure. Any sort of policy development work around information and records management may have a big impact on taxonomy and metadata requirements, and it will also compete with you for the time and attention of operational and senior managers.

Any quality or compliance-oriented project, such as an ISO 9001 accreditation exercise or meeting compliance with Sarbanes-Oxley regulations, will have a big impact on the way that information and documents should be organised and how they are described. Even business continuity projects have an information-about-corporate-information component – the vital records of an organisation such as contracts, plans and records of transactions need to be identified, organised and preserved if the organisation is to be able to reconstitute its business following a major disaster.

In one very large organisation we worked with, the corporate taxonomy team were working on an enterprise-wide taxonomy and a knowledge portal. A year into the project, they started bumping into other similarly semi-mature projects emerging out of the woodwork that had developed competing category systems: a project to collate all the organisation's policy papers into one repository; a collaboration platform for projects involving internal staff and external partners, structured according to another category system; an intranet development project that involved allocating content management responsibilities according to another set of categories; a workflow development application that presented documents to users in a completely different way from the knowledge portal; a new information security policy that allocated access privileges based on another set of categories.

It was obviously too late to call a halt and try to integrate these different perspectives into the corporate taxonomy, so they had to settle for (1) mapping the competing category systems to the corporate taxonomy via a thesaurus; (2) producing taxonomy development and extension guidelines to reduce the differences between the competing systems; and (3) resolving the biggest vocabulary conflicts through negotiating a common standard. In this case, many of these projects had been sponsored and championed by the same senior managers. As is so often the case in infrastructure projects, they simply didn't see the connections. So you may have to probe your project sponsor on what else might be going on because they might not be aware of the potential relevance of such projects.

Identifying these initiatives early gives you three benefits:

- Many of them involve going to the same senior and operational managers to assess current practices and needs, just as your taxonomy initiative will. Identifying them early may mean that you can combine the information-gathering tasks into a single activity and reduce the likelihood of your target managers suffering investigation overload.

- Many of them involve documenting different ways that information is currently being used or should be used. You can reduce the amount of time you need to do your taxonomy field work by getting access to this documentation and mining it for the working vocabularies and organising principles you need.

- You can use these other projects as taxonomy testing grounds and, if working towards a boundary-spanning or common-ground objective (where consistency is important), you will have an opportunity to influence their category systems towards consistency early on before competing category systems get entrenched.

For example, many of our taxonomy projects take place within a broader knowledge management initiative, which frequently includes a knowledge-mapping exercise. In this situation, we can fold much of our needs analysis, scoping and data collection work for taxonomy development into the knowledge-mapping activity, with very little burden of additional explanation or repeated visits.

Step 2: Engage stakeholders

Your meeting with the project sponsor will have given you a map of the stakeholders and key activities that they currently think will be affected by the taxonomy project. The mapping process will have identified or suggested new stakeholders that were not immediately obvious. You will also have your first cut of cues for where the taxonomy project can likely add value, and you have some idea of the technology environment you are working towards and related knowledge and information initiatives.

It's now time to check all this with the people who matter and who know more about what matters – i.e. the work of the organisation across a range of specific contexts. This is where we check the Big Picture against the Babel Instinct.

Using your initial map as a guide, visit the key stakeholders identified in the map and check your understanding of the map with them. You will immediately start picking up different understandings of how activities are structured and how resources are used, as well as missing stakeholders. Within this discussion, you should also be checking for the same range of cues about the kind of taxonomy work that is required that you covered in your meeting with the sponsor.

If you are conducting this exercise in parallel with an information or knowledge audit or through a general knowledge mapping exercise, you will pick up more cues from your discussions with stakeholders about common issues, gaps, problems and opportunities in information and knowledge access. You will be particularly alert to the same issues and themes cropping up in several places. This will help you refine your sense of where the taxonomy need is greatest: between structure-and-organise, common-ground, boundary-spanning, sense-making or discovery.

Lastly, these field visits may also alert you to other knowledge and information infrastructure-related initiatives that your project sponsor may not have been aware of.

Sometimes you will find pockets of the organisation where there are highly localised needs and opportunities. A strategic planning department may be clamouring for a sense-making approach, a research and development division might want a boundary-spanning approach, while everybody else is looking to support common-ground needs at a local level. These possibly competing needs (in terms of resources) will need to be brought back to the project sponsor for balancing and resolution.

Step 3: Refine project purpose

Your validation exercise with the stakeholders will result in a more accurate and complete concept map of key activities and stakeholders supported by the taxonomy project (and will have set the foundation for future communications about the taxonomy project with all concerned – your concept map has become a boundary object). You will also have a fuller picture of common issues and themes and should be able to make a reasoned proposal for the type of taxonomy work that you recommend.

The only potential conflict you may have to resolve is if you have found a demand for sense-making/discovery taxonomy work (which focuses on taxonomy-building *processes* usually among specialists) competing with a need for the other types of taxonomy work (which focus on taxonomy production to support the management of information and knowledge content). The two groups typically involve different distributions of effort and would therefore warrant different project definitions and separate resourcing.

Getting your purpose clear with your project sponsor sets out the groundwork for your communication strategy, and clearly identifies the benefits you want to achieve from your project. In some cases the needs are very well defined and the purpose very clearly expressed. But it is not always so straightforward. Where your client organisation wants to go might not be what it is ready for. In our three case studies below, we illustrate how decisions about taxonomy needs have been made in three quite different contexts. Some details have been changed to preserve confidentiality.

Case study 7.1

The structure-and-organise taxonomy

We were asked to develop a taxonomy for a large training organisation. The project sponsor was the IT manager, and in our initial meeting he explained that they planned to develop a document management system to support the curriculum development process. This involves two different divisions in the organisation: those who do needs analysis and those who do instructional design.

We mapped the key activities covered, who acted on them and the documents produced and consumed in the process, cross-checking with managers from each division. Their current system of development was dependent on Lotus Notes, shared folders and e-mail but because many critical documents were used by both divisions, they wanted to integrate the workflow into a single shared environment.

The mapping exercise demonstrated very quickly that there was a high degree of clarity and consistency in the understanding of the key steps, the vocabularies being used and the purposes for which the documents were used. Although the new system had refined and simplified the old way of doing things, the stakeholders had been engaged in an extensive planning process where they had agreed the detailed steps of the workflow and had reached consensus on vocabulary.

Stakeholders also agreed on the primary purpose of the taxonomy: while developing or validating new curricula and learning materials, different stakeholders in the value chain might want to search for particular examples of previously submitted documents to assist them in a decision of some sort.

This clearly indicated a structure-and-organise approach to the taxonomy, reusing as far as possible existing published vocabularies within the organisation. This was to be a closed system, with no direct access outside the activity areas mapped in the concept maps. There were no boundary-spanning requirements to meet and common ground was already established.

Because this was obviously a taxonomy to support a clearly defined and well understood workflow, the concept map itself generated much of the vocabulary necessary for the taxonomy. But we needed to check whether we had covered all of the possible category perspectives. In an exercise with a range of stakeholders, we asked them to brainstorm four or five different search scenarios in the context of a normal working day for each of the agents identified in the concept maps (including those who would not have direct access to the system, but who might ask an authorised agent for information from it). This revealed that users would not just search by activity and document type, but they might also search by subject being taught or the audience being taught (e.g. part-time, full-time, adult, youth).

We therefore developed a simple taxonomy based on three facets, expressed through the metadata in the document management system:

- document type identified by name of the activity that produced it, as documented in the concept map (e.g. training needs analysis report);
- subject area, as documented in the way that the different training departments and course modules were organised;
- audience type, as documented in the enrolment and certification options described in their promotional literature.

The benefits statement for this project was very simple: the full range of people involved in curriculum development and instructional design would have faster and easier access to previous reference documents to aid them in their daily work.

Losing clarity of purpose

This was a taxonomy project that we consider a failure. It was for a large organisation that specialises in designing and building new technology and equipment. They are highly innovation focused, they employ scientists and engineers in a wide range of very specialised fields and they work the entire knowledge value chain from basic research to the prototyping of equipment.

They had already purchased a large document management system and a very sophisticated enterprise search engine. Then they had discovered belatedly that these systems would not organise their contents for them and that they needed to do some taxonomy work. We were called in to help, with a very tight development timeline because the roll-out of the new system was already scheduled for some two months down the line. Additionally, much of the work of this organisation is secret. We would not get clearance to work with their primary material to help derive the taxonomy. They wanted us to train and guide their KM champions in the evidence gathering and taxonomy construction techniques. We'd design the framework, make our recommendations, do the training and leave them to it.

In our initial scoping meetings, we identified two major needs that they wanted to resolve. Their primary need was that they saw themselves as a highly silo-based organisation, employing scientists and specialists in similar fields but organised by customer type and so scattered across the organisation. Hence there were many knowledge domains and knowledge resources that were effectively being replicated across the organisation and advances in any one area were not being transferred to other specialists who might be able to use them. This indicated a boundary-spanning need.

However, all of these documented knowledge resources resided within the local working folder structures based on shared drives in each division and department. Even within departments, these folder structures were organised inconsistently so that it was often difficult for staff in that department to locate material that they knew was there. This indicated a common-ground need.

Fortunately their document management system supported a very flexible use of metadata. It also represented the primary organisation of content based on the visual metaphor of a folder structure.

So we recommended a faceted taxonomy comprising six facets:

- Document type

- Process
- Things and parts of things
- Project type
- Subject discipline
- Location of project.

To meet the common-ground need, we recommended that the primary visible organising principle expressed in the virtual folder structure should reflect first the organisation structure, and then within each department a common set of document type categories from that facet of the taxonomy. This was based on the observation that organisation structure, even if it changes, is well documented and easily predictable. All new staff are inducted in it.

When we looked at common organising behaviours across departments, organising by document type seemed to be the most consistently adopted principle in a relatively inconsistent environment. Below the top two levels, departments had the flexibility to organise their sub-folders according to their needs, so that localisation to the patterns of work in any given department was, to some extent, possible.

The boundary-spanning need was to be met through faceted browse and search, to be enabled by the enterprise search engine which would leverage all five facets of the taxonomy expressed through metadata. For example, I might be able to search for a technical specification (document type) for some electromagnetic equipment (subject discipline) produced as part of the development phase of the 'Enigma' project (project type).

The taxonomy was, of course, doomed. The belated realisation that significant taxonomy work needed to be done while in the middle of the system implementation, the scope, scale and complexity of the exercise, and a poor understanding of the purpose, all conspired to bring it down. In particular, the project team failed to grasp the way in which virtual folder structures enabled one purpose (common ground) while the use of orthogonal facets expressed through metadata enabled the other purpose (boundary-spanning). In fact, I believe they found it difficult to get beyond the view of a taxonomy as a single organising system in a hierarchy (despite significant effort to persuade them otherwise). This is not uncommon. Facets are not always easily grasped.

Meanwhile, the system implementation was delayed because of integration difficulties, the project sponsor was changed and there was a long period of simply coping in a vacuum. After we had left them, the decision was taken to roll out the system without a taxonomy; when this created difficulty in persuading staff to migrate work to the new system, the project team decided that they needed to address their taxonomy again. However, they decided that since their organisational structure changed so often (an average of one major restructuring every 18 months), it should not be used as the basis for organising content.

Unwittingly thereby they ditched their common-ground purpose and the natural linkages to the way that work is done locally and decided that the virtual folder structure should be used to express the boundary-spanning purpose. They are now, three years on, trying to build a single tree structure to represent the different knowledge domains represented across the organisation. Because their specialisms are deep, so will be their tree, and it will be fiendishly difficult to navigate.

Moreover, because most of their key content is created in the course of daily work within divisions, their repository is going to be a place of secondary storage and resort, because the virtual folder structure no longer represents the natural contours of localised work. They are still doomed to fail.

Our failure here was in not communicating sufficiently clearly to our client the two purposes being served and the different mechanisms through which they were being served. But partly this failure was a function of the organisation trying to move too quickly from what was essentially a mixed Level I and II technology environment to a primarily Level III environment.

Facets are particularly hard to understand where a team has little experience of designing and using metadata to manage information. It's hard to move in one swift step from randomly structured folders on shared drives and the idea that a document is only in one place to a metadata-driven environment that can present the same document in multiple different contexts, particularly when you have that familiar-looking virtual folder structure sitting seductively in the left-hand pane of your screen. It's hard to imagine post-coordination when you've grown up in a pre-coordinated world, and when your environment still looks pre-coordinated.

We took two key lessons from this failure: (1) don't take on impossible projects, because even valiant efforts do not absolve you of blame for failure; (2) don't encourage organisations to move too quickly, even when they are determined that they should. Radical changes in their information environments will simply not take hold. This brings us to our third case study.

Case study 7.3

Evolving purpose

Our third case comes from a public sector organisation that promotes and supports a particular industry. The taxonomy project with them was integrated into a knowledge management strategy-building project, which included drawing up high-level knowledge maps of the key knowledge assets being used to support its business activities. This helped us to fold the taxonomy project scoping, needs analysis and initial evidence gathering into the knowledge mapping activity, and had the strong advantage of keeping the taxonomy project tightly geared to other knowledge and information management initiatives.

In the past, the organisation's various functions had acted as virtually autonomous units, but in recent years a more integrated approach had been required to meet new strategic objectives. Different units needed to coordinate their activities and disbursements more effectively, and many of them performed their functions in relation to the same set of stakeholders, customers and partners.

Our stakeholder visits revealed that this organisation was effectively in a Level I technology environment, even though an early stated intention of the project sponsor was to move to a single document management system to manage all the organisation's information assets. The organisation shared its documents electronically using shared drives and shared folders, but these were wildly inconsistent in their structures. Some were organised by date, some by topic, some by job function or employee names. It was not uncommon to find several organising principles at work within the same folder structure. In one department, a new and different folder structure was generated every year.

In such a chaotic environment it was not surprising that employees engaged intensively in 'information nesting' – printing and compiling files of working reference documents to populate their workstations and storage of soft copies of key documents on local hard disks. This led to problems of duplicated effort, multiple conflicting versions of the same documents and inconsistent information being provided to key stakeholders, customers and partners.

Moreover, since many departments performed different functions in relation to the same set of external agencies, the lack of a coherent internal information management system frustrated the coordination of effort and meant that each department was compiling, sometimes duplicating and sometimes competing versions of information about those agencies.

These factors indicated a very strong need for a common-ground approach to taxonomy work, with some boundary-spanning needs in relation to information about common external partners, customers and stakeholders.

However, in such an undisciplined information environment, we realised very quickly that if this organisation moved immediately to a Level III environment with a document management system, they would simply transfer their confusion from the shared drives into the document management system.

So while we decided to recommend and build a faceted taxonomy based on our analysis of our client's knowledge maps, we recommended that only parts of this taxonomy be used initially, to impose a more consistent structure on the shared drives and folders in a preliminary phase, two years before a document management system should be introduced. Effectively two of the facets were to be used to design a simple tree structure for each department. The two facets were document type and business activity, which between them seemed to account for the most common ways of organising content usefully and predictably on the shared drives.

Our proposal was that department managers would select the top two levels of their folder structure from any combination of terms in these two facets in the taxonomy. Beyond the second level they were free to subdivide according to their own needs, but were encouraged to use terms from the main taxonomy where they were available. From a purist's point of view it might seem heretical to combine two different facets in each level of a tree structure and allow such variation in the choice of terms, but from a pragmatic viewpoint *we judged it better to achieve improved consistency and demonstrate the value of improved consistency than to force complete standardisation* which would have met intense resistance and probably would have reinforced the 'information nesting' activity.

The first phase of the project therefore focused on meeting common-ground needs and on encouraging the evolution of a shared vocabulary and common organising principles by enforcing a degree of consistency but allowing a degree of local choice – which the taxonomy project team could observe and learn from.

Meanwhile two pilot knowledge management projects focused on the coordinated management of common knowledge assets across several departments in relation to two particular types of partner agency – aimed at building a foundation for meeting boundary-spanning needs. The vocabulary and organisation decisions made in these projects were fed back into the taxonomy development.

Hence while the facet framework and top three levels of the taxonomy were determined fairly early in the project, it was recognised that this needed to be an evolutionary taxonomy geared to, and adapting to, the changing information environment of the client organisation. The taxonomy would not meet full maturity or full implementation until greater information consistency and discipline had been achieved and the organisation was ready to reap the benefits of a document management system.

Step 4: Design the approach

With a clear purpose agreed with the project sponsor, it's now time to settle on your approach. To a large extent, the basic methodology for building a taxonomy (as outlined in the next chapter) is fairly consistent. However, there are some big questions you may be asked by various stakeholders, including 'do we build our own taxonomy, or can we buy one?' 'how complex does our taxonomy need to be?'

In Table 7.2 we list the key decision factors expressed as a set of opposites that will influence the approach you take. The cues that you picked up in defining your purpose should give you a clear enough idea of where you are on each scale, and therefore of the likely answers to some of the questions you will be asked.

Table 7.2   Key decision factors in choosing your design approach

Introverted ◄──────────────────────────► Extroverted	
Taxonomy is solely for internal use, there is no need to categorise documents for external parties. Likely that you will need to build your own taxonomy unless you work internally to an industry standard that has a published taxonomy.	Taxonomy supports information exchange with external partners who have metadata or taxonomy standards, or with a professional community that has a taxonomy standard, in which case you might want to buy it. You will still need to check that your internal language matches the external one.
Homogeneous ◄──────────────────────────► Heterogeneous	
The content covered is very homogeneous and consistent, with a well understood and widely followed vocabulary. Your taxonomy project should be relatively straightforward, documenting this language and formalising the organising principles.	The content is heterogeneous, covering many different types of information used for many different purposes. The language to describe it may also vary widely. The taxonomy project will be more complex and will involve a wide range of data gathering and negotiation to a common standard.

Disciplined ◄─────────────────────────► Undisciplined	
A disciplined work environment with strong consistency in how content is produced and organised will have the same impact as a homogeneous content collection, i.e. a simpler, more straightforward taxonomy project.	An undisciplined work environment with little control of how documents are produced and organised will increase the complexity of the taxonomy project and may require an evolutionary approach – e.g. increase consistency step by step in designated areas rather than big bang standardisation.
Mature ◄─────────────────────────► **Emerging**	
If the knowledge domain is very mature and stable, the task will be simpler, and there should be a clear vocabulary and set of organising principles. It may be possible to buy or adapt a taxonomy if this domain occurs on an industry-wide basis. You will still need to check consistency with your internal organisation practices if you buy.	If the knowledge domain is very new, immature or changing rapidly, then your taxonomy approach should be light and evolutionary, identifying a core facet structure and high-level categories, allowing for multiple revisions based on feedback as you develop. The project will be multi-year. Your data collection method may include interactive mapping sessions with experts using techniques such as concept mapping.
Task ◄─────────────────────────► **Discipline**	
If the taxonomy is meant to support operational work then your approach will be to map the contours of that work, and document the working language and organising principles of the key activities and tasks in that area of work. Process mapping may be a useful technique.	If the taxonomy supports a knowledge domain or professional community (e.g. if the subject is taught in a higher education institution, such as engineering) then use the public language of that domain; this may mean buying a taxonomy or adapting the language and structures of, for example, a course curriculum for the subject area. Education or certification in any discipline effectively teaches students the standard taxonomy for that subject.
Explicit ◄─────────────────────────► **Implicit**	
If the content covered is largely information assets contained in documents and databases, then your evidence collection will be easier and will be based on sampling the vocabularies and organising principles for that content.	If the content covered is largely implicit, not captured in documents but embedded in common practices and the knowledge of individuals, then your data collection method will involve more interactive mapping work with groups of people, using techniques such as concept mapping to externalise and standardise the language and organising principles of the domain.
Generalist ◄─────────────────────────► **Specialist**	
If the taxonomy covers content that is useful to the general population but does not cover any subject in great depth, then your taxonomy should be broad and shallow. If there is a large volume of content with a high degree of variety in it, then the only way to keep your taxonomy broad and shallow is to use facets.	If the taxonomy covers content that is very specialised, then you will need a deeper taxonomy. If this is an established, mature discipline (see above) then the taxonomy users will likely have been educated in the structure of the domain and will be able to tolerate deeper taxonomies. Tree structures may work effectively here, and you may be able to buy or adapt published taxonomies.

Step 5: Build the communication plan

Taxonomies touch the intimate details of how we organise and describe our daily work so it is not surprising that taxonomy projects can be unsettling for our colleagues. At the same time, taxonomy development requires periodic intrusions on their time and attention throughout the process, and it often asks them to think and talk about their work in ways they are not used to. And because we are negotiating often conflicting perspectives, we hardly ever give them exactly what they want. Constant, consistent and clear communications are critical to maintain support for the process and trust in the implementation.

There are also two peculiarities of taxonomy work, one of which we touched on in our introduction. Taxonomy design is a skilled, technical discipline founded on a basic human capability, which means that it is possible for anyone to have an opinion and it is not always very clear why the taxonomist's view is a better one or which of the many differing views should prevail. The use of a clearly articulated process and accepted principles for taxonomy development and validation are helpful here, and we will cover these in the next chapter.

The second peculiarity is that stakeholders sometimes 'wake up' to the implications of what they are doing in the taxonomy project very late in the process. You can follow a clear, public process and communicate intensively about what it is you are doing, why you are doing it and the steps involved, and you can have close involvement of your principal stakeholders all the way through. They can review drafts and submit feedback and suggestions, and they can take part in validation exercises, and you may believe that all is going well.

Then your taxonomy comes to implementation and suddenly they panic and it looks all wrong to them. This is a peculiarity of any infrastructure change: it is easy to think about the change in the abstract, even to the point of planning detailed change steps, but because infrastructure is part of the web of things that we take for granted, when the day comes for us to implement the change, we wake up and realise the dangers of what we are doing.

This is simply part of the rules of the game for infrastructure work, so part of your communication strategy is never to be complacent about the apparent buy-in that you have at any stage, and always to be prepared to reset your communications back to the starting point and restate the purpose, recount the process and persuade them to give it a try and evaluate it on its merits. The methodology we propose is designed to expose the project to multiple views from the very beginning (to counteract the panic effect), and to facilitate confidence building through piloting and validation activity, with plenty of feedback and modification along the way.

An obvious defence mechanism faced with this kind of response is to employ a specialist to design your taxonomy, and beyond a preliminary consultation phase to develop your taxonomy in isolation from the workgroups that will use it. This will obviously be a faster and simpler process – at least for the design phase. Unless you are working in the area of a well defined specialist discipline where there are published standards available to draw on, this approach will rarely work when it comes to implementation. The Babel Instinct will ensure that your final taxonomy will be an alien object to everybody in the target audience, and it is likely that they will use compensating and avoidance tactics in its use. There is no alternative to involving and learning from your audience if the taxonomy is to form a common working language for them.

Exactly the same kind of discontinuity in communications and progress will happen if you have major changes in your project team along the way or get a new project sponsor who has not been in the process from the start. Progress can never be taken for granted, nor can the principles that you work to. Be prepared to spell out the same story over and over again, often to the same people.

When it comes to thinking in detail about structuring your communications, it's worth covering three main areas:

- audiences;
- message;
- channels.

Audiences

You have several different audiences to consider, and you need different things from each of them, so you will need to tune your communications to their perspectives.

- *Project sponsors/governance committee.* You will need their support for validation of your purpose and the process that you intend to follow. They will need to back you up during stakeholder panic attacks, assist you in gaining and maintaining senior management support and resourcing, help you get access to the stakeholders that you need to consult, and act as advocates for the taxonomy implementation and adoption. They may not always know what is expected of them, so they will likely need to be reminded from time to time.

- *Project team.* These are the people who will be helping you gather the preliminary material for taxonomy design, and they will be responsible for administering the taxonomy in the long term. They will likely be the first point of contact for communications with taxonomy users, and will collect and respond to feedback. The more they are involved in the taxonomy development process and are educated in the principles for validating a taxonomy (see Chapter 8), the better equipped they will be to support periodic taxonomy evaluation, tuning and revision.

- *Core stakeholders.* These are the people who are your main points of contact and exploration in the needs analysis, design and testing phases. You will need them to teach you how knowledge and information is used in the work areas they represent, provide feedback, lead pilots and act as advocates and taxonomy champions when it comes to implementation. The more they are educated about the process you are following, and the reasons behind it, the more helpful they can be. Core stakeholders are often managers who have a good grasp of how their business areas fit into a bigger whole, and a good sense of how information and knowledge assets support them.

- *Extended stakeholders.* These are the people who will be adopting and using the taxonomy, so they are your main customers. Your communications with them will probably be fairly limited until well into the design phase when you have taxonomy drafts to try out for wider validation.

Message

Although elements of your message need to be tuned to different audiences, much of your message needs to be consistent across audiences. The key elements you will need to cover are:

- what you intend to do (purpose);
- why you intend to do it (benefits);
- how you intend to do it (key steps and activities);
- what is expected from the audience (involvement).

As your project proceeds, you will add:

- what we have done so far;
- what we have achieved;
- what's next.

By following the steps in this chapter so far, you should have a clear statement of purpose, which links directly into benefits. Table 7.3 provides examples.

Your decisions about the purpose will give you the rationale for your approach, and our next chapter will take you through the key steps and activities in which you will likely need to involve your audiences.

Channels

I have seen and tried many different ways of communicating the purpose, rationale, proposed activities and progress of a taxonomy initiative. They have included intranet discussion forums, regular e-mail newsletters, mass staff briefings, training and awareness sessions for champions and activists.

I've learned that it is possible to over-communicate on taxonomy

Table 7.3   Example statements of taxonomy purpose and benefits

Taxonomy purpose	Benefits
Structure-and-organise	Smoother and more efficient workflow, fewer errors, better reuse of information and knowledge within the designated area of work
Common-ground	Better workgroup coordination, better reuse of knowledge and information, faster retrieval of information and knowledge assets within workgroups
Boundary-spanning	Better leverage of knowledge and information assets across workgroups, fewer duplications, conflicts and rework instances, better cross-organisation coordination
Sense-making and discovery	Greater confidence in decision-making, consensus-building and communications across specialist or decision-making teams, greater ability to spot opportunities and risks, enhanced innovation capability

projects, particularly to the larger audience of extended stakeholders, before we have anything tangible to show them or anything concrete for them to do. I've learned that senior managers never remember details. I've learned that the project sponsor and project team need to be rehearsed in the basic purpose, benefits, principles and process over and over again. I've learned that the best time to communicate your message to other stakeholders is just before you need their support or input for a particular phase. It allows them to relate the message to something tangible. I've learned that trust is very important when panic threatens to strike and when you need candid feedback.

This experience, particularly on the importance of trust, has taught me that the best communication channel is face to face, either in a small-group setting such as a meeting or one to one. Your process will introduce uncertainty, it will expose conflicting priorities and perspectives, it will threaten to change the way that work is described and done. If you have no problems in your taxonomy project you should be suspicious. The purpose of your communications strategy is not to pre-empt problems, because problems are endemic to the work – it is to allow them to come to the surface so they can be dealt with openly.

No amount of technical precision in your taxonomy will overcome an inability to communicate a vision of where you want to go and have people take your word on trust. This is why broadcast modes of communicating work less well. More highly appreciated is responsiveness, very targeted, timely and context-specific messages, the ability to take and visibly act on feedback, and a constant visible focus on improving the effectiveness of daily work for your clients – the taxonomy users.

Step 6: Start the governance process

By this stage you will already have a project sponsor, and depending on the scope and scale of the intended project, he or she may or may not be a member of the senior management team. If your project is an enterprise-wide taxonomy, or crosses the boundaries of several departments, then your project sponsor must have sufficient seniority to give you access to the different work areas covered.

And as we saw in Chapter 6, a taxonomy is never a finished product. It is a living thing that needs to adapt constantly to changes in the needs of its stakeholders and to changes in the knowledge domains that it represents. Hence the earlier you can support your project sponsor with a governance team of sufficient seniority and representativeness, the easier many of your tasks will become – in communicating your purpose, securing resources, getting access to the core stakeholders, and so on.

There are three main reasons why the governance of taxonomies needs to be addressed from the start of a taxonomy project.

- *Stakeholder involvement.* Taxonomies must reflect the needs and perspectives of all users, right from the design stage. This means that you need to have easy access to the different stakeholders at each of the critical stages of development and implementation.

- *Change management.* As the content base and content needs change over time (or as the focus of the organisation changes), the taxonomy must also evolve to stay relevant. You need a body of people who can keep you in touch with relevant change in a timely fashion.

- *Ownership.* Full enterprise-wide taxonomies are complex constructs with parts that must remain internally consistent to be effective; hence they require a centralised management function to assure their effectiveness through time. The needs of multiple stakeholders will need to be negotiated and resolved to a common, shared standard, and a representative governance team of sufficient seniority will find it easier to achieve this than a single project sponsor. Such a team would also provide continuity over the lifetime of a taxonomy in a way that a single project sponsor will not.

Suggestions and criteria for nomination to your governance team will include:

- sufficient seniority to influence resources and command access to stakeholders;

- managers representing key domains and stakeholder groups covered by the taxonomy and with a good understanding of the operating environments where the taxonomy will be used;

- IT manager likely to be involved in the technological expressions of the taxonomy;

- records management function;

- knowledge management function;

- CIO or CIO's delegate;

- an enthusiastic advocate;

- a sceptical critic;
- subject-matter experts if covering specialist knowledge domains.

In this chapter I have given an outline of key steps that will give your taxonomy project greater substance, doability, relevance and impact. If it seems overly prescriptive, then I plead the requirement to give clear guidance in a very fuzzy and mutable domain.

In 2006 my colleague Paolina Martin wrote a blog post discussing the relative benefits of using Amaretto versus Cognac when making the Italian dessert tiramisu. Her point was that for certain dishes there are certain core ingredients that must be in place for it to be that particular dish and not another, but other ingredients can be waived or substituted and the sequence of steps and preparation methods may change from case to case. Any individual recipe will give clear, prescriptive guidance, but there are many variations of the recipe, all of them perfectly legitimate (Martin, 2006).

So while the contents of this and the next two chapters do attempt to give linear, prescriptive guidance on how to develop a taxonomy for many different situations, in the real world you may not follow exactly these steps in exactly this linear sequence. For example, in some cases we may conduct the needs analysis and some of the evidence-gathering work from the design stage at the same time to reduce the amount of time and attention we need from core stakeholders. In other cases, there is simply not sufficient access to senior enough people to get the governance process going early on.

Take these chapters then as an unfolding of the key areas to consider and plan for in your taxonomy project. When you implement for yourselves, however, you will improvise, adapt and fold your project to the needs and constraints of your own environment – just as your final taxonomy will.

8

Designing your taxonomy

A manageable work classification scheme works in practice, is not too fine-grained or arcane in its distinctions, and it fits with the way work is organised ... Such a perfect scheme however does not exist. In the real world these areas trade off against each other ... These trade-offs become areas of negotiation and sometimes of conflict.

(Bowker and Star, 1999: 232–3)

When we sit down to build a taxonomy, we are engaging in an ancient human art, and the methods we follow are ancient too. We gather the stuff of our world around us, we sort them into their kinds as they make sense to us and we name the kinds. When we are building a taxonomy to cover knowledge and information assets, our 'stuff' is more abstract, but we engage in essentially the same steps. We gather evidence of the things we want the structure of our taxonomy to support, we put them into groups and we name the groups.

It is, of course, a touch more complicated than that, because we are not Adam and Eve in the never-before-classified Garden of Eden. We have a lot of inherited vocabulary and both implicit and explicit categories embedded in our population and our processes, many of them in competition with each other. This is the additional negotiation and resolution step that Adam and Eve did not have. But the ancient pattern is still there: in any taxonomy project we must gather our evidence, sort it all out in ways that meet our purpose, and figure it out from there (see Figure 8.1).

Figure 8.1   Designing a taxonomy

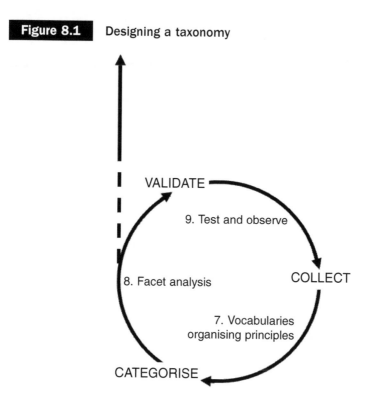

The cognitive constraints on taxonomy design

Ancient as this practice is, there is a basic set of mechanics around how human beings interact with taxonomies, and these relate to the constraints set by our perception and memory. For a taxonomy to work, we need to be able to grasp the shape of the whole, perceive salient details and retain a sense of the whole in our memories. This is how we navigate. We need to understand enough of what we see at any given time to make our next decision, and we need to remember where we have been so that we can find our way back. It turns out that taxonomy building, at one level, is a numbers game.

There are two sets of 'magic numbers' that might give us some clues. The first magic number is the number 7 ± 2, a number proposed by the psychologist George Miller in 1956. He reviewed a number of studies on three cognitive mechanisms that affect our ability to make sense of our environment:

- the span of attention – how many things we can pay attention to at any given time;
- 'immediate memory' (later to be termed short-term memory);
- the number of categories that could be discriminated in any environment.

Miller found that the studies all converged on his 'magical number' of 7 ± 2, although he acknowledged that he had no evidence for a causal connection between what were thought to be three quite distinct cognitive mechanisms. The consistency was compelling, however (Miller, 1956).

Above the number 7, errors in attention, recall and discrimination gradually increased, to an absolute limit of 15 where errors became too frequent in the studies he reviewed and cognition effectively broke down. Miller concluded that we human beings have natural constraints on the amount of information we can process at any given time, but he also noticed that we have strategies for expanding this capacity.

For example, Miller discovered that one strategy for discriminating different categories is to make our judgements based on multiple ways of categorising instead of just one (e.g. size as well as colour), and this extended the range to about 150 categories that could be distinguished with reasonable accuracy. The more ways of categorising that were used, the better overall performance in terms of discrimination, although at a detailed level individual judgements on specific attributes were less accurate. Pattern recognition overall was compensating for specific instances of inaccuracy. Notice that this is effectively a 'facet' strategy. The more facets we use, the more discrete items we can keep track of, even though we may get individual attributes wrong.

Another strategy for memory involves 'chunking', where we substitute a new concept for an entire group of things and therefore start remembering 'chunks' inside which are rolled up the constituent members. This brings short-term memory capacity from an optimal performance of 7 to about 50 (7 chunks of 7), and the breakdown of performance from 15 to about 100–200 items (somewhere between 15 chunks of 7 and 15 chunks of 15).

Miller's magical number has been taken up by pop psychology but, inevitably, harshly judged by his professional successors. A number of studies have shown for short-term memory, for example, that the limits on how many pieces of information can be held in short-term or working memory are much lower than seven, at only three or four items

(MacGregor, 1987; LeCompte, 1999). However, even this is a shifting number, often measured in laboratory conditions, and in abstraction from normal working contexts where multiple factors are being tracked at once.

The value of Miller's original paper was in suggesting that multiple mechanisms (attention, discrimination and memory) seem to operate in combination with each other, and this complementarity can extend the natural cognitive limits we possess. Indeed, long-term memory also comes into play, as prior familiarity with the pieces of information (i.e. long-term memory support) plays a significant role in increasing the number of items that can be retained in working memory at any given time (Hulme et al., 1995). This supports Miller's original observation that we have strategies for getting past our natural cognitive constraints.

For our second set of magical numbers we turn to an evolutionary psychologist by the name of Robin Dunbar. Dunbar became interested in the relationship between brain size and social group size among primates and monkeys – specifically, the size of the neocortex part of the brain, which among other things seems to help us track social relationships. He noticed that there was a correlation between the size of the neocortex and the degree of social complexity in any given species, where social complexity is indicated by average group size.

Social complexity really means the ability of an animal to keep track of its own direct relationships, but also make inferences about third-party relationships. For example, if I know that James is a good friend of Barry, I also know that I cannot count on James to back me up in a fight with Barry – in fact, he might well support Barry against me. Clearly the brain effort involved in keeping track of such alliances and expectations rises exponentially with group size.

Dunbar discovered that there are natural limits imposed on the number of relationships that primates can keep track of – humans included. The first is the 'grooming clique' which consists of the animals who cultivate close, intimate, relationships with each other by engaging in mutual grooming for hours every day. These bonds are important for survival because they provide a 'loyalty buffer' against intimidation, bullying and competition for food from other members of the group. Humans, Dunbar argues, have substituted conversation for physical grooming, but it effectively serves the same purpose. We maintain our close, trusted cliques through conversation. The limit here is the amount of time we can spend in grooming and the number of people we can pay attention to at any given time.

The second set of relationships primates keep track of is the larger set of all the animals in our group. Here we have to keep track of who is who, how they are related to each other, their histories of conflict and behaviour, and so on. This enables them to predict how their peers will behave in different situations, and therefore how one should behave around them. Maintaining such knowledge helps relieve the stress of conflict within the social group; as a group reaches its constraint size, animals become less able to manage their relationships harmoniously and conflicts and stress increase to the point that the group fractures, splits and thereby returns to manageable numbers.

To cut a long story short, the two predicted numbers for human beings, extrapolated from neocortex size, are 12–15 people within a 'grooming clique', and around 150 people (actually a range between 120 and 180 people) for maximum effective group size where everybody knows everybody else. It turns out that this number turns up again and again in human group organisation – in the clan structure of Australian aborigines, village size in agricultural societies, religious communities, 'small world' experiments tracking the average size of urban Americans' circles of friends and modern military formations (Dunbar, 1993, 1996). Above that number, human groups either split, or they put in place infrastructure comprising specific roles, routines and rules to substitute for personal knowledge and interaction. Thus is bureaucracy born.

Just as with Miller's magic number seven, the precise numbers posited by Dunbar have been challenged downwards. Christopher Allen, who has studied online communities for a number of years, reminds us that Dunbar gave his numbers of 12–15 for cliques and 150 for total group size as *maximum* sizes. In the online environment, and studying online collaborative game communities, Allen found that communities plateaued in size much earlier than the Dunbar maximum of 150, averaging about 60 – far short of the supposed 150 limit (Allen, 2004).

But let's bring this back to taxonomy design. Between Miller and Dunbar, we can generate an intriguing set of hypotheses about our cognitive constraints in manipulating a taxonomy as a user. Both Miller and Dunbar suggest that there are two levels of cognitive constraint that we human beings encounter when we try to keep track of multiple things. The first is the 'list' of immediate things we can hold in attention, discriminate effectively and maintain in short-term memory for navigation purposes. Miller suggests this is optimised at 5–9, and breaks down at 15. Dunbar's work suggests that conversational cliques range between four and 15 (although Allen suggests that cliques start breaking down at about nine individuals).

The second constraint is the wider range of things we need to keep in peripheral awareness. Miller posited that 'chunking' – i.e. thinking at one level of abstraction from the concrete thing – allows us to extend the number of items we can easily manipulate in attention and immediate memory, giving us a capacity of somewhere between 100 and 200 items. In Chapter 2 we saw that human beings naturally think in terms of 'basic level categories' so we already know that human beings can naturally think at one level of abstraction from the concrete thing, but not easily beyond that. If we can process these abstractions (such as the concept 'tree') as if they are things, and then apply 'chunking' to them, this gives us a maximum range of 150×15, so a cognitive range covering around 3,375 items.

Dunbar's contribution on maximum group size is important because the so-called 'Dunbar number' is tracking *relationships* between entities – relationships become important when we start chunking because we need to keep in mind the relationship between the items themselves and the abstract concept or category that we have chunked them into. Dunbar's maximum group size is around 150 individuals and keeping track of them involves keeping track of 149 other individuals × 12–15 grooming clique relationships each, which again means that we can keep track of no more than 3,000 relationships or so.

The most basic element of a taxonomy is a list. At the next stage of complexity, a tree organises lists in relation to each other. The tree structure clearly supports our strategy for thinking in 'basic level categories', and also our strategies (such as 'chunking') for getting beyond our natural constraints on the things we can discriminate, follow relationships between and hold in attention and short-term memory. But there are clearly limits of scale to the usefulness of a tree, and the different contributions of Miller and Dunbar suggest some clear heuristics for taxonomy design.

1. Our ability to make sense of lists breaks down above 15 items – hence above 15 items, split the list into separate groups. Fewer is better.

2. Beyond two levels of abstraction (i.e. a three-level tree) our ability to make sense of and navigate the tree starts to break down – hence limit your tree to three levels. Two is better.

These are heuristics, and not hard and fast rules. For example, deep familiarity with the items or with their relationships can extend the lengths of the lists we can manipulate (e.g. lists of country names alphabetically ordered) and the depth of the trees we can easily navigate (e.g. professional engineers who have been entrained in the structure of their subject). Long-term memory does come to the aid of cognition when faced with a taxonomy with which we are familiar or where there are well-established codes for navigation (for instance recognisable names in alphabetical order) (e.g. Hulme et al., 1995).

Our second heuristic about taxonomy depth poses particular problems when it comes to designing taxonomies for large collections of content. Figure 8.2 illustrates the design constraints we must work to when constructing our taxonomies.

The dotted line starting at the bottom left illustrates the effectiveness of a tree-based taxonomy in managing content items. At Level 1 it can only handle a maximum of 15 items, at two levels it can handle 225 and at three levels only just over 3,000. Clearly, for enterprise taxonomies, the scale of content requires greater depth – at five levels of depth, for example, a tree can handle well on the way to a million items of content.

Figure 8.2   Cognitive constraints in navigating a taxonomy

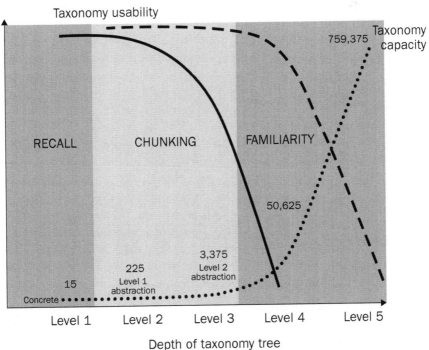

However, the continuous bold line starting at the top left, which represents the ease of use of the taxonomy, is optimised at the first 'list' level, still performs well for 'basic level categories' (Level 2) and can be stretched through 'chunking' those categories to a third level. After that, our ability to manipulate the tree deteriorates rapidly, which means that a tree structure (or a hierarchy) is really not effective above about 3,000 items of content.

We can extend the performance of our taxonomy through two different strategies. One is to rely on user familiarity with the taxonomy structure, terms and relationships, either by reusing a well-entrained 'deep' taxonomy (such as that taught within a professional curriculum) or by reusing implicit operational categories and lists from within the target population. Long-term memory can support taxonomy navigation.

The second strategy is to employ facet analysis. George Miller found that tracking multiple attributes gave better performance and recall than trying to track just one or two attributes. This implicitly supports a faceted approach. Moreover, faceted trees rarely need to go beyond three levels. You may well have half a million documents in your system, but you are unlikely to have more than 3,000 'document types' or aspects of 'engineering' represented in that collection. A facet only tracks one attribute of a document, thereby simplifying the tracking task. Recall is a matter of using facets in combination in a post-coordinated way, and it is through their intersection and overlap that the document itself is retrieved. Multiple facet trees of three or fewer levels each are much better at managing large content collections than deep single trees.

In practice, except in taxonomy projects for very small, well-defined collections of content, both strategies (familiarity and facets) will need to be used in combination. In particular, because familiarity is such a strong enhancer of taxonomy usability, any taxonomy design exercise should always begin with a harvesting activity to uncover the range of vocabularies and categories with which your taxonomy population already works. This is just as true of projects where you are buying in a ready-made taxonomy, where you may need to map the familiarity gaps and compensate for them through customisation, use of a thesaurus or other information architecture design strategies.

Step 7: Collect vocabularies and organising principles

In the collection stage, you are trying to collect as much data as possible in a variety of ways. You need as much evidence as you can collect of the variety of information and knowledge use in your client organisation. In particular, you need to become attuned to the things that are common, taken for granted and familiar within their knowledge landscape. The fact that they are taken for granted may render them virtually invisible to your clients and to you, and this is why this stage needs to be so rigorous and systematic. There are three activities involved in collecting the raw materials of your taxonomy:

- mapping;
- observation;
- evidence gathering.

Mapping

You have already done some preliminary mapping of the knowledge domains at the preparation stage. If this was a high-level mapping process simply to scope out the stakeholder and activity implications, then you'll need to revisit those maps and deepen them. A variety of techniques can be used, depending on the nature of your taxonomy.

Concept mapping is an excellent tool for taxonomies that are closely linked to the activities of a workgroup and for taxonomies that map processes. However, they do not always capture the full depth and range of knowledge assets involved, so we often recommend the use of an input-output knowledge map, constructed around a spine of detailed business activities. This kind of map has good precedents in the information management profession and can be used for a variety of purposes (e.g. Orna, 2004), but for taxonomy applications, we strongly recommend that the maps include more than simply explicit information sources and documents. In my firm we generally try to capture six types of knowledge asset in such maps, influenced strongly by the five-part ASHEN framework developed by David Snowden (2000b) (see Table 8.1). We do this because a simple focus on documents at this stage may be too narrow to adequately capture the full working vocabulary of a domain, and it will probably bias us towards a document-focused taxonomy and we may miss opportunities to include less tangible forms of knowledge in our taxonomy such as expertise maps, competency maps and so on.

Table 8.1 Knowledge asset types

ASHEN framework (Snowden, 2000b)	Knowledge asset types (Straits Knowledge)
Artefacts	Documents – explicit information
Skills	Skills – can be trained
Heuristics	Methods – ways of doing things that are not documented but are communicated within a culture
Experience	Experience – knowledge and expertise gained over time
Natural talent	Talent – 'natural' abilities that cannot be acquired simply through training or experience
–	Relationships – being able to access knowledge and information that other people possess by virtue of having social connections with them

Input-output knowledge maps work on a very simple principle. The central spine of the map is constructed around the key business activities of any given workgroup. Knowledge assets that are required as inputs for that activity are named on the left-hand side of the spine, next to the activity that they support, and knowledge assets that are produced in the course of conducting the activity are listed on the right-hand side of the corresponding activity. They may be colour coded by type of knowledge asset (see above) and they should be named with the commonly used terms used to describe them within the workgroup concerned. An extract from such a knowledge map is given in Figure 8.3.

There are other approaches to knowledge mapping. In Chapter 4, for example, we looked at using process mapping methodology to produce a SIPOC (supplier-input-process-output-customer) knowledge map.

Whatever the specific method we use, we usually prefer to conduct these mapping sessions in groups rather than with individuals, on the principle that a group of people involved in a particular domain are more likely to produce a negotiated map than an idiosyncratic one, and they tend to remind each other of missing items where individuals might easily forget.

Even better, particularly if you have a boundary-spanning objective, if you conduct these knowledge mapping sessions in workshops with

Figure 8.3   Example of input-output knowledge map

Type	Knowledge asset input	Activity	Knowledge asset output	Type
relationships	network of contacts within organisation, including long-serving staff, informal 'company historians'	Corporate Communications – media relations	communicating with external partners in annual reports, corporate presentations, etc.	relationships
relationships	good linkages with newspaper and magazine editors		documentation of corporate achievements	document
skill	media training for key executives		CEO speeches	document
document	SOPs for media enquiry handling; SOPs for press releases		FAQs database, key facts dossier	document
document	media contacts directory		enhanced relationships with key media contacts	relationships
experience	crisis handling experience of Head of Communications		trust of key partners and stakeholders	relationships
method	collection of key facts from internal staff 'knowers', long-time employees		press releases, response tracking report	document
method	lessons learnt, post mortem on press campaigns			
document	detailed programmes of upcoming corporate events			

managers from several different departments, you can ask them to review each other's maps and start to identify common areas, overlaps and sharing opportunities. The process of negotiation that any taxonomy requires starts to become visible and is generated by the managers themselves. This becomes a powerful change management instrument.

Observation

These maps provide both context and a checklist for the next stage of the process, which is to visit each major workgroup wherever possible. A physical visit will reveal to you much of the knowledge and information infrastructure that is taken for granted and not consciously represented in the maps or in accompanying knowledge mapping interviews. It will fill in the gaps, reveal the pain points that your taxonomy is supposed to resolve, and it will alert you to relative priorities in a way that the mapping sessions cannot.

For example, you will see whether different workgroups have different patterns of reliance on physical or electronic documents. You will see the degree to which information 'nesting' is taking place in different parts of the organisation. The labels on laboriously compiled paper files at workstations will tell you which subject areas are the most critical and how they are named. If there are shared collections of physical documents such as in a departmental filing cabinet, you will pick up clues about common-ground categories and vocabularies that are already in place.

You may also want to watch common information and knowledge activities in action, which will give you concrete examples against which to check the 'official story' portrayed in the concept and knowledge maps. Such observations will also indicate to you points of ambiguity, confusion or frustration in locating and accessing information when required.

A variety of methods can be used in the mapping and observation stages – Mike Kuniavsky's compendium *Observing the User Experience* is an excellent place to start for identifying and using appropriate methods – but the main objective is always the same: to gain as full a picture as you can get of the range and diversity of information use across the target population (Kuniavsky, 2003). Because of this it is risky to depend on just a few nominated witnesses or to rely on testimony without complementary observation.

Evidence gathering

In parallel with your visits and observations, you will need to collect evidence of vocabularies, categories and organising principles in use. These will give you strong clues about the implicit and operational taxonomies being used. Examples of items that may give such clues are:

- screenshots of the shared drive folder structure;
- Lotus Notes database structure;
- lists and indexes of common files in the department filing cabinet;

- workflow diagrams and work breakdown structures posted on department noticeboards;
- labels on the spines of commonly used files;
- intranet site maps;
- information resource guides;
- department library classification scheme.

Frequently, no matter how rigorously conducted, your concept maps and input-output knowledge maps may still be quite high level. It is at the evidence-gathering stage that you start to see the real names of folders, documents and implicit categorisation systems in use, so it's a good idea to use your maps as preparation frameworks in advance of your visits to identify particular areas of doubt, ambiguity or clarification that you need to ask questions about and gather evidence on.

Finally, with your maps to structure the landscape and your observations and evidence to ground you in specific details, you are ready to begin the next stage.

Step 8: Facet analysis

In many respects, the facet analysis stage is quite simple and straightforward. As we noted in Chapter 2, very similar candidates for facet analysis crop up across multiple authors and practitioners (see Table 8.2).

Identifying candidates for facet analysis is therefore very easy. The real challenge is in identifying the *salient* facets – the ones that resonate with the majority of your population, the ones that exploit the familiarity of their users and the ones that will prove to be successful structuring mechanisms into the future.

So it's useful to have one or other of these facet frameworks in mind when you are engaged in your mapping, observation and evidence collection activities. In Chapter 3 we surveyed a facet analysis of an incident report, where seven different departments organised the same document in seven different ways – according to seven different facets. These are the details that you will need to notice as you visit the different workgroups in your client organisation. You will learn to recognise when work and information are naturally structured around activity flows, or around groups of customers, or around geographic zone, or around the structure of a technical discipline.

| Table 8.2 | Candidates for facet analysis |

Ranganathan	Straits Knowledge	Rosenfeld and Morville	Tiwana	Wurman
Personality	People and organisations	Audience	–	–
Matter	Things and parts	Product; document type	Form; type; products and services	Category
Energy	Activity cycles	–	Activities	–
Space	Locations	Geography	Location	Location
Time	Time or sequence	–	Time	Time
–	Subject matter	Topic	Domain	–
–	–	Price	–	–
–	–	–	–	Alphabet
–	–	–	–	Hierarchy (scale of magnitude)

Your knowledge maps and evidence collections should give you the best, most straightforward names for the categories and sub-categories within each facet, and for those that are missing you will simply have to draft proposed terms and put them to the test.

Some of your facets will be more straightforward than others. Facets like location lend themselves very easily to lists, for example. So do relatively short lists of well-known organisations which can be arranged alphabetically. Time and sequence can also be represented in lists fairly easily.

Other facets will require a tree or matrix presentation. These are the more complex ones that will be the special focus of your testing phase.

Step 9: Test and observe

Let's assume you have identified your facets and built them out to two or three levels using, as far as possible, the implicit and operational taxonomies you discovered during your collection phase. It's now time to validate your draft. We employ a set of nine key criteria for usable, robust taxonomy structures, as listed in Table 8.3. These criteria complement and reinforce each other, and are intended to ensure that the taxonomy is internally consistent, meaningful to users, easy to navigate and does its principal job of dividing up a large mass of content into easily navigated chunks.

Table 8.3   Key criteria for taxonomy validation

Criterion	Definition
Intuitive (is easy to navigate and use)	Users can successfully predict in which category they are likely to find the content they want, just by looking at the top level. The taxonomy is structured in a way that reflects natural working or usage habits, assumptions or well-known structures (such as organisational structure, workflow, widely entrained syllabus). *Test: Users navigate quickly to the content they need, without getting into blind alleys.*
Unambiguous (does not offer alternates)	Users do not have more than one obvious option for where to place content or find content they need. The taxonomy is structured so that users are presented with a minimum of difficult choices as to where to place content or find content they need. *Test: Users can immediately identify where content should be placed without having to spend time considering alternatives. Different users make consistent decisions using the taxonomy.*
Hospitable (can accommodate all content)	The taxonomy will successfully accommodate probable or foreseen new content, without the need for significant expansion or restructuring. *Test: There are no large bodies of undifferentiated 'general' content. Probable future content can be successfully assigned to existing categories without 'forcing' and without the need to revise the taxonomy.*
Consistent and predictable (provides context)	This complements the principle of intuitiveness. Consistency in how sub-categories are organised (e.g. alphabetically, using logical hierarchies, or familiar structures such as organisation charts) enables users to navigate the taxonomy structure successfully and quickly. One simple consistency rule is that in a tree structure, the principle of subordination at any level should be the same across the whole level, e.g. is a part of, is a kind of, is arranged by date, and so on. *Test: Within any category list, users will navigate quickly to the sub-category they need, without having to read the entire list systematically.*

Table 8.3 *Cont'd*

Criterion	Definition
Relevant (reflects user perspectives)	The taxonomy recognisably reflects common ways of organising information and knowledge in the host organisation. It can also be used as a representation of the organisation's information resources and activity. This complements the principle of intuitiveness. *Test: The information queries that users typically frame in a search can be immediately translated into a part of the taxonomy structure (e.g. 'I'm looking for an after action review on one of our innovation projects last year').*
Parsimonious (no redundancy/ repetition)	The taxonomy structure offers no more and no less than what is required for the content that is to be accommodated. This principle is in tension with the principle of hospitality. *Test: There are no categories that are unpopulated with content. There are no categories that are overpopulated with large amounts of undifferentiated content.*
Meaningful (provides context)	Category, sub-category and topic terms enable users to successfully predict the kind of content to be found behind them. The terms used in the taxonomy reflect common usage. This principle complements the principle of intuitiveness. *Test: Users are not surprised or disappointed by the nature of the content they find inside sub-category or topic folders.*
Durable (will not need frequent change)	The taxonomy does not need frequent change or expansion and rarely requires radical change or reorganisation. A robust taxonomy will generally only require a small audit of effectiveness every year or so unless there are radical and unexpected changes in the nature of content being covered. *Test: There are no serious or repeating complaints about the ability of users to assign content or navigate content using the taxonomy.*
Balanced (even levels of detail/ depth)	When the taxonomy is populated with content, there are relatively even quantities of content across the taxonomy categories. There are relatively even numbers of topic areas per category across the taxonomy. Each level of the taxonomy has broadly consistent degrees of generality and specificity when compared horizontally across the taxonomy. *Test: There are no areas of the taxonomy that are densely populated with large bulges of undifferentiated content while other areas are underpopulated.*

Sometimes, however, you'll see that some principles are in tension with others. The principles of hospitality and parsimony are in clear tension, and the principle of balance, while highly desirable, is very difficult to achieve in practice, especially while still at the design stage.

In fact, these criteria are best treated as heuristics for an effective taxonomy rather than hard and fast rules. Collectively they provide you with signs of health, and they give you tangible, pragmatic things you can test. They are virtually impossible to achieve fully, and not all of them can be tested before you have conducted a pilot.

There are three main stages in validating a taxonomy:

- structural validation;
- validation with people;
- validation with content.

Structural – after design; again after pilot

A structural test is an internal check by your team using the heuristics listed above, seeking to get a sense of balance across the taxonomy. It seeks to remove ambiguity and ensures consistency before exposing your draft to your target population. It also checks that your taxonomy is of the scale and depth that you originally planned, bearing in mind the usability issues in building taxonomies beyond 15 items in a level and beyond three levels in a tree.

With people – pre-pilot

A people test will test for ambiguity, predictability, intuitiveness, relevance and meaningfulness. This can be done systematically with small groups in quick search scenario exercises where users are asked to indicate where they would expect to find a particular document. This will often pick up undetected ambiguities or highlight where a term is not meaningful or familiar to the user population. Some refinements in terminology can be expected here.

With content – during pilot

The real test of any taxonomy is when people have to allocate content to it – i.e. use the taxonomy to categorise content. Before that, even at the people-testing phase, your taxonomy is a theory that represents how people *think* they think around knowledge and information assets. When they start categorising content, you and they will discover the relative effectiveness of your taxonomy across eight of your nine criteria, from ambiguity to balance and hospitality. The only one that you cannot test for in a pilot stage is durability.

With your pilot, you can expect further changes in terminology, perhaps the addition of new categories, and very clear indications of the scope notes that need to be written where you cannot remove ambiguity or avoid variant interpretations of taxonomy terms. A scope note describes in greater detail to the user what kind of content belongs to that category, and sometimes describes what does *not* belong in that category.

Conducting a pilot

Your pilot is important, because you do want to test the taxonomy against its purpose, the full breadth of its target population and a reasonable range of documents. Outsourcing your categorisation tasks within a pilot to non-typical users (e.g. temporary staff hired for the purpose) will tell you very little about the relevance and meaningfulness of the taxonomy terms within your target population. However, while you want representative users and a representative spread of documents, you do not want to commit to testing large quantities of documents in case you need to go back and do substantial revisions. This will then involve extensive rework on recategorising the pilot documents.

It's a good idea to focus your pilot on those facets which are more complex than others – three-level trees, for example, as compared with alphabetical lists – and aim to populate each node of the taxonomy three or four times. A rule of thumb therefore for the number of items to include in your pilot for test categorisation would be four times the number of terms in each taxonomy facet under test.

Pilot categorisation is best conducted under direct observation, because this is the best way to pick up signals of ambiguity, confusion or lack of meaningfulness in the terms. If this is not possible, then feedback sheets with sections framed according to our test criteria are the next best thing. These sheets should be completed immediately after each categorisation session, and where a problematic term is found, the pilot user should be asked to give a preferred suggested term instead.

If resources are available, to guard against being swayed by idiosyncratic feedback, several different users may be asked to categorise the same documents. The feedback is then collated and balanced to identify common issues as well as isolate the more individualistic ones.

Case study 8.1

Facet analysis for a sports organisation

We were tasked with developing a taxonomy for a sports organisation to support a new document management system and intranet redesign. The goals of the project were to help build common ground within departments and to support boundary-spanning needs in certain key areas of collaboration across the organisation.

The facet analysis produced the following list of facets:

- *Document types* – tree structure (two levels) – category names drawn from mapping and evidence-gathering activity.

- *Business activities* – tree structure (three levels) – category names drawn from mapping and evidence-gathering activity.

- *Location* – list – names drawn from International Olympic Committee country list.

- *Sports events* – tree structure (two levels) – category names drawn from evidence-gathering activity followed by lists of official event names.

- *People and organisations* – tree structure (two levels) – category names drawn from evidence-gathering activity, followed by lists of people or organisation names.

- *Sports* – tree structure (two levels) – category names drawn from evidence-gathering and library classification scheme.

The sports facet was the most complex to build, because sports labels did not appear very frequently in our earlier mapping activity – the maps tended to show organisation of content by business activity or document type. The evidence-gathering activity identified several areas where sports-specific vocabulary was being used, but in highly inconsistent ways, and with no single way of organising the content. The organisation's library did have a sports-specific classification scheme, adapted from an alphanumeric classification scheme developed by the Israeli Wingate Institute for Sports and Physical Education. However, this scheme had evidently been grown over time, and so had very little predictable structure to how it organised the various sports in relation to each other. For example, lacrosse, squash and international chess were all adjacent to each other.

Sports classification is an intriguing challenge because different sports can be grouped according to several competing principles: the instrument that is employed (e.g. racquet sports, board sports), the type of activity that is engaged in (e.g. running, climbing), the participants (e.g. team, individual), the objective (e.g. competitive, recreational), their genre (e.g. games, endurance), or the environment they are played in (e.g. water sports, court games).

In this case we chose to organise our facet first of all by the environment in which the sport is played – although in some cases we had to separate clusters of sports by instrument as well as environment. For example, because a very large number of sports are ball games, we ended up with two clusters, one for court-based ball games and one for field- or pitch-based ball games, so as to even out the large number of sports involved.

Although environment is a fairly good principle to discriminate between sports, it is not without its ambiguities – composite sports such as the triathlon may take place across multiple environments, and some sports are a frustrating blend of environments (such as parasailing). New sports, like new religions (and other innovations), often represent a consciously eclectic borrowing of features across pre-existing categories. Obsessive-compulsives do not do well in taxonomy work. Ambiguity always lurks within the cleanest of organising principles. What you want in your main organising principle is a widely applicable principle that produces frequent predictability for the user. Not achieving perfection is okay.

Despite its limitations, we chose the environment principle as the dominant one for two reasons, one structural and one based on the familiarity principle. From a structural point of view, an environment-based classification just happened to spread out our candidate sports much more evenly than any other principle, so that we achieved a 15-term x 3-level structure much more easily than by any other means. From a familiarity point of view, we knew that our client was also responsible for managing a wide range of sports facilities – so from this point of view, we reasoned that the environment in which the sport was played would show up more frequently in their internal information and knowledge content than (say) the equipment with which the sport was played.

For the pilot test of the taxonomy, we planned to focus on just three of the facets: business activities and document types would be tested on a large cross section of documents because these organising attributes showed up much more often in the general document flows of the organisation. The sports facet would be tested on more specific collections of content such as news clippings and archive photographs because the structure of the facet was not self-evident from our earlier investigations and so needed more rigorous testing. The other three facets, location, people and organisations, and sports events, were not involved in the pilot tests because they were both much less controversial and in any case appeared to play relatively minor roles in how people approached and organised their content.

In this chapter we've looked at how to approach the design and testing of a taxonomy. Although we've represented it as a linear set of stages, this can turn out to be an iterative process going through several cycles. This can happen particularly where the organising principles are not self-evident after the first discovery activities of mapping, observation and evidence collection have been conducted.

You may in your first pilot test discover whole new ways of approaching content that force you back to the drawing board. You may simply get your predictions about user behaviour wrong. If you do have some doubt about the robustness of your approach, it is wise not to develop your taxonomy to its full depth, but to sketch it out at a higher level of generality and conduct your tests on that. If it works at a high level, you can cycle back through and deepen the taxonomy, and this time you will be using the classification decisions made by users during your pilot to assess the best way of breaking down your next levels of detail in the taxonomy. Above all, it's important to remember that taxonomy development is a learning, evolving process. No taxonomy worth its salt is born fully formed and ready to roll.

However, if you're lucky, you'll get your taxonomy structure pretty much right first time and with minor refinements you will be ready to go ahead and implement it. That brings us to the topic of our next chapter.

9

Implementing your taxonomy

Between future discounting and the fact that classification is largely for the group, classification is vulnerable to the tragedy of the commons where people prefer looking for classified documents, but don't invest the effort in classification themselves.

(McMullin, 2004)

If you think that most of your work is done when you have your designed taxonomy on the table, then you're in for a disappointment. All you have, valuable though it may be, are the equivalent of the architect's blueprints for how your knowledge and information resources can be structured. There's still a considerable way to go before your taxonomy pays off in information and knowledge infrastructure enhancements that support more effective knowledge use and knowledge flow across the organisation. Until the building is built, the architect's blueprints represent theory, art or fantasy. Only the tangible building itself provides the payoff for the effort involved thus far.

There are three main stages in working through the implementation of a taxonomy. You will already have been thinking through some of the issues inside those stages in your planning phase earlier on, but your planning and design phases may have taken several months to work through. Things will have changed, and you will have learned new things about your client organisation along the way. It's now time to look at how your taxonomy will be implemented in practice, with real people and real content. Throughout the whole process, it's important to keep in mind your original purpose. If necessary (because of new discoveries about opportunities and needs along the way) revisit that purpose with your project sponsor or your governance committee. But it is especially easy in the course of a fairly long project to lose sight of the purpose in the production of a technically demanding artefact – the taxonomy itself. The tail should not wag the dog, and a taxonomy should not wag the organisation. Your purpose should drive all the decisions in the final three steps, illustrated in Figure 9.1, of your project:

- *Step 10: Plan the instantiation of your taxonomy.* How will it be instanced, what tools will you need to support that instantiation and what usability issues do you need to anticipate and provide for?

- *Step 11: Integrate the taxonomy into existing infrastructure.* Your taxonomy is a candidate for addition to your existing information and knowledge infrastructure, but it does not graft itself on to that infrastructure of its own accord. It needs to be deliberately woven into the information landscape, and we'll look at two important ways of doing this.

- *Step 12: Secure the governance process.* You have planned a governance infrastructure, and hopefully leveraged it during your design phase. Now you need to establish a cycle of activity that will ensure your taxonomy remains viable and relevant.

Figure 9.1 The full taxonomy development cycle with implementation steps

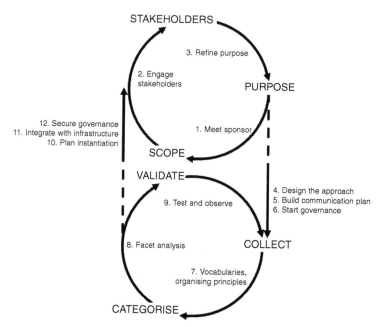

Step 10: Plan the instantiation of your taxonomy

In your planning phase, you will already have anticipated the ways in which your taxonomy will be instantiated, whether through a folder structure, subject guides, a website navigation scheme or metadata-assisted browse and search. Now it's time to turn these plans into reality, and for that you'll need to think through two basic tools of instantiation – a thesaurus and a metadata framework. Even if you are not initially going to use a metadata framework or search engine, as your technology environment matures, you will want to get more value out of the work you have invested in your taxonomy, and these two tools are the means by which you can do that. You will also want to think through practical usability issues. Let's deal with each of these in turn.

Instantiation tools

Your metadata framework presents your intended metadata elements, their definitions and how they will be deployed in a way that helps your technology deployment team to acquire, configure and roll out whatever technology you plan to use. To recap from Chapter 5, metadata can be used in four main ways:

- It *identifies* content – e.g. descriptive metadata captures author and title fields and distinguishes each document from all others.

- It helps systems *manage* content – e.g. administrative and structural metadata capture things like version numbers, archiving date, security and access permissions, links to multiple components in a document, file type.

- It aids *retrieval* of content – e.g. descriptive metadata captures things like taxonomy topics, subject keywords, document description

- Increasingly, it is now being used to *connect* content to other content – behavioural metadata is being captured about the transactions that users have with each document and this is used to infer relationships or connections about the other things the same people transact with, e.g. Amazon's 'other people who bought this book also bought ...'

Metadata content, however important it is behind the scenes, is notoriously difficult to acquire from users. Before you introduced your system, your clients could simply place their documents in a folder of their choosing. Now you're asking them to make a series of decisions about choosing categories, identifying access restrictions and so on. We who know the usefulness of metadata often forget the rude and unnecessary imposition it seems to the people we inflict it on. The simpler we make the metadata task, the better.

All this means that taxonomists need to think beyond just including fields for simple findability inside a metadata framework. The framework will indeed include your taxonomy facets as separate fields, but it will also include other fields to support the other functions of metadata. If you restrict yourself simply to 'your' taxonomy elements and do not consider the entire metadata picture, you will lose opportunities to leverage connections between different elements in the interests of user-friendliness.

For example, records management systems that use a business classification scheme as a taxonomy facet routinely associate retention and disposal decisions with each category within that facet. This means that users who are entering documents into the system do not have to make two sets of decisions. Security and access decisions might well be automatically associated with certain categories in similar ways. Only treating the metadata framework as a whole will present such opportunities to you.

When drawing up your metadata framework, it's important to use a standards-based framework. This will make it easier for the transfer of data across different systems, the use of federated search engines and future migration of content to a new system. For a generalist content collection, the Dublin Core standard is probably your best bet, although for specialised applications, such as for e-learning content (IEEE LTSC, 2002) or records management (NAA, 1999; ISO 23081-1 2006), there are other more detailed metadata standards (or extensions of Dublin Core) that should be looked out for, including the Resource Description Framework (or RDF) for web-based content (W3C, 2006).

To illustrate how metadata is used, a fictional example of a metadata framework for a sports organisation using Dublin Core is given in Table 9.1 (Dublin Core, 2005). The framework contains five taxonomy-related fields, drawing on the sports organisation's taxonomy. Can you spot which ones they are? (If you looked closely enough, you will see that five taxonomy facets are represented here: Sports; Sports Events; Business Activities; Places; Document Types.)

Notice that the Dublin Core field elements can be reused several times (e.g. 'subject' and 'accessRights'), and also that your taxonomy facets

Table 9.1 Example of a metadata framework

Field name	Element name	Definition	Data type or source	Comment
Title	Dublin Core: title	A name given to the resource	Text string	**Compulsory:** Pick up from system – should be in document template
Author	Dublin Core: creator	Name of the person primarily responsible for making the content of the resource	Text string	**Compulsory:** Pick up from system – should be available from login data, allow type-over
Subject area 1	Dublin Core: subject	The topic of the content of the resource	Values come from taxonomy facet: Sport	**Compulsory:** Select from drop-down list (multiple values possible)
Subject area 2	Dublin Core: subject	The topic of the content of the resource	Values come from taxonomy facet: Sports Events	**Compulsory:** Select from drop-down list (multiple values possible)
Subject area 3	Dublin Core: subject	The topic of the content of the resource	Values come from taxonomy facet: Business Activities	**Compulsory:** Select from drop-down list (multiple values possible)
Place	Dublin Core: coverage	Extent or scope of the content of the resource	Values come from thesaurus of geographic names	**Optional:** Select from drop-down list (multiple values possible)
Date	Dublin Core: date	Date the resource was 'published'	Date: use format yyyy-mm-dd	**Compulsory:** Pick up from system by default; (today's date) allow type-over
Document type	Dublin Core: type	The name of the document type	Values come from taxonomy facet: Document Type	**Compulsory:** Pick up from system – should be in document template
Format	Dublin Core: format	File format of the resource	Text string conforming to Internet Media Types (e.g. application/pdf)	**Compulsory:** Pick up from system
Identifier	Dublin Core: identifier	URL or other document identifiers for the resource	Text string	**Compulsory:** Pick up from system
Publisher	Dublin Core: publisher	Entity responsible for making the content available	Values come from list of department names	**Optional:** Use if you want to track content produced by departments – select from drop-down list; this option will involve maintaining list

Table 9.1		Cont'd		
Field name	Element name	Definition	Data type or source	Comment
Security	Dublin Core: accessRights	Information about who can access the resource or an indication of its security status	Values come from drop-down list of security classifications	**Compulsory:** Must be selected according to information security policy
Access	Dublin Core: accessRights	Information about who can access the resource or an indication of its security status	Values come from drop-down list of staff members	**Conditional:** For all documents classified at Confidential and above
Keywords	Abc org: keywords	Additional keywords describing the content for which no equivalent exists in any of the controlled vocabularies above	Text string	**Optional:** Free text entry; keywords entered here can be reviewed periodically for linking to taxonomy through thesaurus

might be provided for by fields other than 'Subject' (e.g. 'coverage' for location name and 'type' for document types). Notice also that we try to ensure that the content of metadata is picked up wherever possible automatically from the system, to reduce user time and effort, and we also try as far as possible to limit free text entry, preferring selection from drop-down lists in order to limit the possibility of errors in typing.

Wherever you have selection from a drop-down list, you need to provide for the maintenance of a database containing your selection lists for each metadata field, and ensure that these lists are updated in the database whenever they change in real life. For example, if your staff list changes, then the master list for *accessRights* will also need to be changed accordingly.

Your second main instantiation tool is your thesaurus. The thesaurus is essentially a dictionary of all the terms in your taxonomy, where for each term its relationships with other terms are explicitly listed. This dictionary of taxonomy terms should be supplemented with other terms that might be used by your target users and are about taxonomy concepts but which are not in the taxonomy. The thesaurus should point the user from those alternate terms towards the authorised taxonomy terms. Table 9.2 is an extract from a thesaurus for a training institution.

Table 9.2   Extract from a thesaurus for a training institution

Term	relationship	Term
aerospace machining	narrower term of	mechanical and manufacturing
aerospace maintenance	narrower term of	engineering services
assessment activities	related term of	lesson plan
assessment instrument	narrower term of	learner engagement plan
assessment lessons	use	assessment scheme
assessment scheme	narrower term of	curriculum design
assessment scheme	broader term of	phase test
assessment scheme	broader term of	test plan
assessment scheme	broader term of	table of specs
assessment scheme	broader term of	OJT task list
assessment scheme	broader term of	SET scope of test
assessment specs	use	assessment scheme

From Table 9.2 we can see that 'assessment lessons' and 'assessment specs' are not authorised terms in the taxonomy but are probably commonly used among the target population. So they are entered into the thesaurus and pointed towards the correct taxonomy terms. The tree relationships are expressed by the 'broader term' and 'narrower term' expressions, and other useful relationships are captured by the 'related term' expression.

A thesaurus will also often have scope notes attached to each authorised term in the thesaurus. This is particularly important for the avoidance of ambiguity and to help users decide on the correct term to assign. In records management applications, precision and lack of ambiguity become very important, and so scope notes become essential tools. An effective scope note will usually contain a brief description of the meaning of the term and guidance on what should be included and excluded under that term.

The main usefulness of a thesaurus is twofold: it can be used as a dictionary to help users decide on the correct category to assign, or it can support delivery of greater relevance in the results from a search engine. If the search engine consults the thesaurus whenever a keyword search is conducted, then it will pick up relevant taxonomy concepts for non-authorised keywords, so long as they have been anticipated in advance.

Apart from the terms within your taxonomy, anticipation of additional likely keywords for your thesaurus can be picked up at several stages. Your initial mapping and evidence-gathering activity will have produced many plausible candidates for alternate terms, since your final taxonomy terms will often be the result of negotiation between several sets of variant terms. Your testing and validation process will also generate evidence of the different terms that people imagine and use when they are searching or classifying content.

Post-implementation, a free text 'keywords' field in a metadata framework (as in our example above) also generates evidence of subject keywords that users associate with particular pieces of content. Regular search log analysis can also reveal frequently used keywords among people using the search function, and frequently used terms should obviously be incorporated into the thesaurus and linked to authorised taxonomy terms. Finally, if your organisation employs 'social tagging' (more about this in the next chapter), then frequently used tags can also be picked up and incorporated into the thesaurus.

A thesaurus can also support a category browse function in an application, as well as other user-support functions, such as suggesting related, more general or more specific content after delivering the primary results of a search.

Usability strategies

It's easy, immersed as we are in our technical issues, to get carried away by enthusiasm for what metadata and thesauri enable us to do, and to forget the world we once lived in, the world of the general user. To the general user, the quality of metadata and the richness of a thesaurus are theoretical benefits quite far removed from the immediacy of laying hands on the right person, information or document at a moment's notice.

Which is to say that the general user, quite reasonably, wants to enjoy the benefits of high-quality metadata and rich thesauri without having to invest in it. They are not, after all, employed as metadata inputters. They have more important roles and tasks to perform – or so their internal scripts often go. Moreover, a great deal of metadata has little direct, obvious benefit for a user. So maintaining metadata, and to a lesser degree thesauri, is seen to impose friction on 'normal' work and is almost universally resented. This leads us to a series of usability heuristics that it's best to keep close to heart:

- *Minimise as far as you can the number of metadata and taxonomy decisions required from users.* This can be done through the autocategorisation examples discussed in Chapter 7, or through linking one metadata decision to another. For example, retention and disposal decisions can be associated with business activities. In our sports taxonomy example, the name of a sports personality can be associated automatically with their sports category via a thesaurus or via an autocategorisation tool.

- *Localise your metadata templates.* A single standard metadata framework for all workgroups and all contexts is probably going to be too big and impractical and compel users to consider metadata elements that are not relevant to their context or content. Once you have your master metadata framework, break it down into mini-frameworks for different contexts that present just the selected metadata elements that are relevant in that context (although it is helpful to maintain a master metadata framework for public access and reference).

- *Reuse your users' effort.* When your users conduct searches they are revealing to you the subject vocabulary that they think in. The very least you can do is use search log analysis to inform your thesaurus development, but you can also invest more effort in tracking the use of content associated with searches, and use this feedback to refine your taxonomy on a regular basis. Observing the behaviour of your target population through your system is often more revealing than asking for feedback or giving them artificial tasks to perform. And when it turns out that your users have to complete the same metadata over and over again for a type of content that recurs frequently, it's time to consider introducing content templates that contain standard default metadata.

Case study 9.1

Metadata strategies and vocabulary control at the BBC

The BBC's mission is 'to inform, educate, entertain and connect Britain'. Employing 25,000 people, it happens, as a by-product, to do pretty much all of that for the rest of the world as well. The BBC's website *bbc.co.uk* has become a central platform in presenting and housing its public content, whether in text, image, video or audio. As at October 2006, the website (which actually comprises 750 subsites) had around 1.5 million webpages (with multiple content items per page), fed by 1,000 new media staff using over 25 different content production systems. At roughly two billion page impressions per month, it is Europe's biggest public draw for content, by a factor of 2 (Loasby, 2006b). In its sheer scale, variety, brand presence and public exposure, it's a content management challenge of titanic proportions.

Metadata has been associated with the BBC's webpage content since the earliest days, but as recently as 2002, the metadata was primarily aimed at driving traffic to the website – i.e. it was tailored for search engine optimisation. Once visitors got to the site, however, metadata support for organising and structuring their experience was sorely lacking. The BBC had no culture of providing structured metadata to support user navigation or connection of related content. Metadata is the key to pulling the latest related content together in the results of a search or in thematic web pages.

By 2004, the landscape was shifting towards user-focused aggregation of content, using strictly enforced controlled vocabularies. Control and precision were important because poorly associated content could have serious brand and credibility implications for the BBC. However, given the scale of the content, the controlled vocabularies were, as Karen Loasby puts it, 'monsters'. Buy-in from contributors was difficult to get, partly because keyword tagging was laborious (despite semi-automatic systems to suggest likely keywords), precision and currency were difficult to achieve in the fast-moving, often ambiguous domain of journalism, and the metadata was only applied to the main content management system and not to other platforms, so it was difficult to achieve site-wide aggregation of content and few people could see tangible benefits from the investment required.

Starting in 2004, the phenomenon of social tagging on the Internet started to gain popularity (see Chapter 10), and the BBC began to experiment with it. In social tagging, the contributor of a document simply adds his or her own keywords as descriptors, without reference to a controlled vocabulary. The system then aggregates all the tags and has ways of presenting the most popular tags. If this feedback is visible to contributors, it often influences the choice of tags towards greater consistency (Mathes, 2004).

Because they are based on individual decisions, social tagging systems are still very weak at removing ambiguity and assuring precision. However, for the BBC they had a great advantage: they were incredibly easy to use for the journalists contributing content and they reflected current usage. Social 'tagsonomies' are always up to date because they represent the latest language of the contributing community.

So they started to experiment with ways of using social tagging to their advantage. They developed, for example, a 'metadata threshold' strategy whereby a term was admitted into the formal controlled vocabularies once a certain amount of content had been tagged with it. Together with semi-automatic term suggestions from controlled vocabularies in the background, this cut the costs of metatagging content dramatically. Meanwhile, interfaces between different content systems are being developed to expand the reach of standardised metadata across repositories and systems.

Attitudes towards metadata have changed partly because it's now much easier to tag content, but also because there has been an increasing focus on audio-video content where added metadata is more obviously the only way to retrieve and organise. It's hard to use the 'Google it' argument which can be applied to text documents. Another contribution to changed attitudes has been the demonstration of metadata's power. Applications such as the BBC's Open Archive now exist that demonstrate to the contributors the value of having structured, consistent metadata. This goes back to a fundamental principle of change management – a tangible example of benefits from the change will trump a 'this will be good for you in the future' argument any day.

The BBC's experience demonstrates the long path that change can take, even among highly content-savvy organisations. Clever strategies for easing the burden of metadata need to go hand in hand with a consistent focus on quality, and the tangible demonstration of need and benefits. The good news is that with patience, persistence and a clear focus, change can be achieved.

Source: Loasby (2006a).

Step 11: Integrate your taxonomy into the infrastructure

When you were planning your taxonomy initiative (Chapter 7) I advised you to go looking for other initiatives in your organisation that touched on your knowledge and information infrastructure and may have involved the development or use of categorisation systems. If you did this well and took them into account, you have by now developed a set of categories and vocabularies that are useful in many different contexts in your organisation and propagation into the infrastructure will be well assured.

But there are two particular domains where special attention is needed, because a taxonomy that does not supply the needs of these two different, critical, infrastructural practices will almost certainly come into competition with them and may well lose. They are the domains of records management and information architecture. Let's take information architecture first, and to do that we need to take a brief side trip into a close relative of taxonomy work – the science of *arrangement*.

A brief history of arrangement

In his well-known book *The Geography of Thought*, Richard Nisbett argues that Western cultures tend to think in categories while East Asian cultures tend to think in contexts. So if an Asian and a Westerner are asked to group associated things from a list comprising monkey, cow, banana and grass, the Asian will tend to connect monkey with banana and cow with grass, while the Westerner will tend to connect the animals with animals and the foods with foods. Asians see connections and contexts, while Westerners see categories (Nisbett, 2003).

Now Nisbett rather over-argues his case, and himself admits that Westerners can think in contexts and Asians can think in categories if they are primed to do so. But his distinction between categorical thinking and contextual thinking is a useful one to pursue.

In the history of taxonomy work, this distinction turns out to be a critical one. Until the 1730s, at least in Europe, the practices of arrangement, classification, categorisation and taxonomy work were all part of the same cluster of concepts. As we saw in Chapter 1, the term *taxonomy* itself literally means habits or laws of arrangement.

By the mid-1770s, however, taxonomy work had already diverged from arrangement work, and this decisive split is exemplified by the conflict between two great biologists – George Louis Leclerc Comte de Buffon and Carl Linnaeus. Born in the same year (1707), Linnaeus and Buffon occupied very different social stations, sat at opposite ends of Europe and set out opposing positions on the ordering and arrangement of knowledge about species.

Linnaeus fought on the side of analysis, categories and controlled nomenclature, while Buffon fought on the side of context, multiple perspectives and understanding through seeing the bigger picture. Though Linnaeus won the field in terms of how taxonomy work became understood, Buffon had a profound though less direct impact on the way in which knowledge was organised for use in subsequent generations. He was the distant ancestor of the disciplines of ecology, information architecture and faceted classification.

To see how this played out, it's necessary to go back in time a couple of centuries. Arrangement is an art that only becomes important when you have a collection of things to arrange. Throughout late antiquity and the Middle Ages, the few people who had the resources to collect diverse things in large quantities were nobles, clerics and royalty, and they did this for prestige, diversion and display. Arrangements of their 'cabinets of curiosities' served to inspire wonder and impress their visitors.

Throughout the fifteenth century, with the spreading of wealth through trade and the growth of scholarship, there was a gradual shift in the purpose behind collection and arrangement. The passion for the collection of 'curiosities' was taken up on a large scale by scholars and scientists across Europe, and their collections were increasingly used as instruments of learning about the natural world. Arrangements of curiosities became part of a larger endeavour to construct a systematic knowledge of the natural world. Collections started to become more systematic and supportive of enquiry, sense-making and discovery. By the beginning of the seventeenth century, writers like Francis Bacon were thoroughly dismissive of the higgledy-piggledy arrangements of the rich and famous:

> There is such a multitude and host as it were of particular objects, and lying so widely dispersed, as to distract and confuse the understanding; and we can therefore hope for no advantage ... unless we put its forces in due order and array by means of proper, and well arranged, and as it were living tables of discovery of these matters which are the subject of investigation ... (Blom, 2003: 46)

As knowledge of the world grew with the expansion of exploration, trade and imperial and economic dominion throughout the seventeenth century, so the collections of the curious grew, and the challenges of sensible arrangement became even more pressing. Bacon's impatience was echoed just over a century later by the methodical Carl Linnaeus who was dismissive of the 'complete disorder' he found in the home of the last great universal collector of his time, Sir Hans Sloane – founder of the collection that became the British Museum. After Sloane, collectors divided themselves into discrete disciplines. The world of knowledge had become too complex to comprehend and represent in one single arrangement (Blom, 2003: 88).

In the midst of this complexity, Linnaeus's great gift to science was threefold. Beginning with his *Systema Natura* in 1735, he introduced a far simpler principle of distinguishing between species based on anatomy than had ever been proposed before. Beginning in 1737 with his *Critica Botanica*, he laid down the rules for his binomial naming system for species which riled his critics immensely (because he substituted so many older naming conventions with his own), but when widely adopted created the first standardised way of describing species. This immeasurably enhanced scientific coordination and collaboration. Finally, his hierarchical, nested classification tree structure turned out to be a perfect vehicle to express the genealogical relationships that gained such prominence during the emerging evolutionary theories of the late eighteenth and early nineteenth centuries (Stearn 2001; Gould, 2000: 80).

Linnaeus's new taxonomic method simplified the task of categorisation, imposed rigorous rules (and therefore consistency), and happened on a form of representation that history turned into a lucky bet. From the point of view of advancing scientific method, his focus on analysis, rules and standardised approaches gave an incalculable advantage.

Buffon by comparison arrived late on the biological scene, only taking up his position of Director of the King's Botanic Gardens in Paris in 1738, when Linnaeus's work on botany was already beginning to reverberate through Europe. He had been a brilliant mathematician, and had at the age of twenty invented the binomial theorem in mathematics (related only in name to Linnaeus's binomial system of nomenclature). But biology turned out to be Buffon's lifelong passion. Beginning in 1749, he began an astonishing forty-year odyssey of publications under the title *Histoire Naturelle, Générale et Particulière* (*Natural History: General and Particular*). Projected to run to 50 volumes, Buffon lived to see 36 of them published, and the series is cited by Stephen Jay Gould as 'one of the most comprehensive and monumental efforts ever made by one man' (Gould, 2000: 78).

Buffon vehemently opposed what he saw as Linnaeus's unhelpful over-simplifications. Buffon recognised the inherent complexity of biological life and insisted that this complexity be represented faithfully. There were many different ways of relating organisms to each other, based on different attributes and principles. They could be grouped according to the environments that they shared (e.g. air, land or water). They could be grouped by function and adaptation (e.g. having wings and flying brings bats closer to birds than mammals whereas anatomy separates the two). They could be grouped by similarity of behaviour, and so on. Anatomy provided one – but only one – way of classifying creatures. The only true test of a species was whether interbreeding between animals was possible so genealogical lineage was also a grouping criterion, leading to Buffon's insight into the instability of species and their adaptations over time (Gould, 2000: 75–90). Buffon was implicitly adopting a faceted approach to the organisation of species.

Linnaeus, as we know, won the war, and it's not hard to understand why. Simplicity and standardisation paid off for the science of the time much more than recognition of complexity, context and multiple ways of looking at things. If ecology had become the mantra of the following century rather than evolution, then Buffon's attention to context, environment and adaptation might have brought his theory back to prominence – indeed, Buffon is now recognised by ecological thinkers as an early forerunner. But it was not to be. In 1774 Buffon had to swallow the Linnaean system when King Louis XV decreed that it be adopted in the King's gardens.

But if Linnaeus successfully appropriated and narrowed the discipline of scientific taxonomy, Buffon's legacy lived on in the arrangements of things for understanding, sense-making and education. Museums, galleries and universities adopted the 'Buffonian system' with enthusiasm, because of its instructive power. The founder of America's first museum, Charles Willson Peale, presented his exhibits with painted backdrops and artificial landscapes, lurking with their environmental neighbours.

At the end of the eighteenth century, the Emperor Franz II constructed a museum in Vienna which was even more lavish than Peale's in its reconstructions of natural habitats, though it sometimes sacrificed accuracy for entertainment.

Also in Vienna in the 1780s, the Hapsburg picture collection was reorganised by Christian van Mechel into chronological order, and suddenly opened up the possibility of art history – identifying styles, schools and periods in art. This vision was brought to fruition in post-revolutionary France right at the end of the eighteenth century when Dominique Denon reorganised the collections of the Louvre on historical principles (Blom, 2003).

Buffon's great gift then was in the recognition that there are many possible ways to organise the same things, and that every arrangement tells a different story. This is what brings us to information architecture.

The inventor of the term 'information architecture' is Richard Saul Wurman, a 'real' architect by training and a vocation, but who has increasingly turned to the design problems involved in providing access to information. Wurman points out (as we noted earlier): 'The ways of organising information are finite. It can only be organised by location, alphabet, time, category, or hierarchy' (Wurman, 2001: 40–1).

But what Wurman also points out is that the same set of things can often be arranged in each of those ways, and each arrangement tells you different things. If you consider an arrangement of pedigree dogs, for example, an arrangement by size displays its own patterns and suggests its own questions (like 'why are there so few large pedigree dogs compared with tiny ones?'). An arrangement by country of origin tells another story, while an arrangement by date of Kennel Club recognition tells a tale of changing tastes over time.

The task of the information architect therefore is to find the arrangements that will be most instructive and useful for any given context of use. Arrangements, not classifications, are the primary name of the game.

This is what the taxonomist, even the faceted taxonomist, is apt to forget if overly focused on the analytical task of discriminating and describing according to fixed principles. Too much attention to the category infrastructure represented by your taxonomy can obscure proper attention to the contexts of use for the information and knowledge assets you cover, and this is why your relationship with the information architects is so important.

The danger is described succinctly by Maish Nichani:

> When it comes to the design of intranets and large websites, the limelight is firmly on issues of taxonomy and navigation (info-seeking) and not so much on the final use (info-using) of the content, known as the target content. (Nichani, 2006)

If your taxonomies are implemented in a way that leaves them seemingly far removed from the contexts in which information and knowledge are naturally used, then you are in trouble. The world of difference between Linnaeus and Buffon expressed itself in a two hundred year divorce between taxonomies for science and arrangements for instruction and learning. The two cannot afford to be separated in an organisational setting, and a faceted taxonomy approach, it turns out, makes it possible to join them.

Usability expert Don Norman recently pointed to some anthropological work conducted in the 1980s on the difference between taxonomy work and arrangement for use.

> Years ago, anthropologists Janet Dougherty and Charles Keller studied how blacksmiths organise their tools. Blacksmiths, they discovered, don't put all the hammers neatly away on the shelves, all together. No, when blacksmiths clean up at night, the hammer goes on the ground, right next to the anvil, and next to the tongs:

all the tools are organised so that they are ready for the job, ready for use. In similar fashion, good carpenters, while working, keep nails near their hammers. In other words, good behavioral organisation reflects human activity structure, not dictionary classification. Dougherty and Keller called this form of organisation taskonomy. (Norman, 2006; see also Dougherty and Keller, 1982)

This observation was confirmed in the mid-1990s by information researchers Barreau and Nardi, who found that users were much more likely to be assisted in their information seeking by contextual cues than by 'logical arrangements' (Barreau, 1995; Barreau and Nardi, 1995). Norman concludes that arrangement for use (taskonomy) is different from logical organisation for well-structured retrieval, where the immediate context of the information or tool is not available (taxonomy). The taskonomy represents the workface, whereas the taxonomy represents the warehouse or stockroom.

It's not that taskonomies are any better than taxonomies – in fact, in any enterprise system, you'll need both taxonomies and metadata to support your taskonomies behind the scenes. But what the taskonomy does is bring the usability of the information being organised closer to the user. Taxonomists cannot remain in the back storeroom keeping the shelves tidy. They also need to venture into the storefront and help their clients get their information organised for use.

Our challenge is that, notwithstanding our consistent user-focus throughout our taxonomy project, what we still have is just a system for logically organising our content (the warehouse), abstracted from its individual contexts of use (the workface). Fortunately, we have in our knowledge and concept maps plenty of examples of contexts in which the target content is used. Our next step therefore is to move from *organisation* of content to *arrangement* for use, from *taxonomy* to *taskonomy* and from the role of *taxonomist* to *information architect*.

We call this particular task *the creation of information neighbour-hoods*. Simply put, taxonomies and metadata provide the scaffolding and structure to start managing our content in meaningful ways, but they are not, as we too often assume, the end of our journey towards usefulness. In the highly task-driven environment of the enterprise, we need to find content which is *organised for use*, in a *usable context*, with *associated stuff* within easy reach.

Information designer Maish Nichani makes some useful distinctions that help us think about information neighbourhoods. The most useful for our purposes is his analysis of how 'target' content gets organised for use. 'Target' content is simply content collected and organised according to common working needs. Within this Maish discriminates between information that is *pertinent* (the direct focus of a visitor's need when they arrive in a given information neighbourhood), *relevant* (other associated material that supports or amplifies or extends the pertinent content) and *action*-oriented (things that you might want to do next, given your target content) (Nichani, 2006).

If we go back to our taxonomy work, all we've really done is created a way of organising a large virtual warehouse of information. Our taxonomy and metadata together with search and browse give us the instruments to locate any item and compile an inventory. But in the midst of a working day, who wants to browse a warehouse or read an inventory?

Maish is describing page structures organised around 'target' content that much more resemble department stores than wholesalers' warehouses. Go to any part of the store and you'll find associated content and ideas for other purchases. Go looking for a fishing rod and you'll find fishing lines and maybe a couple of instruction guides on freshwater fishing. You might even find a knowledgeable salesperson who can explain the differences between different rods and lines, depending on what kind of fishing you want to do. The department store contextualises its content for use and suggests other useful content to you. The warehouse does not.

In constructing an information neighbourhood, the primary tasks of any given workgroup (supported by your earlier concept maps) will help you identify the most obvious *pertinent* content.

Much less clear is how you identify useful *relevant* content – the things that amplify and flesh out the information neighbourhood around your prime reason for being on that web page.

It turns out, however, that faceted taxonomies combined with a Buffonian flexibility about the arrangement of information can come to your rescue. So here are a few suggestions for identifying *relevant* content and building your information neighbourhoods. We use a helpful mnemonic TREASURE to guide us along (see Figure 9.2), and you will recognise the facet analysis as well as discrimination of different knowledge asset types that lies behind it.

The acronym does not mean that you have to find associated content that matches all of these categories. We use it as a checklist to prompt us for possible, useful *relevant* content to put around the *pertinent* content in any given neighbourhood. This is not a mechanical, metadata-driven

Figure 9.2   Checklist for building an information neighbourhood

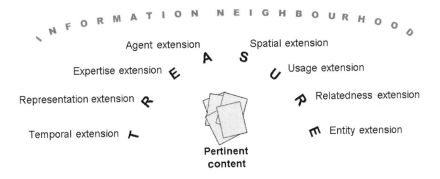

task, though metadata should help (especially if you have a faceted taxonomy behind it).

So here's how the checklist works:

- *Temporal extension.* Might visitors want to scroll backwards through the history of this domain, check previous versions, archives or timelines associated with the pertinent content? Might they want to scroll forward, and anticipate future events or draw up plans, e.g. calendars, templates, planning documents?

- *Representation extension.* What alternative ways of representing this content help you access, understand and use this content? Are there associated images, photographs, video or audio files that would help represent or amplify the content? Are there different points of view on the same domain that need to be represented?

- *Expertise extension.* Does this domain (or part of it) have more detailed specialist knowledge associated with it that should be linked here so that visitors can drill deeper if they need to, e.g. research papers, expertise directories, external specialist sites or subscription databases?

- *Agent extension.* What else might your visitors want to know about any people, groups or organisations represented in your pertinent content, e.g. profiles, directories, lists?

- *Spatial extension.* What else might your visitors want to know about any places and locations mentioned in your pertinent content? Might they want to look at adjacent locations or expand to a regional focus, e.g. maps, location profiles, directories?

- *Usage extension.* In what ways might visitors want to use your pertinent information? What might they want to do next? What actions can you facilitate, e.g. ranking, voting, commenting, making an application, beginning a workflow?

- *Relatedness extension.* What taxonomic categories will be associated with your pertinent content in the visitor's mind? What are likely related topics that they might be interested in? If your taxonomy doesn't tell you, analysis of search and browse patterns of visitors will start to suggest ideas for this.

- *Entity extension.* What else might your visitors want to know about the objects or things or parts of things that may be mentioned in your pertinent content, e.g. machines and machine parts, different types of the same thing, things that can be done with the objects or how they can be used?

This approach takes us a long way from the idea of the information factory/warehouse structured according to a taxonomy and powered by a search engine that we started this chapter with.

For a start, it requires a fairly intimate understanding of the knowledge and information needs and uses of our various constituencies. It requires an ability to identify and prioritise primary uses and contexts of use for information in our organisations for us to be able to plan and build neighbourhoods that work.

It doesn't mean that all the taxonomy and metadata work goes to waste. On the contrary, this work provides precisely the infrastructure that you will require as neighbourhood designers to locate and draw down the information assets you need to populate your respective domains of use.

The end of your journey is not your taxonomy, your metadata and thesaurus, and the warehouse full of content. Journey's end, and the proof of your effort, lies in the neighbourhoods where information gets applied and where the effectiveness of work gets enhanced.

From arrangement to accountability

If information architecture represents the Buffonian end of the ancient opposition between context and categorisation, records management represents the Linnaean end, and just as the information architect will regard you as an interfering conservative, so the records manager will look on you as a dangerous radical.

Records management is important because it is a body of management practices that, in theory at least, preserves and maintains access to a reliable memory of an organisation's activities. This is important for a whole host of reasons, among which are:

- enabling us to see the historical contexts of decisions;
- referring us to plans, designs and specifications that have material or management value for very long periods of time;
- finding out what we actually did in contrast to what we think we did;
- demonstrating to everybody's satisfaction what contracts and agreements we have entered into and what accountabilities we face;
- proving to the satisfaction of a court of law what we did or did not know and do at any particular point in time, and so on.

Records management is about accountability in the old fashioned sense, i.e. giving us the ability to render an account (together with satisfactory evidence) of our actions that is reliable and trustworthy. To do all that we need to process the special class of documents that are records in such a way that we can always retrieve them, so that we know that they are the 'original' unaltered records of the activities and decisions in question, and we need to be able to pull together the records related to any significant action or decision in such a way that we can give an account of the context surrounding that action or decision. We need a taxonomy (among other things), but a taxonomy that is focused on the special features of records and what 'reliable' memory means.

The definition of 'records' is disturbingly vague. The international standard for records management defines it as: 'information created, received, and maintained as evidence and information by an organisation or person, in pursuance of legal obligations or in the transaction of business' (AS ISO 15489.1-2002). It's hard to take that definition and immediately know which documents or datasets need to be managed as records.

Records management specialist Marita Keenan reports that a commonly accepted understanding in the profession is that 'in a business context a record is a by-product of the business transaction.' However, she points out that records may not simply comprise just the direct documentation of the transaction, but also associated documents that provide context to the primary records of that transaction. 'Staff need to think holistically and legalistically in deciding whether the business transaction has any risks connected with it, and hence requiring associated records to be captured into a recordkeeping system' (Keenan, 2006). For example, with the passage of time a given policy document may be difficult to understand without reconstructing the reasoning process involved in formulating that policy, accessed through drafts and minutes of discussions.

Another accessible rule of thumb might be that a record is any document or dataset that allows you to reliably reconstruct any significant action or decision you made in the past. This can be for internal management use or for external purposes, whether in dealing with partners or suppliers or demonstrating that you have met your legal responsibilities, and it encompasses the risk management aspects suggested by Marita Keenan. In some organisations you will also be working in areas that have historical significance, and so your records will at some point be destined for archival status.

This means, from your point of view as an enterprise taxonomist, that a significant part of the content covered by your taxonomy will likely be records. Whether you (or they) like it or not, sooner or later your taxonomy will bump up against the very special requirements of the records management function. Let's look at what that means.

I have used the word 'reliable' several times. Actually in records management, there is a cluster of four very precisely defined concepts that assure the trustworthiness of records over time, each of which has implications for specific records management practices and processes. Again in the slightly stilted language of the records management standard (AS ISO 15489.1-2002):

- *Reliability*. A reliable record is one whose contents can be trusted as a full and accurate representation of the transactions, activities or facts to which they attest and can be depended upon in the course of subsequent transactions or activities. Records should be created at the time of the transaction or incident to which they relate, or soon afterwards, by individuals who have direct knowledge of the facts or by instruments routinely used within the business to conduct the transaction.

- *Integrity*. The integrity of a record refers to its being complete and unaltered. It is necessary that a record be protected against unauthorised alteration. Records management policies and procedures should specify what additions or annotations may be made to a record after it is created, under what circumstances additions or annotations may be authorised, and who is authorised to make them. Any authorised annotation, addition or deletion to a record should be explicitly indicated and traceable.

- *Authenticity*. An authentic record is one that can be proven (a) to be what it purports to be, (b) to have been created or sent by the person purported to have created or sent it, and (c) to have been created or sent at the time purported. To ensure the authenticity of records, organisations should implement and document policies and procedures which control the creation, receipt, transmission, maintenance and disposition of records to ensure that records creators are authorised and identified and that records are protected against unauthorised addition, deletion, alteration, use and concealment.

- *Usability*. A usable record is one that can be located, retrieved, presented and interpreted. It should be capable of subsequent presentation as directly connected to the business activity or transaction that produced it. The contextual linkages of records should carry the information needed for an understanding of the transactions that created and used them. It should be possible to identify a record within the context of broader business activities and functions. The links between records that document a sequence of activities should be maintained.

Records management, even more than librarianship, has a reputation for being a somewhat solipsistic profession, not entirely adjusted to the ordinary needs of the here and now. This is surely partly conditioned by its unique requirement to be accountable to the future and not just the here and now. But when combined with a technical set of processes and rules there has evolved an ethos within the profession that says the 'ordinary user' cannot be entrusted with the sacred tasks associated with preserving the status of records. Records management processes should be undertaken by records management staff.

As the discipline has developed it has focused very much on providing the overriding ability to produce a record when required, especially when required by law. In the paper-based documentary environment this meant ensuring that records were captured quickly into the appropriate files, that files were organised in a structured way so that records staff could locate and retrieve them easily, and that the file movement was carefully controlled.

Hence, while we would expect records managers to be highly attuned to taxonomy work (to organise their records for effective retrieval), in practice what has happened is the opposite. In any given organisation, the number of people actively using the file classification structure *as a taxonomy* is very low (for most people the file reference number is just a number and has no navigational value). Any record-keeping taxonomy that is not exposed to the working needs of a large audience is in great danger of reflecting the very narrow needs of records administrators.

And this is what seems to have happened. Stuart Orr, when studying the use of functions-based classification schemes among organisations in the UK, Canada and Australia, found varying and inconsistent understandings of classification, classification principles and the construction and use of thesauri. While records management theory had relatively sophisticated guidance on the principles according to which records should be classified, in practice records offices diverged considerably and were often hostage to historically accreted schemes.

Despite the rising influence of functional or business activity based classification approaches through the 1990s, interpretations of how this should be done varied considerably, and other classification principles such as organisation structure, record type or record topic were just as common. Orr concluded: 'The understanding of classification in records management has not been as well developed as in library science' (Orr, 2005: 110).

And while 'usability' is one of the four fundamental attributes of a trustworthy record, this does not mean 'usability' in the everyday sense. Records offices have routinely sacrificed ease of use *now* for assuring proper control of the records by properly authorised staff. This worked with varying effectiveness in a paper-based environment, but as a profession, records management has made a poor transition to the high-speed digital environment of multiple electronic copies of every document, decision turnaround times that have accelerated from weeks to minutes, and to transactions by e-mail and instant message that are never captured within records systems. There are notable exceptions to this statement and there are progressive records managers and organisations, but the profession as a whole has done a poor job of adjusting consistently.

Records offices that have existed for years as file processing and file movement logistics departments are poorly equipped to deal with their underlying role – assuring reliable organisational memory of key actions, transactions and decisions, whether expressed on paper or otherwise (it's now mostly otherwise). The speed and volume of information transactions are now simply too much to manage if the records management staff are the sole records processors, so increasingly, reluctantly, but painfully slowly, record-keeping functions are being devolved to the producers and consumers of records – who, unfortunately, frequently have more of a commitment to the now than to the future (McMullin, 2004).

Specifically, in relation to taxonomy work, the profession's limited experience with taxonomy work for large and diverse audiences has resulted in two major (from this book's perspective) mistakes. First, although faceted taxonomy design and the use of metadata are occasionally given polite nods in the literature, it does not seem to be generally understood in practice. Experienced records managers still say, in the words of one recent contributor to a forum, 'in a business classification scheme there should be only one place for a record to be located.' A business classification scheme (BCS) is a common term for the master taxonomy that records managers use to generate their file classification structure – called variously a file plan, a file schema, a records classification plan, and so on.

This commitment to hierarchy has resulted in tree structure record-keeping taxonomies that require extraordinary investments in familiarity – rote learning – to navigate. Orr, for example, found in his study that 12 out of 15 of the practitioners in his sample had more than ten categories at the top level of their taxonomy. One respondent had over two hundred. Eight out of 20 respondents had five or more levels in their taxonomy. Two had nine or more levels which by my calculation would give them a capacity for 38 billion records (Orr, 2005: 99–100).

The second major mistake is the frequent adoption of a 'top-down' approach to taxonomy development. Where record-keeping taxonomies have been developed based on business functions and activities, most records management experts told Orr that a top-down approach working from the mission and objectives of the organisation downwards was the most effective way to build the scheme. Some said that it should be supplemented by checking with users, and there are documented cases of systems and process mapping approaches such as we have described in this book. But over 80 per cent of Orr's expert panel agreed that the top-down analytical approach was the most effective (Orr, 2005: 78–80). In fact, two widely influential approaches to record-keeping classification scheme design, the Australian DIRKs methodology and the British BCS methodology, embed top-down analytical approaches as an explicit part of their guidance (NAA, 2003; National Archives, 2003).

This approach directly contradicts the central thesis of this book, which argues that any taxonomy with a hope of being effective must be grounded in – and built from – the working language of its user population. The issue for us is that the records management approach seems to be still organisation-and-record-centric first and user-centric second.

Small wonder then that the functional classification schemes built on this principle throughout the 1990s seem to have met with considerable user resistance (Orr, 2005: 12; Robertson, 2004). Tina Calabria documented an electronic records management project in a city council in Australia and found that one in two users routinely failed to identify the correct top-level category for their document and found great difficulty in distinguishing between functions. The search terms created by the user population were altogether different from the taxonomy terms, and – perhaps most embarrassing of all – the records managers performed little better than 'normal' users (Calabria, 2004). An emerging trend in records management systems is to provide for two separate metadata fields, one for record-keeping purposes and one for user retrieval purposes – as if the needs of the two parties are permanently irreconcilable (Keenan, 2006).

The problem with you as a taxonomist is that, to the extent that your taxonomy includes items of content that are records, then to that extent you will sooner or later come up against the accountability issues served by records management. This will have implications for your metadata framework, but also directly for your taxonomy, because you may be compelled to use alien categories associated with the organisation's records classification scheme – to which access permissions and retention and disposal rules are all attached. The records classification scheme performs a record control function that cannot be ignored or jettisoned.

Your risk is compounded by the fact that in many organisations the records management function is not highly visible or proactive. The realisation that there are factors you should have considered may well ambush you after your implementation has started. In some cases, records management processes may be lax until your organisation encounters business or regulatory risks associated with its record-keeping (e.g. contract disputes, litigation, official investigations and inquiries, enforcement of regulations such as Sarbanes-Oxley, accreditation in standards such as ISO 9001). The risk of a late ambush is high.

You are likely to face several educational and change management challenges in dealing with these risks because, as we have seen, the records management function, despite good intentions, is on the whole not oriented towards user-centred taxonomy development. The records manager is going to worry much more about whether or not any given record can be produced in a (legally) trustworthy fashion together with all its associated documentation, consistently and reliably every time than about whether Jack down the hall can find readily to hand the piece of information he needs right now to pass on to a customer.

And unlike most of the managers and employees you will deal with, the records manager *thinks* he knows what a taxonomy is. It's called a file plan or a records classification scheme, and the fact that it may follow no consistent taxonomic principles, is not intuitive and almost impossible to use unless you learn it through constant use is not relevant to the purpose, which is to provide a unique pigeonhole with a file reference number for every record that is created. Period.

This is not to say that your goals are at odds with theirs. There is in principle no reason why a faceted taxonomy, especially if it contains a facet that catalogues all the key business activities, should not serve a valid records management function as well. But this facet needs to be integrated (via metadata) with your records control functions that govern retention, disposal and access. This is why in the planning phase we suggested that the records management function be included on your governance committee.

The real challenge is in bridging the psychological distance that many records management practitioners have from the concepts and ideas expressed by the versatile and adaptive information architect. Your role, as the taxonomist, lies between these two poles, servicing arrangements for ready use and simultaneously assuring reliable access over time together with preservation of the key characteristics of a record.

If this presentation of the challenges posed by records management issues seems somewhat jaundiced, it is only because such sharply drawn lines do exist in many organisations, and because taking a stark view will bring the important issues sharply into the foreground. There are also organisations where these issues are recognised and approached in a manner which combines present usability with future accountability, where records managers work with information architects and where taxonomy work supports both. It would be prudent to belong to that class.

It should by now be obvious to you that the taxonomist's task is largely a thankless one from the perspective of the general population. Our role in an organisation is deep in the information and knowledge infrastructure where, if it works, we will not be seen and other actors closer to the outcomes of a good taxonomy (such as information architects and records managers) will take the credit that is due.

Especially when serving the needs of *structure and organise*, *building common ground* and *boundary spanning*, the more visible we are, the less we are really doing our job. As taxonomy processes become more important than taxonomy products, from *sense-making* to *discovery*, we emerge with tools and activities that help people do what they need to do. But we are still enablers rather than primary actors. It's wise to remember this, lest our taxonomic pirouettes distract our clients from what it was they set out to do in the first place – to achieve their objectives, meet their goals, avoid business risk, find new opportunities and improve their effectiveness.

Step 12: Secure the governance process

We have almost reached the end of our journey. In the planning phase of your project you established your governance mechanism, a body of managers representing several key stakeholders (including the records management function). You will have leveraged this group to secure access to the people and domains that you needed to explore, and you will have involved them in the design, validation, communications and change management activities.

Now, post launch, they shift into a new phase. You will have an administrative team that works through whatever technology platform you have selected to maintain your taxonomy, thesaurus, controlled vocabulary lists and metadata framework on a day-to-day basis. Your governance body now becomes a review board, whose responsibility is to ensure the continued relevance and usefulness of your taxonomy.

It's a good idea to perform a systematic review of your taxonomy within six months of implementation, and annually thereafter. This should be guided by the nine criteria (and tests) for an effective taxonomy listed earlier in Chapter 8, and can comprise the following activities:

1. *Collection and analysis of reactive feedback* – analysis of search logs, association of search behaviour with document retrieval, issues and help desk logs.

2. *Collection and analysis of proactive feedback* – surveys, interviews, focus groups, covering quality issues with metadata and categorisation, overall user satisfaction with findability, difficulties with categorisation, suggestions for improvement.

3. *Analysis of content collection* – the evenness of distribution of content across the taxonomy, evidence of categories that are being used as miscellaneous 'catch-alls' because more precise categories are missing, areas of content that are obviously missing from the collection.

4. *Anticipation of business needs* – assessing whether new categories are required to reflect changing activities or knowledge domains, or whether the needs served by the taxonomy are changing (e.g. shifting from boundary-spanning to sense-making needs, or supporting new infrastructural developments).

5. *Structured taxonomy tests* – controlled categorisation or search scenario exercises with sample groups of users to investigate potential issues in greater detail (these issues will be picked up in the steps above).

In all cases, taxonomy change decisions follow the same basic cycle as our initial development process.

- Check the needs and the purpose against stakeholders.
- Plan the most appropriate approach.
- Gather evidence.
- Propose changes.
- Test and validate on a small scale.
- Implement.

In this chapter we covered the processes and challenges inherent in taxonomy implementation. This involves not just the technical implementation issues via thesauruses, technology platforms and metadata, but also the political and pragmatic implementation issues that determine whether or not your taxonomy becomes a useful, living part of your knowledge and information infrastructure.

But what of emerging trends in web technologies, artificial intelligence and social computing? Are the days of the taxonomist numbered? To answer this question we turn to our final chapter.

10

The future of taxonomy work

The reality of life is that order does not survive the advance of time, context confuses categories, and an excessive adherence to structure can prevent new opportunities being seized.

(Snowden, 2005)

There are people who say that the days of structured taxonomies are numbered. There are people who rail in public against the 'industrial age command and control' 'dinosaur' mentality (passion often mixes metaphors) that seeks to structure the management of knowledge and information assets through centrally controlled, designed taxonomies. These people believe passionately that emergent patterns based on individual tagging behaviours will replace structured taxonomy work. Democratic tagging will replace totalitarian taxonomies. Let's call these people the *folksonomists*.

There are other people who also claim that the day of the taxonomy is done. But these people believe that taxonomies do not go far enough to exploit the power of computers to structure and organise information. Why, they ask, should we allow our technical ability to model knowledge to be constrained by the fallible and primitive human capacities of attention, discrimination and cognitive grasp such as we outlined in Chapter 8? Computers can pay attention to far more things, recover them with perfect recall and navigate domains on a much wider scale, infinitely faster, without error. People suck, computers rule. This camp we'll call the camp of the *ontologists*.

I'm guessing, if you have read this far, that you are not completely in either camp, but it's worth finding out why each, for very different reasons, thinks that taxonomy work is passé, and why each is only partly right. If nothing else, the arguments of the folksonomists and the ontologists will likely bounce your way, and so there's value in seeing first what they are talking about, and second where they sit in relation to taxonomy work – not as replacements, but as complementary strategies for specific sets of goals and circumstances. Let's start with the ontologists.

Ontologies and machine intelligence

There's an inherent difficulty simply in the use of the word *ontology*, because it has two very different senses depending on your background and discipline. For anyone who has studied philosophy, ontology means the study of *being* or existence. It is contrasted with epistemology (theory of meaning or knowledge). So ontology is about *thingness* and *things*.

Computer science has a habit of adopting terms from elsewhere and giving them quite different, technical meanings, and the same has happened with the word ontology. Here, the word ontology is used to denote a data model that describes a set of concepts and their relations to each other. It is partly about the things/concepts in the universe of the model, but also about the relationships between the concepts in that model.

It is this sense of ontology that is meant when ontologists challenge the continuing relevance of taxonomies. An ontology is like a much more advanced and flexible thesaurus. It has the same tripartite structure:

Concept A – *relationship* – Concept B

Unlike a thesaurus, an ontology is not limited to three types of relationship (broader term, narrower term, related term). The relationship between two concepts in an ontology can be of any kind, such as 'is a part of', 'is an instance of', 'is a type of', 'is a product of' and so on.

In this sense it's much smarter than a thesaurus or even a tree structure taxonomy, because it can specify the exact nature of the relationship between the two concepts being described. Partly for that reason, but also because ontologies are designed more for machines than humans, they are much more complex than taxonomies or thesauri. Any concept can have any relationships (within the set of relationship types specified by the ontology language) with any other concepts. So an ontology is like a dense network of interconnected concepts, expressing a wide range of relationships. This is what makes it fundamentally different from a taxonomy, because while it fulfils two of the conditions for a taxonomy (connecting related things and semantic expression) it does not fulfil the third condition, which is to map the structure of a domain in a way that is easy to grasp and navigate.

Ontologies, in fact, pride themselves on their precision, and their impenetrability to humans. They are designed as sets of rules and languages that enable the diverse data and information sets of different computer systems to be handled as if they were inhabitants of the same system.

At one level they work as translation engines, mapping diverse vocabularies to a common set of concepts; at another they work as a set of rules that describe the relationships between concepts, thus allowing sophisticated manipulation of information, aggregation of information from different sources, pattern analysis and fairly smart inferences from vast quantities of data that ordinary humans would not be able to handle.

Now obviously this can be very useful in environments where there is a lot to be gained from manipulating large and diverse collections of content, but there are significant costs involved in developing and deploying ontologies.

One cost is simply the effort involved in mapping the concepts and relationship rules that make sense for the possible uses the ontology will serve. This will to some degree parallel the activities involved in building a taxonomy, but at a much larger scale which must involve sampling rather than true mapping and often requires much more intensive intervention by a range of subject-matter experts.

A second cost is that ontologies are very insensitive to naturally occurring ambiguity – i.e. when it is not humanly possible to disambiguate concepts. They work on very precisely specified rules about relationships between concepts, and when their target content moves outside technical domains where precision is relatively high into fuzzy domains of guesswork, human relations and social collaboration, the natural ambiguity of the target content inevitably does not get accommodated within the ontology and must be resolved to something that may be a poor representation of the original. Because an ontology typically operates at a level that is not amenable to human supervision, such ambiguity effects and the resulting margins of error are very difficult to detect and assess.

So ontologies have both strengths and weaknesses. Do they compete with taxonomies? Well, not really. A taxonomy is primarily a device that supports – and depends on – the cognitive abilities of a human being to discriminate and navigate a knowledge domain. An ontology is a device that supports computers in manipulating the knowledge and information resident in large content collections, for specific purposes, with an efficiency and speed that would not be possible for humans. It usually needs taxonomies to help it build its data models and rules, and it must deliver up comprehensible results to its human clients, often through a taxonomy representation.

For this reason, ontologies start to become useful where you have multiple collections of content designed for very different purposes, with multiple taxonomies serving them and their user communities, but where you also want to exploit the content on a wider scale than simply within their own individual platforms.

Let's now turn our attention to the camp of the folksonomists. From the taxonomist's point of view this is a more difficult challenge to unravel, because (1) folksonomies are a much more recent phenomenon and have not yet settled into a mature pattern of use; and (2) because there are several different things going on when people use folksonomies and talk about social tagging, and it's not always easy to disentangle them.

Folksonomies and rich serendipity

The term 'folksonomy' was coined in late July 2004 by Thomas Vander Wal in an online discussion forum devoted to information architecture (Smith, 2004). It proved a catchy term for describing the phenomenon of social tagging, otherwise known as social classification (Smith, 2004), ethnoclassification (Merholz, 2004), tagsonomies (*www.tagsonomy.com*) and social categorisation (Mathes, 2004). Before we get down to strict definitions of what all this means (definitions are always problematic, especially when so many different terms are being used to describe the same phenomenon), let's take a look at what these people were trying to describe.

In the early 2000s, a large number of 'social' websites and businesses blossomed across the Web. Some of these were self-profiling and social networking sites aimed at different target groups such as LinkedIn (*www.linkedin.com*), MySpace (*www.myspace.com*) and Facebook (*www.facebook.com*).

Others grew out of the peer-to-peer filesharing movement started by

Napster and others, and focused on the sharing of resources and content online. Two of the most famous are Delicious (*http://del.icio.us*) for storing and sharing interesting URLs and Flickr (*www.flickr.com*) for storing and sharing photographs. The characteristics of these sites, which developed very large amounts of rich content very quickly, is that the content is created by the visitors to the sites, it is described in tags that are the user's own choice of words, and it is owned by them rather than by the hosts of the site. The content, though contributed for motives that are individualistic (self-profiling, finding connections, easy ways to store photos and URLs), also has social and collaborative spinoffs. If I let other people see my Flickr photos, I get to see theirs. There are rich payoffs for very little personal cost.

The balance between selfish and social motives can change. Other sites, such as the video sharing site Youtube (*www.youtube.com*), are often more about social display than personal content organisation. Yet others, such as the monstrous Wikipedia project (*www.wikipedia.org*), are much more overtly social and collaborative, where the content is painstakingly negotiated by thousands of volunteers. Individual 'ownership' of content does not exist on Wikipedia, but your 'selfish' payoff is your reputation among the inner circle of contributors, editors and authors, and your satisfaction in having put your own stamp on the biggest encyclopedia in history.

What all these sites have in common is the rapid growth of very rich, diverse content collections, contributed by millions of individuals working to a mixture of selfish and social motives, with no centralised controlling mechanism to govern their arrangement or classification. Enter tagging.

In the absence of designed arrangements, the most obvious way to enhance retrieval of content for users (remember, sites such as Delicious and Flickr function as personal storage sites) in a web environment is through description or keyword tagging. This is completely uncontrolled, so if I store some particularly useful knowledge management sites on Delicious I might use generalised terms such as 'knowledgemanagement', 'km', 'mykm', 'plkm', or more specific terms such as 'ksharing', 'taxonomy', 'knowledgeaudit' and so on (only single word tags are allowed). My tags can be publicly comprehensible or very individualistic, they can be highly ambiguous or very precise, very general, or very, very specific.

What makes this tagging activity different from 'free text' keywords entered into optional metadata fields by publishers of content into content management systems? The difference is that in closed content management systems, the 'free text' keywords usually sit unobserved behind the scenes, waiting for a search engine to match them to a search term. In the sites we've described, the tags are exposed to everybody and they become social property. I can do a random search on Delicious or Flickr and find a piece of content I like. I can see the tags and chase those to find other items tagged by the same person with that tag or items tagged by other people using the same tag. If I have permission, I can tag their content with my own tags. If I want my items to come up in the same searches as other people's items that I like, I'll adopt and use their tags.

Socially exposing the tags has some interesting effects, and this is where Thomas Vander Wal's definition of a 'folksonomy' comes into play.

> There [is] tremendous value that can be derived from this personal tagging when viewing it as a collective when you have the three needed data points in a folksonomy tool: 1) the person tagging; 2) the object being tagged as its own entity; and 3) the tag being used on that object ... keeping the three data elements you can use two of the elements to find a third element, which has value. If you know the object (in del.icio.us it is the web page being tagged) and the tag you can find other individuals who use the same tag on that object, which may lead (if a little more investigation) to somebody who has the same interest and vocabulary as you do. That person can become a filter for items on which they use that tag. (Vander Wal, 2005)

If we look at the trail I described from a random keyword search to an object I liked to the tags used on that object to other objects using the same tag, the trail looks like random serendipity (see Figure 10.1). But web searches and hyperlink trails also follow random serendipity, so it's hard to explain the explosion of enthusiasm around social tagging – not an explosion of theoretical interest, but of actual use, implying usefulness. This type of serendipity seems different, more valuable.

The triad of elements that Vander Wal describes in folksonomies (socially exposed personal tagging) seems to hold the key, and the real key is the element in the triad that most observers (especially taxonomists) miss. The really interesting part of a folksonomy is not the content item being described and not the tags that describe the item, but *the person doing the tagging.*

Figure 10.1   Person-mediated serendipity trails in folksonomies

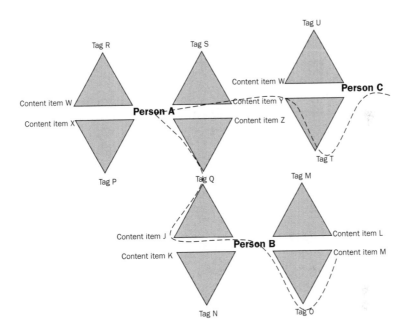

Most taxonomists assume (not incorrectly) that the useful categorisation of content requires the intellectual analysis of that content's subject matter according to the predefined structure of the taxonomy. So the taxonomy itself is an overarching organising framework. But this involves a fairly high cognitive cost in formal categorisation, not to mention possible anxiety over accuracy and precision in using somebody else's categorisation structures and systems (Sinha, 2005; McMullin, 2004).

What Vander Wal realised is that socially exposed tagging for personal use introduces another organising agent that compensates for the ambiguity of its vocabulary with high-value serendipity: *people*. We are much better at picking up information and knowledge cues based on perceived similarities and differences compared to other people than we are at picking up clues from a people-free environment. If people-free environments give us weak serendipity, person-mediated serendipity is much richer.

People are a useful organising agent because they are natural knowledge attractors and aggregators of meaning. People habitually collect and arrange for themselves what Vander Wal calls 'personal infoclouds' and these arrangements reflect a meaningful perspective on knowledge (Vander Wal, 2006). Like the seventeenth-century scientists with their cabinets of curiosities, we all collect – and arrange around us – things that we find interesting and useful. And when we tag them publicly and make the tagged content accessible publicly, we are revealing aspects of our sense-making activity and our information and knowledge landscapes.

Now some of that landscape is shaped, contoured and described in highly individualistic, private, inaccessible ways (the Babel Instinct at work). But other parts are more publicly accessible and will resonate with the interests, common activities and needs of other people. We can learn from other people's structured or semi-structured infoclouds, and as Figure 10.1 shows, we don't need to invest the high cognitive cost of analysis and matching to a predefined structure to do so. I tag for myself, you learn.

I can click on a tag that both you and I used, and it will show me content that has been attached to that tag by anyone, including you and I. If I notice that several content items of interest come from the same few people, I can go look for their personal infoclouds. I can learn their vocabularies and adopt or adapt them if I find them useful. In so doing, I am also exposing my content to them. What we have, effectively, is emergent and naturalistic common-ground and boundary-spanning work going on at the micro, personal level.

Despite the early enthusiasm for folksonomies, there are some heavy costs and constraints built in, however. Rich serendipity requires very large volumes of content and a large, diverse contributing population. With smaller and less diverse volumes of content, and smaller contributing populations, the serendipity payoff weakens, because fewer concentrations of like-interests are possible. Think of the difference between a village and a city in terms of giving access to deep, similar, highly personalised interests.

The cognitive ease of using our own personal categorisation vocabularies (and those that we decide to adopt or adapt from the resonant personal infoclouds of others) and the lack of vocabulary control is a benefit. But this is matched by very high ambiguity in the collective vocabulary of the shared resource and very low precision amounting to meaninglessness in many cases (Mathes, 2004). In October 2006, for example, there were 770,000 photographs hosted on *www.flickr.com* tagged with the word 'me'. This, along with other self-referential tags, are only useful within the personal collections of members and not in the common language space.

Enhancing usefulness in folksonomies

Although the words 'folksonomy' and 'tagsonomy' are a deliberate play on the word *taxonomy*, these shared tagging vocabularies do not have the structures or relationships between terms that a taxonomy brings. They describe a domain, but do not also map it as a taxonomy does. For the first few years, this lack of formal structure was highly touted as a feature of the emergent, 'bottom-up' approach to categorisation. Slowly, however, the 'flat namespace' of social tagging has been evolving different strategies to reduce ambiguity, enhance consistency and create meaningful and useful patterns for its users.

One such strategy is the use of 'tag clouds' to indicate which are the most popular tags. In a tag cloud, the font size of the tag gets larger the more often it is used, so by glancing at a cloud, you will immediately notice the most prominent tags. This works as a feedback device to encourage users to reuse common tags rather than invent non-common personalised ones (Mathes, 2004).

In Wikipedia, an early strategy was to create 'disambiguation pages' which would act as a signpost whenever ambiguous search terms were used that might refer to several different concepts and pages – the page effectively offers scope notes and links to each of the possible destinations.

Relationships between tags can also be inferred using algorithms based on emergent characteristics of the content and user behaviours around it. For example, tags that are frequently assigned together to content objects can have a relationship inferred, and a search engine can suggest possible items based on those inferred associations. This effectively performs a very similar function to a thesaurus, except that the relationships are inferred automatically and continuously as the tagging of content progresses. Flickr, for example, has introduced a 'clusters' feature that allows you to explore the frequently collocated tags for any given tag. Delicious presents a 'related tags' column whenever you browse the results on a particular tag.

There are more complex algorithms to enhance the richness of retrieval. Flickr uses an 'interestingness' algorithm based on a combination of factors such as click-through intensity, comments, ratings, being posted to favourites, and so on. Amazon suggests books that you might be interested in based on your buying patterns combined with the buying patterns of other people who bought the same books as you.

And yes, structures that look suspiciously like taxonomic structures are starting to creep into the social tagging space. Flickr has introduced a geographic location feature which works exactly like a location facet of a taxonomy. Technorati (*www.technorati.com*), which tracks millions of weblogs, uses a very broad set of categories for weblogs (e.g. Business, Entertainment, Technology) in parallel with its tags. RawSugar (*www.rawsugar.com*), a company that provides tagging and searching software, has gone one step further. It allows you to specify parent–child relationships between tags, and presents its tag sets to the user in a two-level hierarchy. If you don't suggest a hierarchy yourself, then when you synchronise your site with RawSugar, it will suggest a hierarchy based on other users' aggregated decisions (which you can change).

Meefedia (*www.meefedia.org*) merges social classification with facets. The editors determine a set of core facets and when users assign tags they assign them to a facet. The content can then be browsed via facets, which immediately reduces much of the ambiguity of a flat namespace. However, large volumes of content start to beg the question of hierarchies within facets to enhance findability and reduce ambiguity and imprecision further (Quintarelli, 2006a).

We can understand why taxonomic structures might start to look attractive. While the flat folksonomy may work well while a content collection is growing (and its ease of use fuels the growth), once a collection starts to mature, people quickly realise that even rich serendipity can be improved. Mature collections cannot be leveraged and exploited systematically without more predictable mechanisms for mapping and navigating the content, and as collections mature, their users become more aware of the potential for exploitation that would come from having more precise finding and navigation aids. So as I write this chapter in late 2006, there is considerable experimental work going on with hybrid folksonomy/taxonomy approaches to achieve this goal. Emmanuele Quintarelli, an active researcher and advocate in this area, believes that social tagging is still in its infancy and that while 'we have early examples of advanced folksonomies usage … the better tools will smoothly mix social tagging, taxonomies and faceted classification in a transparent way for final users to change the way we access information online' (Quintarelli, 2006b).

One approach, proposed by Tom Coates from his experience of social tagging at the BBC, is to aggregate tag clusters based on implicit taxonomic structures surrounding the content being tagged. For example, when radio listeners tag songs, clusters of tags can be aggregated at the radio show level or at the network level. The clusters of most common tags from songs could therefore be used to characterise the flavour of music from the network or the show respectively.

The concept could be extended within organisations to aggregate tags assigned by users at the document level to characterise the knowledge assets at department and division levels. This is an emergent vocabulary grafted onto an implicit external taxonomy (Coates, 2005). Primitive instances of this can be seen already on social networking sites such as imeem (*www.imeem.com*) where you can see the most popular current tags used by each interest group and thereby get a sense of what they are talking about.

Now this doesn't really give you a taxonomy structure. The tags are simply grafted onto an external taxonomy structure and function like descriptive scope notes. They therefore will not give any navigational support as a taxonomy would. Their only merit is that they emerge from common vocabulary used about the domain in question and so represent user perspectives. However, the higher up the tree you go, the less directly relevant to the domain they are – because they are generated from the concrete instances at the bottom nodes of the tree (the song or document) and then aggregated upwards.

Some organisations recognise that social or collaborative tagging gives unique and always current insight into the working vocabularies and basic-level categories of their user population, so they use tagging as a mechanism to collect these vocabularies which they then feed into their controlled vocabularies and taxonomy updating via a thesaurus. For example, Raytheon, a global defence and aerospace systems supplier, has been encouraging free user tagging when its employees make suggestions for useful website links in Raytheon's intranet. The tags are vetted by the corporate librarians and incorporated into the thesaurus wherever they are found to be useful. Often they give much greater insight into the specialised languages of experts that the corporate librarians would not otherwise have encountered except through structured mapping activities such as we have discussed earlier in this book. Christine Connors reported in March 2006:

> These tags are a fantastic resource – users warrant – for keeping the controlled vocabularies up-to-date. They provide us feedback we could get no other way. Given the ease with which people can tag things – and yes, we could argue about whether there should be some cognitive burden for quality's sake – we gain a unique insight via this process. (TaxoCoP, 2006)

Similar efforts have been under way at IBM, this time associated with employee blogging on the intranet (Gibson, 2005a). Actively mapping the tagging vocabularies of different user communities to the corporate language embedded in the official taxonomies and thesauri can be a conscious attempt to break down knowledge silos and build common ground (Gibson, 2005b).

Again, however, this is a somewhat partial approach. The purpose behind the social tagging efforts at Raytheon and IBM (and in the BBC case study we covered in Chapter 9) is not really exploiting the rich serendipity afforded by a folksonomy, i.e. by socially exposing the people, the tags and the content in the way that Vander Wal described. However, making the social tagging easily available within weblogs or in a website suggestion function does help to solve one of the problems of the formal taxonomist, which is staying abreast of the vocabularies and basic-level categories of their user communities – especially important in large distributed organisations in businesses that undergo rapid and constant change. This is the 'pace layering' approach advocated by Campbell and Fast and Peter Morville, where social tagging is deployed as a faster-moving vocabulary layer to reflect current emergent thinking and is used to inform the slower-moving information architecture and taxonomy layers that reflect more stable knowledge and information domains (Morville, 2005: 140–1; Campbell and Fast, 2006). But although the two approaches are being connected, social tagging is being used essentially as a vocabulary collection and updating device rather than a folksonomic discovery device – i.e. it is the servant of the slower taxonomy layer and not a complementary tool in its own right.

Wikipedia takes an approach that has some similarities to RawSugar (i.e. user-generated tags which then have relationships added to them) but is far more flexible. Contributors to articles can create and assign 'categories', using a [[Category: xyz]] tag while editing an article. So far, this is just like collaborative tagging. The key difference in Wikipedia is that categories can also be assigned to other categories, as parents or children, creating the possibility of tree structures. They can also be assigned to multiple categories, resulting in a polyhierarchy rather than a single tree. Like a thesaurus (and unlike RawSugar) related terms can also be linked laterally using pointers from one category page to another (Voss, 2006).

Unlike a traditional thesaurus, however, the Wikipedia category system is not derived from the controlled vocabulary of a predefined taxonomy. As distinct from a designed thesaurus, it is an organic, emergent thesaurus, where categories are related to each other and tied into the category structures after being created. And like the Raytheon example, although the categories are user-generated, the social navigation of tag 'owners' is not possible – the folksonomy triad of content-tag-person is not available for use.

Taxonomies vs folksonomies?

It's worth stepping back a little at this stage and trying to figure out what kind of productive relationship folksonomies can have with taxonomy work, apart from just acting as raw material for user-warranted vocabularies. Folksonomies don't grow because they serve that function for the taxonomists, they grow because they provide socially mediated rich serendipity for the general user in addition to being a personal, individualistic retrieval tool. From that point of view, folksonomies represent and honour the Babel Instinct in all of us. The Raytheon example, and the attempts we have seen to introduce taxonomy-like structures into folksonomies, all fail to transfer the benefits of structure (predictable navigation of a domain) while retaining the rich person-mediated serendipity of the folksonomy. It seems you can only get the one or the other.

To frame this issue in a slightly different way, we might usefully consider a distinction between 'high-context' environments and 'low-context' environments, originally made by the anthropologist Edward T. Hall in the 1970s.

In 'high-context' organisation systems the meaning of things is embedded implicitly in the culture, processes and habits of the organisation. To figure out what's going on, you have to be educated into the original contexts or principles of ordering in order to be able to navigate the environment successfully. A classic example of a high-context culture is that of the Japanese, where a large number of the rules of social etiquette are left unspoken and it takes considerable time to be inculturated and to be able to interpret what's going on around you.

In 'low-context' organisation systems, meaning is explicit and is self-evident as soon as you get into the environment. American culture is (relative to Japan) very low-context, where the rules of the game tend to be very explicit and self-evident and where social transactions based on publicly available information are relatively easy (Hall, 1976).

Translated to the taxonomy domain, folksonomies tend to work as very high-context environments. Tags are directly related to the contexts of use of the people who contribute content, and they are most meaningful to the contributors themselves and progressively lose meaning for other people to the extent that their contexts and perspectives differ.

In Chapter 3 I described an exercise we sometimes do in taxonomy workshops where we ask participants to collect all the different ways they organise their music CDs. So far I think we're up to 20 different ways, including one guy who organised his music in order of the girlfriend he was going out with at the time he bought it. That's also what I'd call a high-context approach, obviously not self-evident to the general user (in fact, there's probably a postmodernist Casanova movie idea in there somewhere).

But formal taxonomic systems can also be high-context and can still work quite well – specialised engineering or scientific taxonomies, for example, where users can tolerate deep and specialised taxonomic hierarchies because they have been educated into them or have built up significant familiarity with them.

This issue of idiosyncratic or high-context taxonomies isn't new. The bookish eighteenth-century US president Thomas Jefferson (who reconstituted the Library of Congress with his personal collection after the British destroyed the original library) compiled reading lists for law students organised by the time of day that they should be read, on the principle that the mind has different energy levels at different times: Religion, Ethics and Law in the morning, Politics and History in the afternoon, and Literature in the evening (Wilson, 1996: 34–5). Without knowing these assumptions about energy levels, the classification is difficult to comprehend and predict.

Jefferson also built less high-context taxonomies. In fact he was a prodigious taxonomist: the classification schemes he devised for his own personal library, the congressional library, the University of Virginia and the College of William and Mary were so diverse 'that they might well have been the products of different minds' (Wilson, 1996: 42). Jefferson was an ardent foe of the Comte de Buffon on a number of fronts, but he displayed the same pragmatic taxonomist's insight into the need for different arrangements for different needs, and some of those arrangements were decidedly high-context.

While folksonomies and some taxonomies can both be high-context, folksonomies tend to be more impenetrable, especially at low volumes of content, because they represent aggregates of several personal contexts which may be very diverse and idiosyncratic. The 'me', 'here' and 'mybooks' tags represent a higher proportion of the whole in small-volume collections. Jess McMullin has suggested that folksonomies represent 'a low-investment bridge between personal classification and shared classification' (McMullin, 2004) and it is true that at least at high volumes, with lots of visible feedback about how other people are tagging, idiosyncrasy is diminished and clear and meaningful patterns about those contributing contexts can emerge – indeed this is what provides the rich serendipity trails that we have discussed. But at low volumes, and in the absence of strong feedback on tagging patterns, multiple personal tagging habits can be more confusing than single personal systems.

By contrast, a taxonomy that is high-context tends to represent the context of a single, distinct homogeneous community and so is theoretically much easier to interpret and read if you learn the background context and have sustained access to the knowledge community, even where there are fairly low volumes of content.

If a taxonomy needs to serve a boundary-spanning purpose in any way, then it needs to become much more publicly accessible and low-context. Ramana Rao puts it most eloquently when speaking about information architecture:

> Use the 'grain of the wood'. Information has inherent structure, a grain. Trees, tables, time, documents, calendars, these are the spines that organise information. By designing tools based on such canonical information structures, they become potentially applicable in a wide range of situations. (Wurman, 2001: 167)

Rao could easily be describing low-context taxonomies when he refers to 'canonical information structures' – take one look, and pretty much everyone will know how they work and how they can be navigated. Unless working for a very specialised and closed community, much of the corporate taxonomist's work, as we've seen in previous chapters, must be in discovering the shape of these canonical information structures within an enterprise and shaping their taxonomies around them.

So on balance the aggregated high contexts of the folksonomy do seem to be opposed to the dynamics of coordination, collaboration and common language served by taxonomies. To a degree, as we have seen, at high volumes of activity and content, and with strong feedback on tagging activity, tagging patterns can emerge that influence the formation of something like common ground, but this is a much less certain outcome than in a structured taxonomy exercise.

This can be qualified slightly. As we noted earlier, and as Clay Shirky observed so accurately at the birth of the social tagging boom, the hierarchical taxonomy works fine on small-content collections but becomes increasingly unwieldy as the scale of content and community amplifies. Social tagging, on the other hand, amplifies ambiguity and confusion on small scales, but produces beneficial patterns to support rich serendipity at very large scales with diverse content collections and with diverse user communities (Shirky, 2005).

This suggests that folksonomies and taxonomies deliver their benefits in different ways and in different types of situation, and that they can often coexist fruitfully as alternative and complementary aspects of knowledge and information infrastructure. As Emmanuele Quintarelli puts it:

> Folksonomies are not the solution to every modern problem of classification and they are not alternative to the traditional classification schemes librarians have designed over the years. They are more simply a powerful and innovative tool that should be applied only under the right circumstances and considering their own specific properties and the differences in respect to other classification schemes as taxonomies and faceted classification. (Quintarelli, 2005)

When content collections and user communities are small, well defined or relatively homogeneous then formal taxonomic structures supporting well defined user needs are likely to deliver most value; as communities and content collections grow in scale and diversity, and as the value of rich serendipity grows, then social tagging as a functionality – in particular the folksonomic person-mediated serendipity scent trails it provides – becomes more valuable as a complement to increasingly strained formal navigation aids (see Figure 10.2). This was certainly the reasoning behind the decision by IBM to adopt folksonomies within their global intranet. Serving over 300,000 employees their formal taxonomy contains 3,700 nodes and millions of documents, well beyond easy cognitive grasp (as we saw in Chapter 8), and therefore requiring significant familiarity building among its users (Gibson, 2005a).

Figure 10.2   Social tagging as a complement to taxonomy work

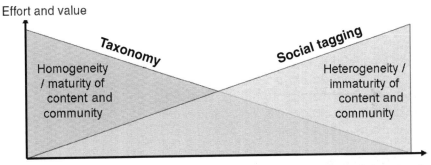

Effort and value

Taxonomy

Social tagging

Homogeneity / maturity of content and community

Heterogeneity / immaturity of content and community

Scale of content and active community

Towards an array of knowledge infrastructure tools

The enthusiasm of recent converts or the confidence of technical expertise often creates a rhetoric that privileges one approach over others. The perceived incumbents or arbiters of power (such as the centrally positioned taxonomist with his or her controlled vocabularies and rules for addition and exclusion) are often targets for such rhetoric. I hope we've shown, however, that both folksonomies and ontologies exist as part of an array of devices that support different ways of exploiting knowledge and information collections for different purposes.

Both ontologies and folksonomies work best with large, heterogeneous collections, the one by formally specifying the key attributes of a domain and depending on precision and machine processing, and the other by leveraging the much less precise but often more interesting discoveries afforded by natural human networks and sense-making activity. Taxonomies occupy a middle ground, attempting to balance design with discovery, precision with serendipity. Metadata powers them all.

Peter Morville expresses this position very eloquently:

> ... that's the beauty of the boundary object we call metadata. We don't have to choose. Ontologies, taxonomies and folksonomies are not mutually exclusive. In many contexts, such as formal websites, the formal structure of ontologies and taxonomies is

worth the investment. In others, like the blogosphere, the casual serendipity of folksonomies is certainly better than nothing. And in some contexts, such as intranets and knowledge networks, a hybrid metadata ecology that combines elements of each may be ideal. (Morville, 2005: 139)

Figure 10.3 pulls together what we have discovered. On the left-hand side, we have the open, inexpensive and expressive folksonomy. It is high in ambiguity and does not support purposeful domain navigation to any useful extent, but in the right conditions it is rich in supporting serendipitous discovery.

Figure 10.3   An array of knowledge infrastructure tools

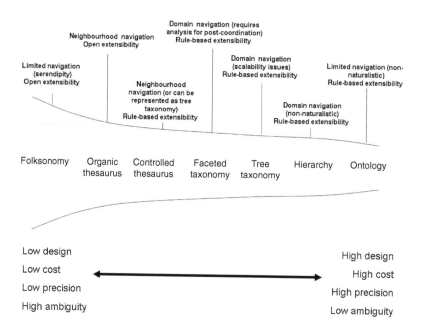

Next up we have what we've called the 'organic thesaurus' such as the Wikipedia example discussed earlier in this chapter. Categories and relationships can be added at will by the user community, and to this extent purposeful navigation can be improved and ambiguity reduced, though ambiguity and imprecision are inevitable consequences of an uncontrolled and not explicitly negotiated aggregation of individual decisions. Although a thesaurus does not give the ability to visually navigate an entire knowledge domain (in the way that a taxonomy does), it can, with the right visualisation tools, provide the ability to navigate the immediate neighbourhoods of any given concept.

Thinkmap's visual thesaurus, illustrated in Figure 10.4, is one such visualisation tool. The tool provides you with the immediate neighbourhood of the term you are searching on – i.e. the concepts that are directly related, by parent–child or associative relationships. If you click on any of those related terms, that term will move to the centre of the map and its neighbourhood will be displayed instead. So immediate neighbourhood navigation is possible, but purposeful navigation of the entire knowledge domain represented by the thesaurus is not. The tool does not give any sense of the structure of the whole, as a taxonomy does.

The organic thesaurus in Figure 10.3 is followed by the suite of tools that we have focused on in this book: the controlled thesaurus and the faceted, tree and hierarchical taxonomy forms. Each requires an incremental investment in design and control mechanisms, and with that investment comes an improvement in support for purposeful navigation and precision of retrieval. However, alongside that comes a cost in terms of representing naturalistic categorisation patterns. Tree taxonomies run into issues of scale that faceted taxonomies avoid, but faceted taxonomies increase the number of decisions that a searcher or a classifier has to make and the content needs to be analysed and decomposed into facets and the different types of attributes identified.

At the far right of Figure 10.3, design and precision are paramount in the ontology, but with that comes the loss of navigation power for humans. It is costly to design and maintain, and this needs to be justified in the value it brings to its clients.

Each of these tools in Figure 10.3 provides different benefits and costs, and each is suitable for different kinds of environment and purpose. None of them solves all of our knowledge infrastructure needs for all circumstances. Our final section makes a case for a balanced use of taxonomies and a portfolio approach to the use of the tools we have described here.

The benefits of diversity in knowledge and information infrastructure

Unless your taxonomy project is very focused upon a highly circumscribed community and context of use, your taxonomy work will usually need to

Figure 10.4   Thinkmap's Visual Thesaurus

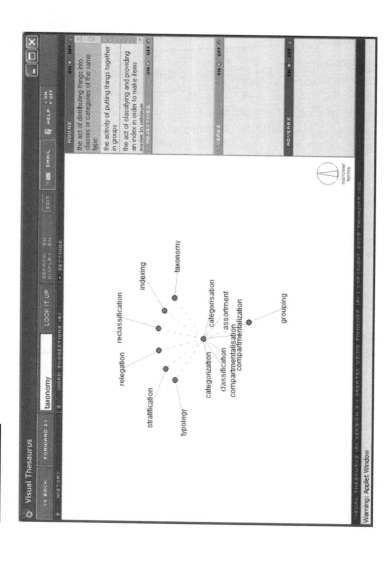

Source: www.visualthesaurus.com

weave itself into the broader knowledge and information infrastructure in your client organisation and may form a major component within it. If you have invested considerable effort in a taxonomy initiative, it is tempting to try to leverage that effort as widely and as deeply as possible. This is especially true where your taxonomy work is focused on building common ground or acting as a boundary object.

We frequently encounter clients who are eager to apply their taxonomy structures to a variety of uses, including navigation structures in websites, general search and browsing in an intranet and application to specialised content repositories. The taxonomy becomes a standard vocabulary to which all applications must conform.

While there is considerable benefit to be gained from developing consistency and standards in vocabulary and categories across an organisation (because it underpins knowledge sharing and coordination), too much standardisation can be a very destructive thing. It is, in fact, the Linnaean trap of assuming that a single system can support all knowledge needs.

Knowledge and information infrastructure is much more like a complex ecosystem than a designed environment, and it has to be so because it needs to cater for a wide variety of uses and activities, past, present and future. It must support not just a diversity of tasks, but a diversity of interests and knowledge domain specialisations, not to mention the ability to reconstruct historical events, generate new applications and innovations, and reflect and support work types that change at different velocities. Financial procedures tend to change slowly, for example, while manufacturing or technology-related work may change rapidly. The infrastructure must support all of these different purposes, paces and people.

In this respect, an information and knowledge environment such as a portal or intranet should ideally resemble a city in the way that it works, as described in Jane Jacobs' masterpiece, *The Death and Life of Great American Cities* (Jacobs, 1992).

> One principle emerges so ubiquitously, and in so many and such complex different forms, that [it] becomes the heart of my argument. This ubiquitous principle is the need of cities for a most intricate and close-grained diversity of uses that give each other mutual support, both economically and socially. (Jacobs, 1992: 14)

Healthy knowledge environments are like healthy cities: they support a range of primary work activities across an organisation, together with secondary activities that spin off from or are afforded by these primary activities. These are our knowledge neighbourhoods, arranged for different uses. They also support a diverse range of different knowledge activities, from storing and retrieving personal information clouds to collaboration and coordination activity, communications and knowledge sharing, idea creation, serendipitous knowledge discovery and innovation. Their ability to support such a wide variety of use creates a constant and varied traffic, and this traffic leaves its mark in more intensive and valuable knowledge and information transactions and residues.

It is simply not possible for a single vocabulary and category set to deliver consistent value for all those needs. Inevitably, just as in a city, over-standardisation may bring efficiency, but it suppresses diversity of use. In consequence the knowledge environment must privilege a few key activities over others, and it becomes a destination for hit and run raids and a limited range of functional transactions (Jacobs, 1992: 212–13). It becomes a dead space rather than a living space. Unfortunately, this is more often true than false once we move from the raunchy variety of the Internet to the static, over-designed and homogenised spaces of corporate intranets.

Moreover, the over-homogenisation of language and categories can severely prejudice the diversity of specialisation and perspective that is necessary across a community for learning, innovation and the recognition of new risks.

The task of the taxonomist or information architect is *not* to provide absolute consistency and standardisation, maximum tidiness and complete information efficiency. Optimising efficiency in a complex system, as Jacobs noted in regard to cities, destroys the resilience of that system and its capacity to adapt to new circumstances. It also suppresses serendipity (Snowden, 2005). So the task of the taxonomist or information architect is not to optimise efficiency, but to optimise effectiveness, and that *always* means sub-optimal efficiency. *Consistency and standardisation must be sufficient for effectiveness and the meeting of your goals – and no more than sufficient.*

To remain resilient and adaptive, a knowledge environment must always also be hospitable to alternate mechanisms of knowledge organisation, access and use – which to a degree will compete for attention with the formally privileged mechanisms such as taxonomies.

So it is not especially healthy to try to bend folksonomies to the needs of taxonomies as vocabulary harvesting devices and leave it at that. If the conditions are right to support healthy folksonomies, then the organisation will get far greater value by actively exploiting their potential for providing rich serendipity. They can by all means be used to harvest vocabularies, but this is just icing on the cake, not the substance of the cake.

So how much consistency and standardisation is the right amount? We might answer with Jane Jacobs (and with Abraham Lincoln before her):

> The answer to this is something like the answer Lincoln gave to the question, 'How long should a man's legs be?' Long enough to reach the ground, Lincoln said. Just so [the correct answers must be] a matter of performance. They cannot be based on abstractions ... (Jacobs, 1992: 208)

The degree of consistency imposed by a taxonomy versus the degree of competition among different taxonomies or alternate knowledge organisation tools must be determined by the overall performance objectives of an organisation, where it wants to go, what it wants to achieve and how it defines its effectiveness.

The balance will be more on the side of the dominant boundary-spanning taxonomy when it is striving to overcome stagnant knowledge silos and improve cross-organisation coordination. It will be more on the side of diverse knowledge organisation mechanisms when it is trying to break down groupthink and create greater innovation capabilities.

In all circumstances, competing mechanisms should always be allowed to coexist with a taxonomy, and should never be allowed to die out completely, because that will kill the value that a taxonomy brings. A taxonomy thrives on the bed of the Babel Instinct, and dies once it is cut off from that source of new insight, new perspectives and new ways of looking at things. The whole essence of taxonomy work is to constantly repair the fragmentation caused by the Babel Instinct, and to weave the social fabric that allows collectives of people to work together effectively, to organise and exploit their knowledge for common use and to discover new things. The taxonomy, ironically, is the servant of Babel, not the master of it, and it cannot survive the complete death of Babel's diversity. An effective taxonomy sits *between* Chaos and Order and mediates the two; it does not, as its so often assumed, represent the domain of Order unequivocally.

To see an example of this plethora of competition between knowledge organisation devices we need go no farther than online bookseller Amazon. Look at any Amazon page for a given book and you will find a taxonomy (represented by formal subject categories), user-contributed tags, links to other books bought by other people who bought this book, booklists compiled by users on related topics and suggestions for other books based on a complex algorithm combining your past behaviours and those of others, and so on. All of these mechanisms for purposefully finding – or serendipitously discovering – books coexist and compete. You can bet that Amazon watches the intensity of use of each of these mechanisms, and as any single instrument gets used more or less intensively, Amazon will adjust its investment in supporting it accordingly. As Amazon has grown, so has the number of ways of locating and suggesting books. Taxonomies form only part of this complex web, and rightly so.

If we neglect this principle and insist on complete standardisation and totalitarian taxonomy rule, then Jane Jacobs' savage indictment of city planning in her time will come back to haunt our intranets, portals and document management systems – indeed, in many cases, it has done so already:

> It follows that the exuberant variety inherent in great numbers of people, tightly concentrated, should be played down, hidden, hammered into a semblance of the thinner, more tractable variety or the outright homogeneity often represented in thinner populations. It follows that these confusing creatures – so many people gathered together – should be sorted out and stashed away as decently and quietly as possible, like chickens on a modern egg-factory farm. (Jacobs, 1992: 220)

Spimes and the future of taxonomies

The relegation of taxonomies to one among many knowledge organising strategies is not to say that *taxonomy work* will become less and less important as we discover new ways of organising and connecting people to knowledge. The structured mediation of diversity and the breaking of redundant categories are functions that human beings will always need.

To see why, we look ahead to the futuristic idea of *spimes*, invented by science fiction writer Bruce Sterling in 2004 (Sterling, 2004, 2005). A spime is a smart artefact that essentially collects its own metadata about itself and its history. It could be a shirt that collects metadata about how often it is worn, how it is washed and ironed with what detergents, and the locations its wearer has brought it to. It could be a book that carries its own history of who has read it, and where, and how many people have read all the way to the end or given up half way.

If this seems far-fetched, it's worth remembering that RFID (radio frequency identification) tags in artefacts can already be linked up to geographical positioning systems (GPS), so that they can always know where they are at any given time. The Amazon feature of 'people who bought this book also bought' is a primitive but powerful spime-like behaviour. It's metadata gathered by the book title about what other people have done around the purchase of this book.

Obviously spime-like behaviours provide extraordinary knowledge and information possibilities for figuring out patterns of artefact use, and how these patterns can be anticipated, changed, influenced, leveraged or provided for. Will this new power remove the taxonomist's role? Not at all.

How will we determine which types of information spimes should collect, and why? How will we design systems that aggregate, integrate and interpret the information from this auto-collected metadata? If we think about it, both tasks are primary functions of the taxonomist – the first being facet analysis, and the second mapping the contexts of use or application of the knowledge.

So while the taxonomy as an artefact (especially as a slow-moving artefact) may well recede in relative importance as we get smarter around the interfaces between technology and information, it is unlikely to disappear completely, and taxonomy work as a discipline and as a skill set has an assured future. So long as we do not construe taxonomy work as solely being about the construction of slow-moving and standardising taxonomies, so long as we recognise the full range of activities that can make up taxonomy work in support of organisational effectiveness, and so long as we remember that we do not hold all the answers and must accommodate competing approaches, then we shall still have productive work ahead.

Bibliography

Allee, Verna (1997) *The Knowledge Evolution: Expanding Organisational Intelligence*. Oxford: Butterworth-Heinemann.

Allen, Christopher (2004) *The Dunbar Number as a Limit to Group Sizes*. See: *http://www.lifewithalacrity.com/2004/03/the_dunbar_numb.html* (accessed 14 July 2006).

AS ISO 15489.1-2002 *Records Management Part 1: General*. Sydney: Standards Australia.

Bailey, Kenneth D. (1994) *Typologies and Taxonomies: An Introduction to Classification Techniques*. Thousand Oaks, CA: Sage.

Baker, Wayne (2000) *Achieving Success Through Social Capital: Tapping the Hidden Resources in Your Personal and Business Networks*. San Francisco: Jossey-Bass.

Barreau, D.K. (1995) 'Context as a factor in personal information management systems', *Journal of the American Society for Information Science*, 46 (5): 327–39.

Barreau, D. and Nardi, B.A. (1995) 'Finding and reminding: file organisation from the desktop', *SIGCHI Bulletin*, 27 (3): 39–43.

Berreby, David (2005) *Us and Them: Understanding Your Tribal Mind*. New York: Little, Brown.

Blom, Philipp (2003) *To Have and to Hold: An Intimate History of Collectors and Collecting*. New York: Overlook Press.

Blom, Philipp (2005) *Enlightening the World: Encyclopédie, the Book that Changed the Course of History*. New York: Palgrave Macmillan.

Blunt, Wilfrid (ed.) (2001) *Linnaeus: The Compleat Naturalist*. Princeton, NJ: Princeton University Press.

Bowker, Geoffrey C. and Star, Susan Leigh (1999) *Sorting Things Out: Classification and Its Consequences*. Cambridge, MA: MIT Press.

Bukowitz, Wendi R. and Williams, Ruth L. (1999) *The Knowledge Management Fieldbook*. London: Pearson Education.

Burt, Ronald (2001) 'Bandwidth and echo: trust, information, and gossip in social networks', in Alessandra Casella and James E. Rauch (eds), *Networks and Markets: Contributions from Economics and Sociology*. New York: Russell Sage Foundation.

Byrne, Bill (2001) 'Turning GUIs into VUIs: dialog design principles for making web applications accessible by telephone', *VoiceXML Review*, 1 (6). See: *http://www.voicexmlreview.org/Jun2001/features/dialog_design.html* (accessed 6 January 2006).

Calabria, Tina (2004) *Evaluating Caloundra City Council's EDMS Classification.* See: *http://www.steptwo.com.au/papers/kmc_caloundracouncil/pdf/KMC_CaloundraCouncil.pdf* (accessed 21 December 2005).

Campbell, D. Grant and Fast, Karl V. (2006) *From Pace Layering to Resilience Theory: The Complex Implications of Tagging for Information Architecture.* Paper presented at the IA Summit 2006, Vancouver, 23–27 March. See: *http://iasummit.org/2006/files/164_Presentation_Desc.pdf* (accessed 6 October 2006).

Coates, Tom (2005) *How to Build on Bubble-up Folksonomies.* See: *http://www.plasticbag.org/archives/2005/09/how_to_build_on_bubbleup_folksonomies/* (accessed 3 October 2006).

Crandall, Beth, Klein, Gary and Hoffman, Robert R. (2006) *Working Minds: A Practitioner's Guide to Cognitive Task Analysis.* Cambridge, MA: MIT Press.

Cross, Rob and Parker, Andrew (2004) *The Hidden Power of Social Networks: Understanding How Work Really Gets Done in Organisations.* Boston: Harvard Business School Press.

Dale, Adrian (2001) 'Taxonomies in action at Unilever Research', with commentary by Jean Graef, *Montague Institute Review*, February.

Davenport, Thomas H. and Marchand, Donald A. (2000) 'Is KM just good information management?', in Donald A. Marchand and Thomas H. Davenport (eds), *Mastering Information Management.* London: Financial Times Prentice Hall, pp. 165–9.

Davenport, Thomas H. and Prusak, Laurence (1997) *Information Ecology: Mastering the Information Environment.* New York: Oxford University Press.

Davenport, Thomas H. and Prusak, Laurence (1998) *Working Knowledge: How Organisations Manage What They Know.* Boston: Harvard Business School Press.

Dixon, Nancy M. (2000) *Common Knowledge: How Companies Thrive by Sharing What They Know.* Boston: Harvard Business School Press.

Dougherty, Janet W.D. and Keller, Charles M. (1982) 'Taskonomy: a practical approach to knowledge structures', *American Ethnologist*, 9 (4): 763–74.

Douglas, Mary (1992) *Risk and Blame: Essays in Cultural Theory*. London: Routledge.

Dublin Core (2005) *DCMI Metadata Terms*. See: *http://dublincore .org/documents/dcmi-terms/* (accessed 26 June 2006).

Dunbar, Robin (1993) 'Co-evolution of neocortex size, group size and language in humans', *Behavioral and Brain Sciences*, 16 (4): 681–735.

Dunbar, Robin (1996) *Grooming, Gossip and the Evolution of Language*. London: Faber & Faber.

Durkheim, Emile and Mauss, Marcel (1963) *Primitive Classification*. London: Cohen & West.

Dwyer, Jim (2002) 'What went wrong that day? Few seem determined to find out', *New York Times*, 11 September.

Earley, Seth (2005) *Developing Enterprise Taxonomies*. See: *http://www .earley.com/Earley_Report/ER_Taxonomy.htm* (accessed 17 January 2006).

Edols, Liz (2001) 'Taxonomies are what?', *Free Pint*, October, no. 97. See: *http://www.freepint.com/issues/041001.htm#feature* (accessed 16 November 2006).

Fleisher, Craig S. and Bensoussan, Babette E. (2003) *Strategic and Competitive Analysis: Methods and Techniques for Analyzing Business Competition*. Upper Saddle River, NJ: Prentice Hall.

Gibson, Bud (2005a) *IBM's Intranet and Folksonomy*. See: *http:// thecommunityengine.com/home/archives/2005/03/ibms_intranet_ a.html* (accessed 3 October 2006).

Gibson, Bud (2005b) *Using Mapped Folksonomy to Break Corporate Silos*. See: *http://thecommunityengine.com/home/archives/2005/02/ using_mapped_fo.html* (accessed 3 October 2006).

Gilad, Ben (2001) 'Industry risk management: CI's next step', *Competitive Intelligence Magazine*, May–June. See: *http://www .bengilad.com/pdfs/s_Next_Step.doc* (accessed 16 November 2006).

Goodwin, Kim (2001) 'Perfecting your personas', *Cooper Interaction Design Newsletter*, July/August. See: *http://www.cooper.com/ newsletters/2001_7/perfecting_your_personas.htm* (accessed 30 June 2005).

Gould, Stephen Jay (2000) *The Lying Stones of Marrakech: Penultimate Reflections in Natural History*. New York: Three Rivers Press.

Graef, Jean (2001) 'Managing taxonomies strategically', *Montague Institute Review*, March.

Graef, Jean (2004) 'An architecture for information', *Montague Institute Review*, November.

Graef, Jean (2005) Personal e-mail communication, 19 December.

Hall, Edward T. (1976) *Beyond Culture*. New York: Anchor.

Hamilton, Stewart (2000) 'Information and the management of risk', in Donald Marchand (ed.), *Competing with Information: A Manager's Guide to Creating Business Value with Information Content*. Chichester: John Wiley.

Henczel, Susan (2001) *The Information Audit: A Practical Guide*. Munich: K.G. Saur.

Horovitz, Jacques (2000) 'Information as a service to the customer', in Donald Marchand (ed.), *Competing with Information: A Manager's Guide to Creating Business Value with Information Content*. Chichester: John Wiley.

Hulme, C., Roodenrys, S., Brown, G. and Mercer, R. (1995) 'The role of long-term memory mechanisms in memory span', *British Journal of Psychology*, 86: 527–36.

IEEE LTSC (2002) *WG12: Learning Object Metadata*. See: *http://ltsc.ieee.org/wg12/* (accessed 11 October 2006).

ISO 23081-1 (2006) *Information and Documentation – Records Management Processes – Metadata for Records – Part 1: Principles*. Geneva: ISO.

Jacka, J. Mike and Keller, Paulette (2002) *Business Process Mapping: Improving Customer Satisfaction*. New York: John Wiley.

Jacobs, Jane (1992) *The Death and Life of Great American Cities*. New York: Vintage.

Jensen, Rolf (1999) *The Dream Society: How the Coming Shift from Information to Imagination Will Transform Your Business*. New York: McGraw-Hill.

Keenan, Marita (2006) Personal communication, 7 October.

Kipfer, Barbara Ann (2001) *The Order of Things: How Everything in the World Is Organised into Hierarchies, Structures, and Pecking Orders*, revised edn. New York: Random House.

Klein, Gary (1998) *Sources of Power: How People Make Decisions*. Cambridge, MA: MIT Press.

Krebs, Valdis (2003) *Divided We Stand???* See: *http://www.orgnet.com/leftright.html* (accessed 3 July 2006).

Krebs, Valdis (2004) *Divided We Stand*. See: *http://www.orgnet.com/divided.html* (accessed 3 July 2006).

Kuniavsky, Mike (2003) *Observing the User Experience: A Practitioner's Guide to User Research*. San Francisco: Morgan Kaufmann.

Kurtz, Cynthia F. and Snowden, David J. (2003) 'The new dynamics of strategy: sense-making in a complex-complicated world', *IBM Systems Journal*, Fall: 462–83.

Kwasnik, Barbara H. (1999) 'The role of classification in knowledge representation and discovery', *Library Trends*, 48 (1): 22–47.

Lakoff, George (1987) *Women, Fire, and Dangerous Things: What Categories Reveal About the Human Mind*. Chicago: University of Chicago Press.

Lambermont-Ford, Jean-Paul (2005) 'Searching for a global solution', *Knowledge Management Magazine*, 8 (1); reprinted in Jason Schofield (ed.) (2005) *Taxonomies: Structuring Corporate Information*. London: Ark Group, pp. 22–7.

Laming, Lord (2003) *The Victoria Climbié Inquiry: Summary and Recommendations*. London: HMSO.

Lave, Jean and Wenger, Etienne (1991) *Situated Learning: Legitimate Peripheral Participation*. Cambridge: Cambridge University Press.

LeCompte, D. (1999) 'Seven, plus or minus two, is too much to bear: three (or fewer) is the real magic number', *Proceedings of the Human Factors and Ergonomics Society*. Santa Monica, CA: HFES, pp. 289–92.

Loasby, Karen (2006a) 'Changing approaches to metadata at bbc.co.uk: from chaos to control and then letting go again', *Bulletin of ASIS&T*, October/November. See: *http://www.asis.org/Bulletin/Oct-06/loasby .html* (accessed 11 October 2006).

Loasby, Karen (2006b) Personal communication, 11 October.

McArthur, Tom (1986) *Worlds of Reference: Lexicography, Learning and Language from the Clay Tablet to the Computer*. Cambridge: Cambridge University Press.

McDermott, R. and O'Dell, C. (2001) 'Overcoming cultural barriers to sharing knowledge', *Journal of Knowledge Management*, 5 (1): 76–85.

MacGregor, J.N. (1987) 'Short-term memory capacity: limitation or optimization?', *Psychological Review*, 94 (1): 107–8.

Mackenzie, John (2005) Interview, 8 June.

Mackenzie, John (2006) Personal communication, 27 January.

McMillan, John (2005) *Inquiry into the Circumstances of the Vivian Alvarez Matter*. Canberra: Commonwealth Ombudsman.

McMullin, Jess (2004) *The Cognitive Cost of Classification*. See: *http://www.interactionary.com/index.php?cat=7* (accessed 6 October 2006).

Marchand, Donald (ed.) (2000) *Competing with Information: A Manager's Guide to Creating Business Value with Information Content*. Chichester: John Wiley.

Martin, Paolina (2006) *Amaretto or Cognac – Which Tastes Better in Tiramisu?* See: *http://www.greenchameleon.com/gc/blog_detail/*

amaretto_or_cognac_which_tastes_better_in_tiramisu (accessed 8 September 2006).

Mathes, Adam (2004) *Folksonomies: Cooperative Classification and Communication Through Shared Metadata*. See: *http://www .adammathes.com/academic/computer-mediated-communication/ folksonomies.html* (accessed 23 September 2006).

Merholz, Peter (2004) *Ethnoclassification and Vernacular Vocabularies*. See: *http://www.peterme.com/archives/000387.html* (accessed 3 October 2006).

Milgram, Stanley (1992) 'Psychological maps of Paris', in John Sabini and Maury Silver (eds), *Individual in a Social World: Essays and Experiments*, 2nd edn. New York: McGraw-Hill.

Miller, George A. (1956) 'The magical number seven, plus or minus two: some limits on our capacity for processing information', *Psychological Review*, 63: 81–97.

Morville, Peter (2005) *Ambient Findability*. Sebastopol, CA: O'Reilly.

Moser, Ingunn (2004) *Does Information Flow? Managing Information Flow and Fluidity in Medical Practice*. See: *http://effin.org/ Dokumenter/Does_information_flow.pdf* (accessed 18 August 2005).

Mui, Ylan Q. (2006) *Wal-Mart Web Site Makes Racial Connections: DVD Shoppers Get Offensive Referrals*. See: *http://www.msnbc.msn .com/id/10736265/* (accessed 11 October 2006).

NAA (1999) *Recordkeeping Metadata Standard for Commonwealth Agencies*. Canberra: National Archives of Australia. See: *http://naa.gov.au/recordkeeping/control/rkms/summary.htm* (accessed 11 October 2006).

NAA (2003) *The DIRKS Manual: A Strategic Approach to Managing Business Information*. Canberra: National Archives of Australia. See: *http://www.naa.gov.au/recordkeeping/dirks/dirksman/dirks.html* (accessed 11 October 2006).

National Archives (2003) *Business Classification Scheme Design*. London: National Archives. See: *http://www.nationalarchives.gov.uk/ documents/bcs_toolkit.pdf* (accessed 11 October 2006).

Ng, Daniel (2005) *Communicating a Knowledge Management Strategy: CAAS Experience*. Paper presented at the Annual iKMS Conference, Singapore, 14 October.

Nichani, Maish (2006) *Taming Your Target Content*. See: *http://www .pebbleroad.com/article/taming_your_target_content/* (accessed 18 July 2006).

Nisbett, Richard (2003) *The Geography of Thought: How Asians and Westerners Think Differently ... and Why*. New York: Free Press.

Nonaka, I. and Takeuchi, H. (1995) *The Knowledge-Creating Company: How Japanese Companies Create the Dynamics of Innovation.* Oxford: Oxford University Press.

Norman, Don (2006) *Logic Versus Usage: The Case for Activity-Centered Design.* See: *http://www.jnd.org/dn.mss/logic_versus_usage_t.html* (accessed 8 August 2006).

O'Dell, Carla and Grayson, C. Jackson (1998) *If Only We Knew What We Knew: The Transfer of Internal Knowledge and Best Practice.* New York: Free Press.

Ohara, Hiroshi (2004) 'Experience and review of SARS control in Vietnam and China', *Tropical Medicine and Health*, 32 (3): 235–40.

Orna, Elizabeth (2004) *Information Strategy in Practice.* Aldershot: Gower.

Orr, Stuart Anthony (2005) *Functions-Based Classification of Records: Is It Functional?* MSc dissertation, University of Northumbria.

Osmond, Dennis H. (2003) 'Epidemiology of HIV/AIDS in the United States', *HIV InSite Knowledge Base Chapter.* San Francisco: UCSF Center for HIV Information. See: *http://hivinsite.ucsf.edu/InSite?page=kb-01-03* (accessed 2 January 2006).

Palmer, M.J. (2005) *Inquiry into the Circumstances of the Immigration Detention of Cornelia Rau.* Canberra: Attorney General's Department.

Pauker, Benjamin and Whitaker, Joel (2000) *Strategic Intelligence: Providing Critical Information for Strategic Decisions.* Washington, DC: Corporate Strategy Board.

Perrow, Charles (1999) *Normal Accidents: Living with High-risk Technologies.* Princeton, NJ: Princeton University Press.

Pitts, Angela (2005) 'A taxonomy for the Homeland Security Digital Library', with commentary by Jean Graef, *Montague Institute Review*, October (online).

Portes, A. (1998) 'Social capital: its origins and applications in modern sociology', *Annual Review of Sociology*, 24: 1–24.

Pruitt, John and Prudin, Jonathan (2003) *Personas: Practice and Theory.* American Institute of Graphic Arts. See: *http://www.aiga.org/resources/content/9/7/8/documents/pruitt.pdf* (accessed 30 June 2005).

Quintarelli, Emmanuele (2005) *Folksonomies: Power to the People.* Paper presented to the ISKO Italy-UniMIB meeting, Milan, 24 June. See: *http://www.iskoi.org/doc/folksonomies.htm* (accessed 3 October 2006).

Quintarelli, Emmanuele (2006a) *Folksonomies 2.0 – The Chaotic Order.* See: *http://www.infospaces.it/wordpress/topics/information-*

architecture/74 (accessed 3 October 2006).

Quintarelli, Emmanuele (2006b) *Tagging Ecologies*. See: *http://www .infospaces.it/wordpress/topics/information-architecture/95* (accessed 3 October 2006).

Ranganathan, S.R. (1967) *Prolegomena to Library Classification*, 3rd edn. London: Asia Publishing House.

Rath & Strong (2000) *Rath & Strong's Six Sigma Pocket Guide*. Lexington, MA: Rath & Strong.

Reuters (1996) *Dying for Information: A Report on the Effects of Information Overload in the UK and Worldwide*. London: Reuters.

Ripley, John (2003) *Unilever HPC: Our Path to Growth*. Chicago: Unilever pdf presentation. See: *http://www.unilever.com* (accessed 8 December 2004).

Robertson, James (2004) *Rolling Out a Records Management System*. See: *http://www.steptwo.com.au/papers/kmc_recordsmanagement/ pdf/KMC_RecordsManagement.pdf* (accessed 21 December 2004).

Robertson, James (2006) *Nine Ways to Fix Intranet Search*. See: *http://www.steptwo.com.au/papers/kmc_fixingsearch/index.html* (accessed 29 July 2006).

Rogers, Everett (1995) *Diffusion of Innovations*, 4th edn. New York: Free Press.

Rosenfeld, Lou and Morville, Peter (2002) *Information Architecture for the World Wide Web*. Sebastopol, CA: O'Reilly.

Rusanow, Gretta (2003) *Knowledge Management and the Smarter Lawyer*. New York: ALM Publishing.

Saffo, Paul (2005) *Farewell Information, It's a Media Age*. See: *http://www.saffo.com/essays/index.php* (accessed 3 July 2006).

Schein, E. (1985) *Organisational Culture and Leadership*. San Francisco: Jossey-Bass.

Sen, Amartya (2006) *Identity and Violence: The Illusion of Destiny*. New York: W.W. Norton.

Shirky, Clay (2005) *Ontology Is Overrated: Categories, Links, and Tags*. See: *http://shirky.com/writings/ontology_overrated.html* (accessed 3 October 2006).

Sinha, Rashmi (2005) *A Cognitive Analysis of Tagging (or How the Lower Cognitive Cost of Tagging Makes It Popular)*. See: *http://www.rashmisinha.com/archives/05_09/tagging-cognitive.html* (accessed 3 October 2006).

Smith, Gene (2004) *Folksonomy: Social Classification*. See: *http://atomiq .org/archives/2004/08/folksonomy_social_classification.html* (accessed 3 October 2006).

Snowden, David J. (2000a) 'The art and science of story or "Are you sitting uncomfortably?" Part 1: gathering and harvesting the raw material', *Business Information Review*, 17 (3): 147–56.

Snowden, David J. (2000b) 'The ASHEN model: an enabler of action', *Knowledge Management*, 3 (7); revised version of article available at: *http://www.cognitive-edge.com/articledetails.php?articleid=7* (accessed 16 November 2006).

Snowden, David J. (2005) 'Stories from the frontier', *E: CO*, 7 (3-4).

Snowden, David J. (2006) Personal communication, 3 August.

Spence, Jonathan D. (1984) *The Memory Palace of Matteo Ricci*. London: Faber & Faber.

Star, Susan Leigh and Griesemer, James R. (1989) 'Institutional ecology, "translations" and boundary objects: amateurs and professionals in Berkeley's Museum of Vertebrate Zoology, 1907–39', *Social Studies of Science*, 19: 387–420.

Star, Susan Leigh and Ruhleder, Karen (1996) 'Steps towards an ecology of infrastructure: design and access for large information spaces', *Information Systems Research*, 7 (1): 111–34.

Stearn, William T. (2001) 'Linnaean classification, nomenclature, and method', in Wilfrid Blunt (ed.), *Linnaeus: The Compleat Naturalist*. Princeton, NJ: Princeton University Press, pp. 246–52.

Sterling, Bruce (2004) *When Blobjects Rule the Earth*. Paper presented at SIGGRAPH Los Angeles, August. See: *http://www.boingboing.net/images/blobjects.htm* (accessed 11 October 2006).

Sterling, Bruce (2005) *Shaping Things*. Cambridge, MA: MIT Press.

Sunstein, Cass (2002) *Republic.com*, new edn. Princeton, NJ: Princeton University Press.

Svenonius, Elaine (2000) *The Intellectual Foundation of Information Organisation*. Cambridge, MA: MIT Press.

TaxoCoP (2005) Postings from Meredith Levine, Denham Grey, Seth Earley, Katherine Bertolucci, Leonard Will and David Eddy on the Taxonomy Community of Practice discussion forum. See: *http://groups.yahoo.com/groups/TaxoCoP* (accessed 18–19 December 2005).

TaxoCoP (2006) *The Value of Social Tagging in a Corporate Setting*. See: *http://taxocop.wikispaces.com/Social+tagging* (accessed 3 October 2006).

Taylor, Arlene G. (2004) *The Organisation of Information*, 2nd edn. Westport, CT: Libraries Unlimited.

Thomas, J., Kellogg, W. and Erickson, T. (2001) 'The knowledge management puzzle: human and social factors in knowledge management', *IBM Systems Journal*, 40 (4): 863–84.

Tiwana, Amrit (2002) *The Knowledge Management Toolkit*, 2nd edn. Upper Saddle River, NJ: Prentice Hall PTR.

Tsoukas, Haridimos (2005) *Complex Knowledge: Studies in Organisational Epistemology*. Oxford: Oxford University Press.

Vander Wal, Thomas (2005) *Folksonomy Definition and Wikipedia*. See: *http://www.vanderwal.net/random/entrysel.php?blog=1750* (accessed 23 October 2006).

Vander Wal, Thomas (2006) *Exposing the Local Infocloud*. See: *http://www.personalinfocloud.com/2006/05/exposing_the_lo.html* (accessed 23 October 2006).

Vaughan, Diane (1996) *The Challenger Launch Decision: Risky Technology, Culture, and Deviance at NASA*. Chicago: University of Chicago Press.

Vitt, Elizabeth, Luckevich, Michael and Misner, Stacia (2002) *Business Intelligence: Making Better Decisions Faster*. Redmond, WA: Microsoft Press.

von Clausewitz, Carl (1999) *On War*, Vol. 1. Project Gutenberg e-text.

von Oech, Roger (2001) *Expect the Unexpected (or You Won't Find It)*. New York: Free Press.

Voss, Jakob (2006) *Collaborative Thesaurus Tagging the Wikipedia Way*. Paper presented at the WWW2006 Conference, Edinburgh, 23–26 May.

W3C (2006) *Resource Description Framework (RDF)*. See: *http://www.w3.org/RDF/* (accessed 11 October 2006).

Weick, Karl E. (1995) *Sensemaking in Organisations*. Thousand Oaks, CA: Sage.

Wenger, Etienne (1998) *Communities of Practice: Learning, Meaning and Identity*. Cambridge: Cambridge University Press.

Williamson, Matt (2003) *Even a Clown Can Do It: Cirque de Soleil Recreates Live Entertainment: Case B*. Fontainebleau: INSEAD Euro-Asia Centre.

Wilson, Douglas L. (1996) *Jefferson's Books*. Monticello, MN: Thomas Jefferson Foundation.

Wurman, Richard Saul (2001) *Information Anxiety 2*. Indianapolis: Que.

Yates, Frances (1984) *The Art of Memory*. London: Ark Paperbacks.

Index

Alvarez, Vivian, 56, 85

Amazon.com, 101, 147, 209, 245, 259–61

ambiguity, xvi, 6, 7, 17, 20–6, 35–7, 46–7, 107, 111, 133, 135, 143, 159, 162, 196–7, 199, 201–2, 204, 213, 216, 239, 241–6, 252, 254, 261

anthropology and taxonomies, 4, 38, 60, 88–9, 93, 125

archetypes, 87–90, 118–22

arrangement, taxonomies and, 4, 42, 161–2, 164, 218–26, 241, 243–4, 250, 258

ASHEN framework, 193–4

autocategorisation, 72, 73, 161–3, 215

Babel Instinct, xv, 57–61, 127, 147, 153, 167, 178, 244, 249, 259

Barings Bank, 55

basic level categories, 16, 190–2, 247–8

BBC, 215–17, 246–7, 248

BCG Matrix, 26, 28–9, 78, 130

biology and taxonomies, xvii, 4–5, 15, 20, 24, 71, 125, 131, 218–21

boundary object, boundary spanning, 49, 61–6, 72–3, 111–12, 123, 128–9, 133, 137–8, 147–8, 156, 158, 160–1, 166–72, 174, 180, 194, 203, 234–5, 244, 251, 253, 257, 259

Bowker, Geoffrey, xiii, 15, 62, 64, 70, 71, 123, 127, 129, 145, 185

British Council, 108–12

Buffon, Comte de, 218–22, 250

build or buy decision, 150–1, 175–6

Cabot Corporation, 114–15, 122, 128

Camillo, Giulio, 9–10

caste system, 18–20

category busting, 91, 105, 107–8, 124

category discovery, 83, 88, 91, 95, 102

change management, 6, 50, 52, 64–5, 101–2, 112, 116–22, 148–9, 172, 173–5, 177–83, 195, 214–17, 232, 234

Chevron, 98–9, 113

Cirque du Soleil, 91, 133

Civil Aviation Authority of Singapore, 118–22, 131

classification, xiii, xv, xvii, 4–6, 8, 11, 13, 23, 24, 25, 30–1, 33–5, 37, 42, 70–1, 78, 97, 99, 114, 123, 129, 141, 145, 150, 185, 197, 203–5, 207, 210, 218, 220, 222–3, 230–3, 240–1, 246, 250–2

Climbié, Victoria, 50–7, 65–6,
138
Club Med, 88, 90, 131
collecting, 10, 72–4, 131, 218–19,
224, 243–4
Colon Classification scheme, 33–5
common ground, 105, 117–18,
124, 127–9, 133, 137–8, 140,
147–8, 150, 158–61, 166, 167,
169–72, 174, 180, 196, 203,
234, 244, 248, 251, 257
communication strategy, 177–81
communities of practice, xiv, 45,
106–7, 112–13
competency mapping, 108–12, 194
concept maps, xiii, 44, 48, 107,
121, 155–7, 167–9, 176, 193,
196–7, 223–4
content management, xvii, 10, 94,
99, 100–2, 105, 122, 146,
159–63, 165, 209, 215–17,
223–6, 241–2
controlled vocabulary, 6–7, 99,
160–1, 164, 212, 216–17, 234,
247, 248, 253
cost management, 74–81, 124
customers, 81–90, 124, 131
Cynefin Framework, 134–51

Dale, Adrian, xiv, 92–4, 132
Department of Homeland Security,
72–4, 129, 138–9
Dewey Decimal Classification, 5,
30, 33, 35
disposable taxonomies, 92–4,
132–3, 158
Dublin Core, 210–12
Dunbar, Robin, 188–91

Earley, Seth, xiv, 63
echo chambers – see silos

evolutionary approach, 72–4, 139,
143, 173–6, 245, 248
expert–novice gaps, 38, 47, 123,
129, 138, 148
expertise, 44, 93, 103–4, 106–8,
119–21, 134, 138, 146, 163,
165, 176, 183, 194, 225, 239,
247

facets, 10, 33–42, 47, 59, 63,
73–4, 75, 80, 102, 114–15,
122, 127, 129, 137–8, 143,
161, 162, 169, 170–2, 174–5,
176, 187, 192, 197–8, 202,
203–5, 210–12, 218, 220, 222,
224–5, 231, 233, 246, 252,
254–5, 261
findability – see information
retrieval
folksonomies, 6, 102, 139, 214,
216, 237–8, 240–54, 258
Ford, 99

governance of taxonomies, 102,
149, 154, 178–83, 207–8,
233–5
Graef, Jean, xiv, 18, 94, 100, 102

hierarchies, 10, 13, 18–25, 38, 40,
42, 46, 59, 130–1, 143, 171,
199, 220, 246, 250, 252, 254–5
HIV AIDS, 70–1, 99, 133

IBM, 89, 248, 252
implicit taxonomies, xv, 78, 79,
89, 151, 185, 192, 196–8,
246–7, 249
incident reports, 62–4, 197
information architecture, 26, 41,
192, 217–26, 233, 240, 248,
251

information management, 1–3, 29, 36, 53, 55, 64–5, 68, 99, 101, 103–6, 122, 124, 138, 148, 155, 161, 164–5, 173, 193

information neighbourhoods, 223–6, 258

information nesting – see silos

information retrieval, xvii, 3, 7, 11, 29, 47, 58, 64, 72, 81, 95, 98–101, 105–6, 113, 122, 124, 127, 136, 161–4, 180, 192, 209–10, 217, 223, 227, 229–32, 234, 241, 245–6, 249, 255, 258

infrastructure, xiii, xiv, 36, 49, 54, 55, 64–6, 90–1, 94–5, 101–2, 104, 117–18, 123, 147, 155, 164–7, 177, 189, 196, 207–8, 217, 226, 233, 235, 252–60

innovation management, 28–9, 68, 80, 90–4, 107, 117, 124, 132–4, 135, 180, 257–9

International Classification of Diseases, 70, 129

Jacobs, Jane, 257–60

Jefferson, Thomas, 250

Keenan, Marita, xiv, 227–8, 232

knowledge articulation, 54–6, 59, 64–5, 115, 117, 127, 129, 146, 149

knowledge lens framework, 102–8

knowledge management, xiii, xvi–xvii, 2–3, 11, 23–4, 48, 53, 55, 59, 61, 97–122, 125, 138, 145, 155, 165–6, 173–4, 182

knowledge maps, 5, 8, 24–5, 42, 74, 76, 97, 102, 106–7, 113, 121, 155, 158, 166–7, 173–4, 193–8

Kwasnik, Barbara, xiii, 13, 19, 26, 42

Leeson, Nick, 55

librarianship, xiii, xvii, 4, 6, 19, 22, 24, 26, 33–5, 97, 99, 125, 153, 229–30, 247, 250, 252

Library of Congress Classification, 33, 35

Linnaeus, Carl, xiii, 131, 218–22, 257

lists, 4, 10–11, 13–15, 18–19, 37–40, 43, 46, 48, 86, 100, 102, 189, 190, 192, 198, 202, 203, 211–12, 234

Loasby, Karen, xiv, 215–17

Mackenzie, John, xiv, 108–12

maintenance of taxonomies, 132, 137, 139, 149, 179, 182, 200, 211, 212, 215, 234–5, 255

Martin, Paolina, xiv, 183

Maslow, A.H., 19–20

matrices, 10, 25–33, 37–8, 40, 42, 47, 78, 83–4, 89, 125, 130, 137, 139, 161, 162, 198

memory, taxonomies and, 8–10, 16–17, 48, 127, 145, 186–92

Mendeleev, D.I., 26–7, 29, 130–1

metadata, 37, 40, 47, 72, 98, 100–2, 160–5, 169, 170–2, 175, 209–17, 223–6, 231–4, 241, 253–4, 260–1

Miller, George, 186–92

mind-maps, 44, 48, 93

Moor Hall Health Club, 83–6

NAICS, 5, 6, 129

navigation, taxonomies and, 8, 10, 14, 25, 29, 31, 33, 37–8, 47,

80, 83, 86–7, 138, 159–64, 172, 186, 189–92, 199–200, 209, 216, 222, 230–1, 239–40, 246–7, 249, 251–2, 254–5, 257

negotiation, taxonomy work as, xvi, 11, 59–61, 64, 94, 111, 114, 129, 137, 158, 164, 166, 175, 177, 182, 185, 194–5, 214, 254

Ng, Daniel, xiv, 118–21

Nichani, Maish, xiv, 222–4

nomenclature, 43, 133, 218, 220

Nursing Interventions Classification, 145

OLAP, 84–5

ontologies, 237–40, 253–5

operational taxonomies, 126, 137, 196, 198

organisational effectiveness, 49–50, 123–34, 234, 261

parsimony in taxonomies, 13, 200–1

periodic table, 26–7, 29–30, 130

personas – see archetypes

piloting a taxonomy, 178–9, 201–5

Pitts, Angela, xiv, 72–4

polyhierarchies, 10, 25–6, 37, 47, 80, 114, 125, 137, 161–2, 248

post-coordination, 35, 38, 40, 47, 161–2, 172, 192

power, 14, 18, 123, 141, 143–6, 253

pre-coordination, 34–6, 38, 159, 161–2, 172

private taxonomies, 59–61

process maps, 44–5, 48, 74–8, 102, 113, 176, 194, 231

racism, 123, 141–3, 163

Ranganathan, S.R., 33–5, 40, 198

Raytheon, 247–9

records management, xiv, 6, 24, 36, 75, 99, 101, 146, 153, 165, 182, 210, 213, 226–34

relationships between concepts, 3, 5–7, 8, 10, 14–15, 17, 18, 20, 24–5, 26, 33, 40, 42–3, 46, 73, 89, 101, 122, 127, 139, 156, 190–2, 209, 212–13, 238–9, 245–6, 248, 254–5

research and development, 90–4, 128–9, 133, 147–8, 167, 170–2

risk management, 50, 67–74, 83, 90, 124, 130, 132–5, 144, 164, 180, 228, 232, 234, 258

Robertson, James, xiv, 163, 232

Rwandan massacres, 141–3

salience, 130–3, 139, 145, 186, 197

Sarbanes-Oxley, 36, 165, 232

SARS, 69–70, 135–6

science and technology mapping, 91–2

scope notes, 7, 85, 202, 213, 245, 247

search engine, 7, 37–40, 72, 93, 99, 102, 160–4, 170–1, 209–10, 213–16, 224, 226, 234, 242, 245

segmentation, 83–6, 88–9

sense-making, 1, 3, 26, 33, 47, 69, 91, 102, 105, 117, 122, 124, 130–7, 158, 167–8, 180, 219, 221, 234–5, 244, 253

serendipity, 94, 101, 139, 240–4, 246, 248–9, 251–4, 258–60

silos, 56, 107, 125, 141, 147–8, 170, 173–4, 196, 248, 259

Snowden, David, xiii, 89, 90, 133–5, 193, 237
social capital, 117
social network mapping, 106–7, 113
social tagging – *see* folksonomies
spimes, 260–1
sports taxonomy, 203–5, 210–12, 215
stakeholders, 60, 75, 146, 150–1, 154–8, 165–9, 173–5, 177–83, 193, 234–5
standardisation, xvi, 5, 11, 33, 60–1, 64–5, 76, 78, 83, 85, 95, 97, 101, 102, 105, 109, 111–12, 115, 128–9, 132, 136–8, 150, 158, 166, 174, 175–6, 178, 182, 210, 215, 217, 220–1, 257–9, 260–1
Star, Susan Leigh, xiii, 15, 49, 61, 62, 63, 64, 70, 71, 123, 127, 129, 145, 185
storytelling, 89–90, 107, 119, 121
system maps, 10, 14, 42–5, 48

taskonomy, 222–3
taxonomy, definition, 4–10
taxonomy work, xiii, xv–xvii, 11, 49, 57, 65, 67, 78–9, 83, 90–2, 94–5, 98–9, 101–2, 105, 118, 122, 123–4, 130–40, 149, 161, 164–8, 177, 204, 218, 222, 224, 231, 233, 237–8, 259–61
technology environment, 155, 158–64, 170–5, 209, 235, 237
thesaurus, 6–7, 15, 56, 73, 94, 97, 100, 139, 166, 192, 209, 212–15, 226, 230, 234, 238, 245, 247, 248, 254–6
tree structures, 10, 13–25, 29–31, 37–8, 40, 42, 44, 46–8, 59, 63, 73, 80, 86–7, 94, 102, 114, 122, 125, 130–1, 136–7, 143, 160–2, 172, 174, 176, 190–2, 198, 199, 201–2, 203, 213, 220, 231, 238, 247, 248, 251, 254–5
trust, 2, 53, 117, 128, 147, 177, 181, 188, 228
typology, 25–6, 83, 89, 105, 118–22, 131, 143

Unilever, 80–1, 92–4, 107, 125, 132
usability, 14, 40, 87, 138, 153, 172, 186–92, 199–201, 208–9, 214–15, 222–3, 230, 233

validation of taxonomies, 111, 139, 154, 167, 177–80, 198–203, 214, 234–5
Vander Wal, Thomas, 240–4, 248
visibility, taxonomies and, xvi, 36, 47, 49, 64, 70–1, 78, 95, 124, 132–3, 137, 139–40, 144–6, 149, 154, 193, 195, 216, 234, 251
voicemail, 86–7
von Clausewitz, Carl, 8

Wal-Mart, 163
Wenger, Etienne, xiv, 112–13, 116
Wikipedia, 241, 245, 248, 254

Yahoo!, 99–100